Great Players in Notre Dame Football

The best players of any football program in the nation

The book is written for those of us who love Notre Dame Football and all the outstanding players we have watched perform over the years. Since we cover ND football from the first game in 1887, there surely are some great players highlighted in this book which none of us know.

The book first tells the story about how college football began and then on to the first American football game in 1867. From there, the progression leads, to Notre Dame's first football team and its first game in 1887, then to the first Notre Dame team with a coach in 1894. Moving through the years we cover the team of players who served the great immortal Notre Dame coaches-- Rockne, Leahy, Parseghian, Devine, and Holtz, to the current season with Coach Brian Kelly. The emphasis within this book is the players and we take time our regularly to report on great games in which those great players excelled. You're going to love it. It will be like football season is year-round.

This book captures the great players in Notre Dame Football. It takes the reader through introductions for Notre Dame's 31 coaches but concentrates on the great players who played like champions today and in days gone by. There are great stories in here about 128 years' worth of great games (1234 games). The book often stops in time and talks about a particular super player such as Johnny Lujack, Paul Hornung, Angelo Bertelli, Gus Dorais, Golden Tate, Knute Rockne, Tony Rice, Jerome Bettis, Vegas Ferguson, Tom Clements, Tommy Rees, George Connor, Nick Buoniconti, & Terry Brennan.

You will not be able to put this book down!

Brian Kelly

Copyright © February 2017, Brian W. Kelly Editor: Brian P. Kelly
Great Players in Notre Dame Football Author: Brian W. Kelly

All rights reserved: No part of this book may be reproduced or transmitted in any form, or by any means, electronic or mechanical, including photocopying, recording, scanning, faxing, or by any information storage and retrieval system, without permission from the publisher, LETS GO PUBLISH, in writing.

Disclaimer: Though judicious care was taken throughout the writing and the publication of this work that the information contained herein is accurate, there is no expressed or implied warranty that all information in this book is 100% correct. Therefore, neither LETS GO PUBLISH, nor the author accepts liability for any use of this work.

Trademarks: A number of products and names referenced in this book are trade names and trademarks of their respective companies.

Referenced Material: *Standard Disclaimer:* The information in this book has been obtained through personal and third party observations, interviews, and copious research. Where unique information has been provided or extracted from other sources, those sources are acknowledged within the text of the book itself or in the References area in the front matter. Thus, there are no formal footnotes nor is there a bibliography section. Any picture that does not have a source was taken from various sites on the Internet with no credit attached. If resource owners would like credit in the next printing, please email publisher.

Published by: LETS GO PUBLISH!
Editor in Chief Brian P. Kelly
Email: info@letsgopublish.com
Web site www.letsgopublish.com

Library of Congress Copyright Information Pending
Book Cover Design by **Brian W. Kelly**

Editor—Brian P. Kelly

ISBN Information: The International Standard Book Number (ISBN) is a unique machine-readable identification number, which marks any book unmistakably. The ISBN is the clear standard in the book industry. 159 countries and territories are officially ISBN members. The Official ISBN For this book is

978-0-9986282-6-4

The price for this work is: $ 14.99 USD

10   9   8   7   6   5   4   3   2   1

Release Date: February 2017

Notre Dame Season Records from 1887 through 2017

Year	Coach	Record	Champs	Year	Coach	Record	Champs	Bowl col 2
1887	No coach	0–1		1952	Frank Leahy	7–2–1		
1888	No coach	1–2		1953	Frank Leahy	9–0–1		
1889	No coach	1–0		1954	Terry Brennan	9–1		
1890	No games	0–0		1955	Terry Brennan	8–2		
1891	No games	0–0		1956	Terry Brennan	2–8		
1892	No coach	1–0–1		1957	Terry Brennan	7–3		
1893	No coach	4–1		1958	Terry Brennan	6–4		
1894	J.L. Morison	3–1–1		1959	Joe Kuharich	5–5		
1895	H.G. Hadden	3–1		1960	Joe Kuharich	2–8		
1896	Frank E. Hering	4–3		1961	Joe Kuharich	5–5		
1897	Frank E. Hering	4–1–1		1962	Joe Kuharich	5–5		
1898	Frank E. Hering	4–2		1963	Hugh Devore	2–7		
1899	James McWeeney	6–3–1		1964	Ara Parseghian	9–1		
1900	Pat O'Dea	6–3–1		1965	Ara Parseghian	7–2–1		
1901	Pat O'Dea	8–1–1		1966	Ara Parseghian	9–0–1	Champs	
1902	James Farragher	6–2–1		1967	Ara Parseghian	8–2		
1903	James Farragher	8–0–1		1968	Ara Parseghian	7–2–1		
1904	Louis Salmon	5–3		1969	Ara Parseghian	8–2–1		Lost Cotton
1905	Henry J. McGlew	5–4		1970	Ara Parseghian	10–1		Won Cotton
1906	Thomas Barry	6–1		1971	Ara Parseghian	8–2		
1907	Thomas Barry	6–0–1		1972	Ara Parseghian	8–3		Lost Orange
1908	Victor M. Place	8–1		1973	Ara Parseghian	11–0	Champs	Won Sugar
1909	Frank Longman	7–0–1		1974	Ara Parseghian	10–2		Won Orange
1910	Frank Longman	4–1–1		1975	Dan Devine	8–3		
1911	John L. Marks	6–0–2		1976	Dan Devine	9–3		Won Gator
1912	John L. Marks	7–0		1977	Dan Devine	11–1	Champs	Won Cotton
1913	Jesse Harper	7–0		1978	Dan Devine	9–3		Won Cotton
1914	Jesse Harper	6–2		1979	Dan Devine	7–4		
1915	Jesse Harper	7–1		1980	Dan Devine	9–2–1		Lost Sugar
1916	Jesse Harper	8–1		1981	Gerry Faust	5–6		
1917	Jesse Harper	6–1–1		1982	Gerry Faust	6–4–1		
1918	Knute Rockne	3–1–2		1983	Gerry Faust	7–5		Won Liberty
1919	Knute Rockne	9–0		1984	Gerry Faust	7–5		Lost Aloha
1920	Knute Rockne	9–0		1985	Gerry Faust	5–6		
1921	Knute Rockne	10–1		1986	Lou Holtz	5–6		
1922	Knute Rockne	8–1–1		1987	Lou Holtz	8–4		Lost Cotton
1923	Knute Rockne	9–1		1988	Lou Holtz	12–0	Champs	Won Fiesta
1924	Knute Rockne	10–0 Won Rose	Champs	1989	Lou Holtz	12–1		Won Orange
1925	Knute Rockne	7–2–1		1990	Lou Holtz	9–3		Lost Orange
1926	Knute Rockne	9–1		1991	Lou Holtz	10–3		Won Sugar
1927	Knute Rockne	7–1–1		1992	Lou Holtz	10–1–1		Won Cotton
1928	Knute Rockne	5–4		1993	Lou Holtz	11–1		Won Cotton
1929	Knute Rockne	9–0	Champs	1994	Lou Holtz	6–5–1		Lost Fiesta
1930	Knute Rockne	10–0	Champs	1995	Lou Holtz	9–3		Lost Orange
1931	Hunk Anderson	6–2–1		1996	Lou Holtz	8–3		
1932	Hunk Anderson	6–2–1		1997	Bob Davie	7–6		Lost indep.
1933	Hunk Anderson	3–5–1		1998	Bob Davie	9–3		Lost Gator
1934	Elmer Layden	6–3		1999	Bob Davie	5–7		
1935	Elmer Layden	7–1–1		2000	Bob Davie	9–3		Lost Fiesta
1936	Elmer Layden	6–2–1		2001	Bob Davie	5–6		

Year	Coach	Record		Year	Coach	Record		Bowl
1937	Elmer Layden	6–2–1		2002	Tyr Willingham	10–3		Lost Gator
1938	Elmer Layden	8–1		2003	Ty Willingham	5–7		
1939	Elmer Layden	7–2		2004	Ty Willingham	6–5		
1940	Elmer Layden	7–2		2004	Kent Baer	0–1		Lost Insight
1941	Frank Leahy	8–0–1		2005	Charlie Weis	9–3		Lost Fiesta
1942	Frank Leahy	7–2–2		2006	Charlie Weis	10–3		Lost Sugar
1943	Frank Leahy	9–1	Champs	2007	Charlie Weis	3–9		
1944	Ed McKeever	8–2		2008	Charlie Weis	7–6		Won Hawaii
1945	Hugh Devore	7–2–1		2009	Charlie Weis	6–6		
1946	Frank Leahy	8–0–1	Champs	2010	Brian Kelly	8–5		Won Sun
1947	Frank Leahy	9–0	Champs	2011	Brian Kelly	8–5		Lost Sports
1948	Frank Leahy	9–0–1		2012	Brian Kelly	12–1		Lost BCS
1949	Frank Leahy	10–0	Champs	2013	Brian Kelly	9–4		Won Pinstripe
1950	Frank Leahy	4–4–1		2014	Brian Kelly	8–5		Won Music
1951	Frank Leahy	7–2–1		2015	Brian Kelly	10–3–0		Lost Fiesta
Total: 892 Wins		314 L	42 Ties	2016	Brian Kelly	4-8-0		

Total Wins   896   Total Losses   320
Total Ties   42   * Prior to Overtime Rules
Stats from   1887   * Through January 2017

In November 2016, it was announced by the NCAA that due to an academic scandal, Notre Dame would be forced to vacate all victories from both the 2012 season and the 2013 season. ND lost 21 wins all-time. We used the NCAA's official Football Records book.

Before vacation of wins:

Rank	Program	Years	Wins	Losses	Ties	Games
1.	Michigan	137	935	332	36	1292
2.	Notre Dame	128	896	320	42	1247
3.	Texas	124	891	359	33	1272
4.	Nebraska	127	889	370	40	1288
5.	Ohio State	127	885	321	53	1248
6.	Alabama	122	875	326	43	1233
7.	Oklahoma	122	870	321	53	1233

After vacation of wins:

Rank	Program	Years	Wins	Losses	Ties	Games
1.	Michigan	137	935	332	36	1292
2.	Texas	124	891	359	33	1272
3.	Nebraska	127	889	370	40	1288
4.	Ohio State	127	885	321	53	1248
5.	Notre Dame	128	875	320	42	1247
6.	Alabama	122	875	326	43	1233
7.	Oklahoma	122	870	321	53	1233

Dedication

I dedicate this book to my wonderful wife Patricia; our three wonderful children Brian, Michael and Katie; and our friendly friends—Angel Ben our once very happy dog, and Buddy, our cheerful cat.

Thank You All!

Acknowledgments:

I appreciate all the help that I received in putting this book together, along with the 62 other books from the past.

My printed acknowledgments were once so large that book readers needed to navigate too many pages to get to page one of the text. To permit me more flexibility, I put my acknowledgment list online at www.letsgopublish.com. The list of acknowledgments continues to grow. Believe it or not, it once cost about a dollar more to print each book.

Thank you all on the big list in the sky and God bless you all for your help.

Please check out www.letsgopublish.com to read the latest version of my heartfelt acknowledgments updated for this book. Thank you all!

In this book, I received some extra special help from many avid Notre Dame supporters including Jack Lammers, Bruce Ikeda, Dennis Grimes, Gerry Rodski, Charles and Marilyn Gallagher, Joseph F. McKeown, Melvin Manhart, Red Jones, Michael McKeown, Wily Ky Eyely, Angel Irene McKeown Kelly, Angel Edward Joseph Kelly Sr., Angel Edward Joseph Kelly Jr., Ann Flannery, Angel James Flannery Sr., Mary Daniels, Bill Daniels, Robert Gary Daniels, Angel Sarah Janice Daniels, Angel Punkie Daniels, Joe Kelly, Diane Kelly, Brian P. Kelly, Mike P. Kelly, Katie P. Kelly, Angel Benjamin Kelly, and Budmund (Buddy) Arthur Kelly.

References

I learned how to write creatively in Grade School at St. Boniface. I even enjoyed reading some of my own stuff.

At Meyers, High School and King's College and Wilkes-University, I learned how to research, write bibliographies and footnote every non-original thought I might have had. I learned to hate ibid, and op. cit., and I hated assuring that I had all citations written down in the proper sequence. Having to pay attention to details took my desire to write creatively and diminished it with busy work.

I know it is necessary for the world to stop plagiarism so authors and publishers can get paid properly, but for an honest writer, it sure is annoying. I wrote many proposals while with IBM and whenever I needed to cite something, I cited it in place, because my readers, IT Managers, could care less about tracing the vagaries of citations. I always hated to use stilted footnotes, or produce a lengthy, perfectly formatted bibliography. I bet most bibliographies are flawed because even the experts on such drivel do not like the tedium.

I wrote 103 books before this book and several hundred articles published by many magazines and newspapers and I only cite when an idea is not mine or when I am quoting, and again, I choose to cite in place, and the reader does not have to trace strange numbers through strange footnotes and back to bibliography elements that may not be readily accessible or available.

Yet, I would be kidding you, if in a book about the great players in Notre Dame Football, I tried to bluff my way into trying to make you think that I knew everything before I began to write anything in this book. I spent as much time researching as writing. I might even call myself an expert of sorts now for all the facts that I have uncovered.

Without any pain on your part you can read this book from cover to cover to enjoy the stories about the many great moments in Notre Dame Football.

It took me about two months to write this book. If I were to have made sure a thought that I had was not a thought somebody else ever had, this book never would have been completed or the citations pages would exceed the prose.

I used ND Season summaries from whatever source I could to get the scores of all the games. I verified facts when possible. There are many web sites that have great information and facts. Ironically most internet stories are the same exact stories. While I was writing the book, I wrote down a bunch of Internet references that I show you below and when you finish reading this book, you may click and enjoy them.

My favorite source has been the Notre Dame Student Magazine called Scholastic which has been published almost from day one at the university. It stopped publishing football issues under its name for some reason at some point and began different publications that highlight football in the same fashion as Scholastic.

Yearly season football summaries were not included in Scholastic until 1901, so it won't help to look for 1887 articles in this magazine. Articles about football are in many of the many of the older issues of Scholastic that were published each year. As an example, in the April edition of 1931, there is major coverage of Knute Rockne's Tragic Death.

http://scholastic.nd.edu/about/

About

Scholastic is the student news magazine of the University of Notre Dame. Founded in 1867, Scholastic is the United States' oldest continuously running collegiate publication. In its history, Scholastic has served first as Notre Dame's weekly student newspaper and now as a monthly news magazine. Scholastic publishes an annual Football Review, printed every February. This issue recaps the Notre Dame Football season with game summaries and in-depth commentary.

Scholastic is a multiple winner of the "News Magazine of the Year" award from the Indiana Collegiate Press Association (ICPA) and the Pacemaker, a national journalism award given by the Associated Collegiate Press.

The offices of Scholastic are located in the basement of the South Dining Hall at Notre Dame, and the mailing address is 315 LaFortune Student Center, Notre Dame, IN 46556.

While I was writing this book, because I was not sure that my citations within the text would be enough, and I was not producing a bibliography, I copied URLs into the book text of areas on the Internet in which I had read articles or had downloaded material and had brought articles or pieces of articles into this book. Hopefully, this will satisfy any request for additional information.

Preface:

I like to begin my books about Notre Dame with this quote:

"We shall always want Notre Dame men 'to-play-to win' so long as there is a Notre Dame to win cleanly according to the rules ... because Notre Dame men are reared here on the campus in this spirit and because they exemplify this spirit all over the world, they are the envy of the nation."
- ■ Rev. John J Cavanaugh C.S.C; 14th president of the University of Notre Dame.

Knute Rockne may be the finest coach who ever lived. He is certainly the most revered of all coaches in ND football. I bet fewer people know who the first great player was in Notre Dame football. Back in the 1880's and early 1900's there were no formal groups with authority to select the best players in the nation.

Walter Camp was from the Midwest and he was the most respected selector. Yet, the dominance of Ivy League players on Camp's All-America teams led to criticism over the years that his selections were biased against players from the leading Western universities, including Chicago, Michigan, Minnesota, Wisconsin, and Notre Dame.

Pioneer ND Coach Jesse Claire Harper had a few fine lads on his squad that seemed more dedicated and better performers than any that had come before. These were Gus Dorais (QB) and Knute Rockne, End. When Dorais threw, it was usually Rockne who was the guy catching the ball. The forward pass had just become legal. Dorais and Rockne practiced so hard that when they played their games, they performed with such ease that it seemed that they were cheating. But it was simply hard work.

Once Rockne and Dorais graduated and Rockne became the head coach, Dorais was his assistant coach. At that time, super-heroes and super-players were much more easy to spot and record than when Walter Camp and a few other selectors decided which players should receive the nation's recognition.

Most writers who are intrigued as I about great football players figure out the greatest player and then slot him at # 1 on the list and then they find their next best guy and slot him at #2, and so on and so on. I am not going to do that in this book.

Anybody who was playing football for Notre Dame in 1887 as far as I am concerned was great. The same goes for the tough guys who played for Coach Jesse Harper including Rockne and Dorais. So, when I find a good one for sure, there will be a mention of him in this book. So, this nook does not have the top fifty from one to fifty or the top 100 players from 1 to100. Instead, the great players are listed within the football season they played from season 1 in 1887 to season 127 in 2017. In other words, the seasons are examined chronologically and the players are highlighted within the seasons in which they played. I sure hope you enjoy this unique approach.

In this way, you get to read about the players who few people know before you find the players from today that everybody knows. Since there are few game films from way back, there will be no voting on greatest since these old timers who appear to be the greatest based on the writings of the times are deemed great and they get a fair look. I am sure I will miss some and perhaps in a subsequent edition I will create a second volume for the forgotten ND players from over the ages.

In other ND books that I have written, I made sure I wrote about the ND playing fields. We lightly cover this ground again in this book. Besides Rockne and Dorais, for example, it is fun to know that when the House that Rock Built was built and actually played in – in 1930, the Irish enjoyed its first encounter with their new stadium on October 4,1930 beating SMU W (20–14). Knute Rockne was the coach in his last year.

The first Notre Dame touchdown in the stadium was scored by "Jumping on a 98-yard kickoff return. The official dedication was a week later on October 11 against Navy, and Savoldi scored another three touchdowns and he was cited as "the first hero in the great lore of Notre Dame Stadium. How many of you have ever heard of "Jumping Joe?" Nor did I until I started my book projects.

Once the stadium was constructed and opened, every Notre Dame Football Team with all the greatest players of all time walked down the same tunnel right before every home game. In the mid-1990s, many know that Notre Dame's red-bricked arena underwent a $50 million expansion and renovation that added more than 21,000 seats.

My kids, who were all less than ten years old at the time snuck in during construction, before there was danger of a construction accident, on a summer visit to the campus. The stadium was wide open. The kids, Brian, Mike, and even Katie scored touchdowns on the same field upon which the greatest scored; but my kids did not even have a whiffle ball to carry. Then, unopposed, they scored touchdowns the other way and back again. When they were tired out. We all went back to the Morris Inn for some lunch.

Notre Dame is at it again building something wonderful. The Campus Crossroads Project is underway now and it will reshape the stadium again with about four thousand new seats and some great new campus buildings. It is all coming soon in a mammoth $400 million-dollar project

The football program from day one competed under the nickname "Catholics" and for a time it was widely known as the "Ramblers." Coach Harper's and Coach Rockne's teams were often called the Rovers or the Ramblers and there were no compliments intended. ND would travel anywhere to get a game. They roamed and rambled far and wide, an uncommon practice before the advent of commercial airplanes.

After the 1909 game v Michigan, Sportswriter E.A. Batchelor, who had overheard ND teammates encouraging each other to fight hard because they were Irish and the team needed to fight hard to win the game, is credited with first using the moniker "Fighting Irish" in the written word. University president Rev. Matthew Walsh, C.S.C., officially adopted "Fighting Irish" as the Notre Dame nickname in 1927. So, now, it is official.

You'll learn a lot about Notre Dame and its players in this new book by Brian Kelly. It highlights the <u>Great Players in Notre Dame Football</u> and it walks the reader briskly through every major time-period in ND history, even a few in which there was not a coach to be seen.

Brian Kelly (not the football coach) would like you to know that when football season closes in the second week of January each year, there is now a great football item—this book—that is available all 52 weeks of the year and in fact all 365 days each year. It does not rely on the stadium gates being open.

It is now available for you to add to your Notre Dame football experience and your book collection. Once you get this book, it is yours forever unless, of course you give it away to one of the many who will be in awe, and who will accept it gladly.

The book takes a quick look at a number of the great players in Notre Dame history, some famous, and some not so famous but historical nonetheless. Admittedly, the book devotes many more pages for the more famous players than the less.

As tough as it may be to believe for some of the more recent Notre Dame supporters, not all Notre Dame coaches are named Rockne and not all Notre Dame great players are named Montana or Bettis.

Lest we forget, it was not just the players on the best teams but all Notre Dame Football teams that were Irish Tough. Paul Hornung, for example, won a Heisman Trophy in a year that Notre Dame had a tough time winning a game.

The book opens with its first story about the very beginning of college football as a sport in America. It then moves on to the players and their great seasons—all the way to Coach Brian Kelly's last game. It tells a story about the football seasons and the players from the first game in 1887 right to the beginning of the 2017 season. It is written for those of us who love Notre Dame Football.

I predict that you will not be able to put this book down

You are going to love this book because it is the perfect read for anybody who loves Notre Dame and Notre Dame Football and wants to know more about the most revered athletic program of all time.

Few sports books are a must-read but Brian Kelly's <u>Great Players in Notre Dame Football</u> will quickly appear at the top of Americas most enjoyable must-read books about sports. Enjoy!

Sincerely,

Brian P. Kelly, Editor in Chief
I am Brian Kelly's eldest son

Table of Contents

Chapter 1 Introduction to the Book.................................1

Chapter 2 The Beginning of College Football 3

Chapter 3 Notre Dame's First Football Team.................. 25

Chapter 4 ND Football – The No Coach Years 31

Chapter 7 ND Football – The Second Seven Years........... 41

Chapter 8 First 12 ND Football Seasons of 20th Century..... 51

Chapter 9 Coach Jesse Harper 1913-1917 77

Chapter 10 Coach Knute Rockne 1918-30....................... 89

Chapter 11 Post Rockne: Coach Hunk Anderson 1931-33..115

Chapter 12 Post Rockne: Coach Elmer Layden 1934-40 125

Chapter 13 Coach Frank Leahy 1941-1953.....................133

Chapter 14 Coach Terry Brennan: 1954-1958 171

Chapter 15 Coach Joseph Kuharich: 1959-1963 181

Chapter 16 Coach Ara Parseghian: 1964-1974 189

Chapter 17 Coach Dan Devine 1975-1980......................227

Chapter 18 Coach Gerry Faust: 1981-1985.....................253

Chapter 19 Coach Lou Holtz: 1986-1996 261

Chapter 20 Coach Bob Davie: 1997–2001 287

Chapter 21 Coach Tyrone Willingham: 2002 – 2004.........293

Chapter 22 Coach Charlie Weis: 2005–2009...................299

Chapter 23 Coach Brian Kelly 2010–2016 319

Books by Brian W. Kelly...344

About the Author

Brian Kelly retired as an Assistant Professor in the Business Information Technology (BIT) Program at Marywood University, where he also served as the IBM i and Midrange Systems Technical Advisor to the IT Faculty.

He is one of the leading authors in America with this, his 105th published book. Brian is an outspoken and eloquent expert on a variety of topics and he has also written several hundred articles on topics of general interest to most Americans.

Most of his early works involved high technology. Later, Brian wrote a number of patriotic books and most recently he has been writing human interest books such as *The Wine Diet* and *Thank you, IBM*. His books are always well received.

Brian's 105 books are all highlighted at www.letsgopublish.com. They are for sale at www.bookhawkers.com, Amazon, Kindle, Barnes & Noble & other fine booksellers. One day perhaps, even the famous Notre Dame Book Store will agree to host this book.

Brian was a candidate for the US Congress from Pennsylvania in 2010 and he ran for Mayor in his home town in 2015. He loves Notre Dame and was an Irish fan long before some other guy with the same name happened to come to South Bend, Indiana.

Chapter 1 Introduction to the Book

Notre Dame celebrates its 125th year.

Brian Kelly, ND Coach Leading the Fighting Irish

In 2012, Notre Dame celebrated its 125th year of football. As part of the celebration, the University built a web site that fans of Notre Dame should find quite enjoyable— http://125.nd.edu. The site has many enjoyable items to tickle the imagination and it provides a very real look at Notre Dame over its 125-year history (as of 2012). The very first item that I viewed on this site was at the following web address: http://125.nd.edu/moments/first-game-in-notre-dame-football-history/

Enjoy the Sept 22 2012 125th anniversary game panorama picture at http://125.nd.edu/pano/

This book celebrates Notre Dame's great football players and the university's long-lasting impact on American life. People like me, who love Notre Dame, will love this book. Those not quite such admiring fans as I, will sneak it off the shelf at their doctor's office or their barber's like Bob Yanelavage, and read it quietly in the corner.

We kick off the football part of the book in Chapter 2 with the founding of college football and we move on to the founding of the football program at Notre Dame in 1887. From there we look at many of the great players who form the great football teams in ND history.

In defining the format of the book, we chose to use a timetable that is based on a historical chronology. Within this framework, we discuss some the great players in ND Football history, and there are many great players who have made football exciting at Notre Dame.

No book can claim to be able to capture all the great moments, as it would be a never-ending story, but we give it a try. It is amazing the number of well-known great players that have walked through Notre Dame's championship portal.

Thanks for choosing to take this fun ride with us through Notre Dame Football History. The great players noted in this book are part of the great legacy of Notre Dame University and its world class football program.

Chapter 2 The Beginning of College Football

Lots of playing before playing became official

The official agreed upon date for the first American-style college football game is November 6, 1869. If you can find a replay of this game someplace in the heavens, however, you would find it would not look much like football as we know it. But, it was not completely soccer or rugby either.

Before this game, teams were playing a rugby style like that played in Britain in the mid-19th century. At the time in the US, a derivative known as association football was also played. In both games, a football is kicked at a goal or run over a line. These styles were based on the varieties of English public school football games. Over time, as noted, the style of "football" play in America continued to evolve.

On November 6, 1869, the first football game in America featured Rutgers and Princeton. Before the teams were even on the field it was being plugged as the first college football game of all time. Notre Dame did have a rugby team at the time, but nobody at Notre Dame, from what I could find, was even thinking about the game of football.

The first game of intercollegiate football was a sporting battle between two neighboring schools on a plot of ground where the present-day Rutgers gymnasium now stands in New Brunswick, N.J. Rutgers won that first game, 6-4.

There were two teams of 25 men each and the rules were rugby-like, but different enough to make it very interesting and enjoyable.

Like today's football, there were many surprises; strategies needed to be employed; determination exhibited, and of course the players required physical prowess.

1st Game Rutgers 6 Princeton 4 College Field, New Brunswick, NJ

At 3 p.m. the 50 combatants as well as 100 spectators gathered on the field. Most sat on a low wooden fence and watched the athletes discard their hats, coats and vests. The players used their suspenders as belts. To give a unique look, Rutgers wore scarlet-colored scarfs, which they converted into turbans. This contrasted them with the bareheaded boys from Princeton.

Two members of each team remained stationary near the opponent's goal in the hopes of being able to slip over and score from unguarded positions. Thus, the present day "sleeper" was conceived. The remaining 23 players were divided into groups of 11 and 12. While the 11 "fielders" lined up in their own territory as defenders, the 12 "bulldogs" carried the battle.

Each score counted as a "game" and 10 games completed the contest. Following each score, the teams changed direction. The ball could be advanced only by kicking or batting it with the feet, hands, heads or sides.

Rutgers put a challenge forward that three games were to be played that year. The first was played at New Brunswick and won by Rutgers. Princeton won the second game, but cries of "over-emphasis" prevented the third game in football's first year when faculties of both institutions protested on the grounds that the games were interfering with student studies.

This is an excerpt of the Rutgers account of the game on its web site. A person named Herbert gave this detailed account of the play in the first game:

"Though smaller on the average, the Rutgers players, as it developed, had ample speed and fine football sense. Receiving the ball, our men formed a perfect interference around it and with short, skillful kicks and dribbles drove it down the field. Taken by surprise, the Princeton men fought valiantly, but in five minutes we had gotten the ball through to our captains on the enemy's goal and S.G. Gano, '71 and G.R. Dixon, '73, neatly kicked it over. None thought of it, so far as I know, but we had without previous plan or thought evolved the play that became famous a few years later as 'the flying wedge'."

"Next period Rutgers bucked, or received the ball, hoping to repeat the flying wedge," Herbert's account continues. "But the first time we formed it Big Mike came charging full upon us. It was our turn for surprise. The Princeton battering ram made no attempt to reach the ball but, forerunner of the interference-breaking ends of today, threw himself into our mass play, bursting us apart, and bowing us over. Time and again Rutgers formed the wedge and charged; as often Big Mike broke it up. And finally, on one of these incredible break-ups a Princeton bulldog with a long accurate, perhaps lucky kick, sent the ball between the posts for the second score.

It was at this point that a Rutgers professor could stand it no longer. Waving his umbrella at the participants, he shrieked, "You will come to no Christian end!"

Herbert's account of the game continues: "The fifth and sixth goals went to Rutgers. The stars of the latter period of play, in the memory of the players after the lapse of many years, were "Big Mike" and Large (former State Senator George H. Large of Flemington, another Princeton player) ...

Notre Dame-Army Football

The University of Notre Dame did not get into the football act until the late 1880's. At this time, the rules of rugby kept changing to accommodate the infatuation for the Americanized style of "football" play that would ultimately become the American game of football.

Walter Camp: the father of American football?

Walter Camp was a very well-known rugby player from Yale. In today's world, he would have been characterized as a rugby hero. It was his love of the game, his knowledge of the game as it was played, and his innovative mind that caused him to take the evolution of football even further. He pioneered the changes to the rules of rugby that slowly transformed the sport into the new game of American Football.

The rule changes that were introduced to the rugby and association style of play were mostly those authored by Camp, who was also a Hopkins School graduate. For his original efforts, Walter Camp today is considered to be the "Father of American Football". Among the important changes brought to the game were the introduction of a line of scrimmage; down-and-distance rules; and the legalization of interference (blocking).

There was no such thing in those days as a forward pass and so the legalization of interference in 1880 football permitted blocking for runners. The forward pass would add another dimension to the game that made it much different than rugby or association football.

Soon after the early football changes, in the late nineteenth and into the early twentieth centuries, more game-play type developments were introduced by college coaches. The list is like a who's who of early American College Football. Coaches, such as Eddie Cochems, Amos Alonzo Stagg, Parke H. Davis, Knute Rockne, John Heisman, and Glenn "Pop" Warner helped introduce and then take advantage of the newly introduced forward pass. College football as well as professional football, were introduced prior to the 20th century. Fans were lured into watching again and again once they saw the game played.

College football especially grew in popularity despite the existence of pro-football. It became the dominant version of the sport of football in the United States. It was this way for the entire first half of the 20th century. Bowl games made the idea of football even more exciting in the college ranks. Rivalries grew and continued and the fans loved it! This great football tradition brought a national audience to college football games that still dominates the sports world today.

In researching this chapter, I found that Edgar Allan Poe was an All-American for Princeton in 1889, the first-year players were named.

Edgar Allan Poe – No kidding!

Edgar Allan Poe served as Attorney General of the State of Maryland from 1911 to 1915. Born in Baltimore, Poe was named

for his second cousin, twice removed, the celebrated
author Edgar Allan Poe, who died in 1849.

The great athlete Poe attended Princeton University, where he played quarterback of the 1889 varsity football team, which finished with a perfect 10-0 record. Poe was named the quarterback of the very first 1889 College Football All-America Team.

A cute anecdote of the season was that After Princeton beat Harvard, 41–15, a Harvard man is said to have asked a Princeton man whether Poe was related to the great Edgar Allan Poe. According to the story, "the alumnus looked at him in astonishment and replied, 'He is the great Edgar Allan Poe.'"

What number is he?

Another interesting tidbit on the formation of football is that teams played without uniform numbers. Nonetheless somehow the players were identified. Just two years after Notre Dame formed its team, in 1887, the first All-America team was named in 1989 There is some scuttle about that as Walter Camp and some others picked players from the big Eastern Colleges almost exclusively and so there were few All Americans at Notre Dame in the early years.

Gus Dorais was the first consensus All-American for Notre Dame in 1913. He was a Quarterback who loved throwing touchdowns to Knute Rockne, an end on the team who made All-American but not consensus. Additionally, in 1913, Ray Eichenlaub, the ND fullback also received non-consensus All-American honors. All three played on a great team and were coached by Jesse Harper.

ND's next consensus All-American was Frank Rydzewski, who played Center on Jesse Harper's 1917 team. Notre Dame's third All-American came in 1920 when the Gipper won the honor as a halfback, though George Gipp played numerous other positions. Gipp's coach at the time was Knute Rockne in his third year.

In 1889, numbers to identify individual players were not recommended. It took until 1915 that they were recommended. But, it wasn't until 1937 that numerals were required on both the front and back of game jerseys. In 1967 this rule was further modified to require numbering according to position, with offensive players ineligible to receive forward passes assigned numbers in the 50-79 range.

This book has little to do with pro-football or any other sport. However, there is no denying that the greatest college football players more often than not eventually found their fortunes in professional football. Pro football can be traced back to the season that Notre Dame brought forth a real football team after a two-year lapse from its last half-Rugby season in 1889. It was 1892 when William "Pudge" Heffelfinger signed a $500 contract to play for the Allegheny Athletic Association against the Pittsburgh Athletic Club.

Twenty-eight years later, the American Professional Football Association was formed. This league changed its name to the National Football League (NFL) just two years later. Eventually, the NFL became the major league of American football. Originally, just a sport played in Midwestern industrial towns in the United States, professional football eventually became a national phenomenon. We all know this because from August to February, in America, many of us are glued to our TV sets or chained to our seats in some of the most intriguing pro-football stadiums in America.

Rules and Penalties

The big problem players from different teams and different geographies had when playing early American-style football in college was that the style of play was not standardized. The rulebooks were not yet written or were at best incomplete and disputable.

A rule over here, for example, would be a penalty over there. And, so in the 1870's there was a lot of work to try to make all games to be played by the same rules. There were minor rule changes such as team size was reduced from 25 to 20 but of course over the years, this and all other rules continued to evolve. For years, there was no such thing as a running touchdown. The only means of scoring was to bat or kick the ball through the opposing team's goal.

Early rugby rules were the default. The field size was rugby style at 140 yards by 70 yards v 120 X 53 1/3 (including end zones) in today's football game. There was plenty of room to huff and puff and almost get lost. There were no breaks per se for long periods. Instead of fifteen minute quarters, the game was more like Rugby and Soccer with 45 minute halves played continuously.

In 1873 to put some order to the game, Columbia, Princeton. Rutgers, and Yale got together in a hotel in New York City and wrote down the first set of intercollegiate football rules. They changed a few things along the way but the end product was a much more standard way of playing football games. Rather than use the home team's rules, all teams then were able to play by the same rules

Harvard did not to comply with rules

For its own reasons, Harvard chose not to attend the rules conference. Instead, it played all of its games using the Harvard code of rules. Harvard therefore had a difficult time scheduling games. In 1874, to get a game, Harvard agreed to play McGill University from Montreal Canada. They had rules that even Harvard had never seen. For example, any player could pick up the ball and run with it, anytime he wished.

Another McGill rule was that they would count tries (the act of grounding the football past the opponent's goal line. Since there was no end zone, which technically makes a football field of today 120 yards long, a touchdown gave no points. Instead, it provided the chance to kick a free goal from the field. If the kick were missed, the touchdown did not count.

In 1874 McGill and Harvard played a two-game series. Each team could play 11 men per side. This was in deep contrast to the even earlier days of college football before standard rules when games were played with 25, 20, 15, or 11 men on a side.

The first game was played with a round ball using what were known as the "Boston" rules (Harvard). The next day, the teams played using the McGill rules, which included McGill's oval ball which was much like an American football, and it featured the ability to pick up the ball and run with it. Harvard enjoyed this experience especially the idea of "the try" which had not been used in American football. Eventually, the try evolved into the American idea of a touchdown and points were given when a try was successful.

Not all the rules lasted the duration and some were very strange by today's standards. One of the most perplexing rules was that a man could run with the ball only while an opponent chose to pursue him. When a tackler abandoned the ball-carrier, the latter had to stop, and was forced to kick, pass or even throw away what was called "his burden."

McGill has a great account of this match on their web site. Type *McGill web site football against Harvard* into your search engine.

Their players wore no protective pads. Woolen jerseys covered the torso, while white trousers encased the players' legs. Some trousers were short and some were long. It did not seem to matter for the game. A number of the men wore what they called black "football turbans" which were the ancestors of the modern helmet; others chose to wear white canvas hats.

The Harvard players wore undershirts made of gauze. Think about that for a while. They also wore what were called *full length gymnasium costumes.* They also wore light baseball shoes. Most of the team wore handkerchiefs, which were knotted about their heads.

The gauze undershirts were a trick. There was strategy in this choice of top uniform. When a player was first tackled, the gauze would be demolished and the next opponent would have nothing to grab other than "slippery human flesh." Harvard won the game: score = 3-0.

The next go at playing by the rules was when Harvard took on Tufts University on June 4, 1875. This was the first American college football game played using rules similar to the McGill/Harvard contest. Tufts won this game. Despite the loss, Harvard continued pushing McGill style football and challenged Yale.

The Yale Bulldogs team accepted under a compromise rule set that included some Yale soccer rules and Harvard rugby rules. They used 15 players per team. It was November 13, 1875 for this first meeting of Harvard v Yale. Harvard won 4-0. Walter Camp attended the game and the following year he played in the game as a Yale Bulldog.

Camp was determined to avenge Yale's defeat. Onlookers from Princeton, who saw this Harvard / Yale game loved it so much, they brought it back to Princeton where it was quickly adopted as the preferred version of football.

Once Walter Camp caught onto the rugby-style rules, history says he became a fixture at the Massasoit House conventions. Here the rules of the game were debated and changed appropriately. From these meetings, Camp's rule changes as well as others were adopted.

Eleven players instead of fifteen

Having eleven players instead of fifteen aided in opening the game and it emphasized speed over strength. When Camp attended in 1878, this motion was rejected but it passed in the 1880 meeting. The line of scrimmage and the snap from center to the quarterback also passed in 1880. Originally the snap occurred by a kick from the center, but this was later modified so the ball would be snapped with the hands either as a pass back (long snap) or a direct snap from the center.

It was Camp's new scrimmage rules, however, which according to many, revolutionized the game, though it was not always to increase speed. In fact, Princeton was known to use line of scrimmage plays to slow the game, making incremental progress towards the end zone much like today during each down.

Camp's original idea was to increase scoring, but in fact the rule was often misused to maintain control of the ball for the entire game. The negative effect was that there were many slow and unexciting contests. This too would be fixed with the idea of the first down coming into play.

In 1982, at the rules meeting, Camp proposed that a team be given three downs to advance the ball five yards. These rules were called the down and distance rules. Along with the notion of the line of scrimmage, these rules transformed the game of rugby into the distinct sport of American football.

Among other significant rule changes, in 1881, the field size was reduced to its modern dimensions of 120 by 53 1/3 yards (109.7 by 48.8 meters). Camp was central to these significant rule changes that ultimately defined American football. Camp's next quest was to address scoring anomalies. His first cut was to give four points for a touchdown and two points for kicks after touchdowns; two points for safeties, and five points for field goals. The notion of the foot in football /rugby explains Camp's rationale.

In 1887, game time was fixed at two halves of 45 minutes each. Additionally college games would have two paid officials known as a referee and an umpire, for each game. In 1888, the rules permitted tackling below the waist and then in 1889, the officials were given whistles and stopwatches to better control the game.

An innovation that many list as most significant to making American football uniquely American was the legalization of blocking opponents, which back then was called "interference." This tactic had been highly illegal under the rugby-style rules and in rugby today, it continues to be illegal.

The more those who know soccer and football find rugby to be more like soccer.

Though *offsides* is a penalty infraction today, *offsides* in the 1880's in rugby was very much the same as *offsides* in soccer. The prohibition of blocking in a rugby game is in fact because of the game's strict enforcement of its *offsides* rule. Similar to soccer, this rule prohibits any player on the team with possession of the ball to loiter between the ball and the goal. Blocking continues as a basic element of modern American football, with many complex schemes having been developed and implemented over the years, including zone blocking and pass blocking.

Camp stayed active in rule making for most of his life. He had the honor of personally selecting an annual All-American team every year from 1889 through 1924. Camp passed away in 1925. The Walter Camp Football Foundation continues to select All-American teams in his honor.

With many rule changes as noted, as American style rugby became more defined as American football, more and more colleges adopted football as part of their sports programs. Most of the schools were from the Eastern US. It was not until 1879 that the University of Michigan became the first school west of Pennsylvania to establish a bona-fide American-style college football team.

Back then, football teams played whenever they could in the fall or the spring. For example, Michigan's first game was in late spring, near the end of what we would call the academic year. On May 30, 1879 Michigan beat Racine College 1–0 in a game played in Chicago. In 1887, Michigan and Notre Dame played their first football game, which did not benefit from Camp's rules.

The first night time game

It was not until September 28, 1892 that the first nighttime football game was played. Mansfield State Normal played Wyoming Seminary in Mansfield, Pennsylvania.

These schools are close to where I live. The game ended at a "declared" half-time in a 0–0 tie. It had become too dark to play.

Wyoming Seminary was not a college and to this day it is not a college. I live about five miles from the school. It is a private college preparatory school located in the Wyoming Valley of Northeastern

Pennsylvania. During the time-period in which the game was played, it was common for a college and high school to play each other in football—a practice that of course has long since been discontinued.

The reason that it got too dark to play, ironically was not because the game began at dusk. Mansfield had brought in a lighting system that was far too inadequate for game play. This historical game lasted only 20 minutes and there were only 10 plays. Both sides agreed to end at half-time with the score at 0-0. Though it may seem humorous today, for safety reasons, the game was declared ended in a 0-0 tie after several players had an unfortunate run-in with a light pole.

Mansfield and Wyoming Seminary are thus enshrined in football history as having played in the first night game ever in "college football." History and football buffs get together once a year to celebrate the game in what they call "Fabulous 1890's Weekend." This historic game is reenacted exactly as it occurred play by play just as the actual game is recorded in history. Fans who watch the game are sometimes known to correct players (actually actors) when they deviate from the original scripted plays. Now, that shows both a love of the game and a love of history.

Mansfield and Wyoming Seminary's game added additional fame to both schools when the 100th anniversary of the game just happened to occur on Monday, September 28, 1992. Monday Night Football celebrated "100 years of night football" with its regularly scheduled game between the Los Angeles Raiders and the Kansas City Chiefs at Arrowhead Stadium. The Chiefs won 27–7 in front of 77,486 fans. How about that?

More football history was recorded when Army played Navy in 1893. In this game, we have the first documented use of a football helmet by a player in a game. Joseph M. Reeves had been kicked in the head in a prior football game. He was warned by his doctor that he risked death if he continued to play football. We all know how tough the Midshipmen and Black Nights (Cadets) are regardless of who they may be playing. Rather than end his football playing days prematurely. Reeves discussed his need with a shoemaker in Annapolis who crafted a leather helmet for the player to wear for the rest of the season.

Football conferences

Things were happening very quickly in the new sport of football. Organization and rules became the mantra for this fledgling sport. It was being defined while it was being played. Formal college football conferences were just around the corner. In fact, the Southeastern Conference and the Atlantic Coast Conference both got started in 1894.

The forward pass

None of Camp's rules for American Football included the most innovative notion of them all – the forward pass. Many believe that the first forward pass in football occurred on October 26, 1895 in a game between Georgia and North Carolina. Out of desperation, the ball was thrown by the North Carolina back Joel Whitaker instead of having been punted. George Stephens, a teammate caught the ball.

Despite what most may think or surmise, it was Camp again when he was a player at Yale, who executed the first game-time forward pass for a touchdown. During the Yale-Princeton game, while Camp was being tackled, he threw a football forward to Yale's Oliver Thompson, who sprinted to a touchdown. The Princeton Tigers naturally protested and there appeared to be no precedent for a referee decision. Like many things in football including a game-beginning coin-toss, the referee in this instance tossed a coin, and then he made his decision to allow the touchdown.

Hidden ball trick

Some one-time tricks have not survived football. For example, on November 9, 1895 Auburn Coach John Heisman executed a hidden ball trick. Quarterback Reynolds Tichenor was able to gain Auburn's only touchdown in a 6 to 9 loss to Vanderbilt. This also was the first game in the south that was decided by a field goal.

1895 Auburn Tigers football

The team executed a "hidden ball trick" in the game against Vanderbilt

Coach John Heisman is in the second row in the middle wearing glasses.

The trick was simple but would be illegal today. When the ball was snapped it went to a halfback. The play was closely masked and well screened. The halfback then thrust the ball under the back of the quarterback's (Tichenor) jersey. Then the halfback would crash into the line. After the play, Tichenor "simply trotted away to a touchdown."

The end of college football?

Football was never a game for the light of heart. You had to be tough physically and tough mentally to compete. Way back in 1906, for example complaints were many about the violence in American Football. It got so bad that universities on the West Coast, led by California and Stanford, replaced the sport with rugby union. At the time, the future of American college football, a very popular sport enjoyed by fans nationwide was in doubt. The schools that eliminated football and replaced it with rugby union believed football would be gone and rugby union would eventually be adopted nationwide.

Soon other schools followed this travesty and made the switch. Eventually, due to the perception that West Coast football was an inferior game played by inferior men when compared to the rough and tumble East Coast, manhood prevailed in the West over the inclination to make the game mild. The many tough East Coast and Midwest teams had shrugged off the loss of the few teams out West and they had continued to play American style football.

And, so the available pool of rugby union "football" teams to play remained small. The Western colleges therefore had to schedule games against local club teams and they reached out to rugby union powers in Australia, New Zealand, and especially, due to its proximity, Canada.

The famous Stanford and California game continued as rugby. To make it seem important. The winner was invited by the British Columbia Rugby Union to a tournament in Vancouver over the Christmas holidays. The winner of that tournament was rewarded with the Cooper Keith Trophy. Nobody in America cared. Eventually the West Coast came back to football.

Nonetheless the situation of injury and death in football persisted and though there was a lot of pushback, it came to a head in 1905 when there were 19 fatalities nationwide. President Theodore Roosevelt, a tough guy himself, is reported as having threatened to shut down the game nationwide if drastic changes were not made. Sports historians however, dispute that Roosevelt ever intervened.

What is certified, however, is that on October 9, 1905, the President held a meeting of football representatives from Harvard, Yale, and Princeton. The topic was eliminating and reducing injuries and the President according to the record, never threatened to ban football. The fact is that Roosevelt lacked the authority to abolish football but more importantly, he was a big fan and wanted the game to continue. The little Roosevelts also loved the sport and were playing football at the college and secondary levels at the time.

Theodore Roosevelt, Jr. after breaking his ankle during a Harvard football game.

Meanwhile, there were more rule changes such as the notion of reducing the number of scrimmage plays to earn a first down from four to three in an attempt to reduce injuries. The LA Times reported an increase in punts in an experimental game and thus considered the game much safer than regular play. Football lovers did not accept the new rule because it was not "conducive to the sport."

Because nobody wanted players injured or killed in a game, on December 28, 1905, 62 schools met in New York City to discuss major rule changes to make the game safer. From this meeting, the Intercollegiate Athletic Association of the United States, later named the National Collegiate Athletic Association (NCAA), was formed.

The forward pass is legalized

One rule change that was introduced in 1906 was devised to open up the game and thus reduce injury. This new rule introduced the legal forward pass. Though it was underutilized for years, this proved to be one of the most important rule changes in the establishment of the modern game.

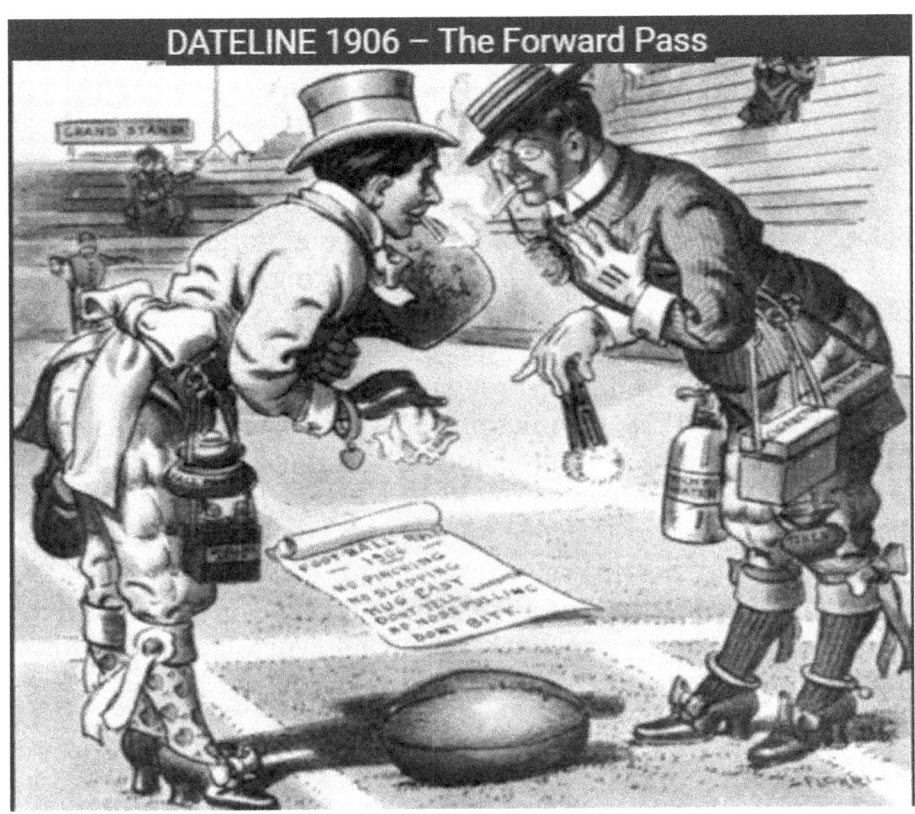

Because of these 1905-1906 reforms, mass formation plays in which many players joined together became illegal when forward passes became legal. Bradbury Robinson, playing for visionary coach Eddie Cochems at St. Louis University, is recorded as throwing the first legal pass in a September 5, 1906, game against Carroll College at Waukesha.

Later changes were in the minutia category but they added discipline and safety to the game without destroying its rugged character. For example, in 1910, came the new requirement that at least seven offensive players be on the line of scrimmage at the time of the snap, that there be no pushing or pulling, and that interlocking interference (arms linked or hands on belts and uniforms) was not allowed.

These changes accomplished their intended purpose of greatly reducing the potential for collision injuries.

As noted previously, great coaches emerged in the ranks who took advantage of these sweeping changes. Amos Alonzo Stagg, for example, introduced such innovations as the huddle, the tackling dummy, and the pre-snap shift. Other coaches, such as Pop Warner and Notre Dame's Knute Rockne, introduced new strategies that still remain part of the game.

Many other rules changes and coaching innovations came about before 1940. They all had a profound impact on the game, mostly in opening up the passing game, but also in making the game safer to play without diminishing its quality.

For example, in 1914, the first roughing-the-passer penalty was implemented. In 1918, the rules on eligible receivers were loosened to allow eligible players to catch the ball anywhere on the field.

The previously more restrictive rules allowed passes only in certain areas of the field. Scoring rules also changed which brought the scoring into the modern era. For example, field goals were lowered from five to three points in 1909 and touchdowns were raised from four to six points in 1912.

Star Players

Star players emerged in both the collegiate and professional ranks including Jim Thorpe (shown on next page,)

Jim Thorpe, Circa 1915

Red Grange, and Bronko Nagurski were also big stars. These three in particular were able to move from college to the fledgling NFL and they helped turn it into a successful league. Notable sportswriter Grantland Rice helped popularize the sport of football with his poetic descriptions of games and colorful nicknames for the game's biggest players, including Notre Dame's "Four Horsemen" backfield and Fordham University's linemen, known as the "Seven Blocks of Granite."

Adding to the lore, University football team's offensive line under head coach "Sleepy" Jim Crowley was one of the four horsemen from Notre Dame fame and his assistant was Frank Leahy who won four National Championships as head coach of Notre Dame after his stint at Fordham.

The Heisman

Jay Berwanger (on the prior page) was the 1st Heisman Winner. In 1935, New York City's Downtown Athletic Club awarded its first Heisman Trophy to University of Chicago halfback Jay Berwanger (left).

He was also the first ever NFL Draft pick in 1936. The trophy continues to this day to recognize the nation's "most outstanding" college football player. It has become one of the most coveted awards in all of American sports.

Notre Dame is proud to note that a record seven of its greatest football players have won the Heisman trophy. ND has also produced 97 consensus All-Americans, 33 unanimous All-Americans, and 50 members of the College Football Hall of Fame. All of these are NCAA records. With 486 players so far selected, Notre Dame is second to USC in the number of players chosen by NFL teams in the professional football draft.

As professional football became a national television phenomenon, college football did as well. In the 1950s, Notre Dame, which had a large national following, formed its own network to broadcast its games, but by and large the sport still retained a mostly regional following.

New formations and play sets continued to be developed by innovative coaches and their staffs. Emory Bellard from the University of Texas, developed a three-back option style offense known as the wishbone. Bear Bryant of Alabama became a preacher of the wishbone.

The strategic opposite of the wishbone is called the spread offense. Some teams have managed to adapt with the times to keep winning consistently. In the rankings of the most victorious programs, Michigan, Texas, and Notre Dame are ranked first, second, and third in total wins.

And so, that is as far as we will take it in this chapter about the early evolution of football. With so many conferences and sports associations as well as pro, college, high school, and mini sports, something tells me we have not yet seen our last rule change.

Chapter 3 Notre Dame's First Football Team

1887: Nearly 45 years from the founding

In a book about Great Players in Notre Dame Football, in the ND early years if the University and the pundits kept better records back then, I bet we would have a few great candidates for the best player/coach at Noted Dame until the first coach arrived. The ND players coached themselves in the beginning until 1894.

On Nov. 23, 1887, nearly 45 years to the day after Rev. Edward Sorin, C.S.C., arrived in northern Indiana, the University of Notre Dame fielded a collegiate football team. There is nobody who can tell the History of Notre Dame Football better than Notre Dame itself. So, I will use the following brief account which was originally published in Scholastic, Notre Dame's internal student magazine.

The quoted narrative from Scholastic describes the scene of the inaugural contest between Michigan and Notre Dame. Following a quick depiction of the game, I have included several additional pictures for your enjoyment and edification. All of these photos are free for the viewing on the Internet.

" For some days, previous to Wednesday, great interest had been manifested by our students in the football game which had been arranged between the teams of the Universities of Michigan and Notre Dame. It was not considered a match contest, as the home team had been organized only a few weeks, and the Michigan boys, the champions of the West, came more to instruct them in the points of the Rugby game than to win fresh laurels.

1887 Champion Michigan Wolverine football team

"The visitors [Michigan] arrived over the Michigan Central RR., Wednesday morning, and were at once taken in charge by a committee of students. After spending, a few hours in "taking in" the surroundings, they donned their uniforms of spotless white and appeared upon the seniors' campus. Owing to the recent thaw, the field was damp and muddy; but nothing daunted, the boys "went in," and soon Harless' new suit appeared as though it had imbibed some of its wearer's affinity for the soil of Notre Dame.

At first, to render our players more familiar with the game, the teams were chosen irrespective of college. After some minutes' play, the game was called, and each took his position as follows:

"**Univ. of M**. – Full Back: J.L. Duffy; Half Backs: J.E. Duffy, E. McPheran; Quarter Back: R.T. Farrand; Centre Rush: W.W. Harless; Rush Line: F. Townsend, E.M. Sprague, F.H. Knapp, W. Fowler, G.W. De Haven, M. Wade.

"**Univ. of N.D**. – Full Back: H. Jewett; Half Backs: J. Cusack, H. Luhn; Quarter Back: G. Cartier; Centre Rush: G.A. Houck; Rush Line: F. Fehr, P. Nelson, B. Sawkins, W. Springer, T. O'Regan, P.P. Maloney.

"On account of time, only a part of one inning was played, and resulted in a score of 8 to 0 in favor of the visitors. The game was interesting, and, notwithstanding the slippery condition of the ground, the Ann Arbor boys gave a fine exhibition of skillful [sic] playing. This occasion has started an enthusiastic football boom, and it is hoped that coming years will witness a series of these contests.

"After a hearty dinner, Rev. President Walsh thanked the Ann Arbor team for their visit, and assured them of the cordial reception that would always await them at Notre Dame. At 1 o'clock carriages were taken for Niles, and amidst rousing cheers the University of Michigan football team departed, leaving behind them a most favorable impression." **End of Scholastic Excerpt**

Modern ND Football

Originally posted Sep 4, 2013. http://mvictors.com/teaching-them-modern-football-1887/
Thank you to the Michigan Athletic Association for making this piece, shown in its entirety below, publicly available:

> "With all the talk on the historical significance of the Michigan-Notre Dame rivalry, I'd thought I'd share a little bit on the original meeting in 1887. Women, prepare to swoon.

DeHaven and Harless

So, you've heard that Michigan taught Notre Dame how to play this game. This is true of course, and the details of that meeting are chronicled up front in John Kryk outstanding book Natural Enemies.

Kryk explains that the origins of the fateful meeting in South Bend over 125 years ago, can be attributed to three men: students George DeHaven, Billy Harless and Notre Dame's prefect Patrick 'Brother Paul' Connors.
In a nutshell, DeHaven and Harless were former Notre Dame students in the mid-1880s who, in 1886, enrolled at Michigan. Both were exceptional athletes and suited up for the U-M 1887 varsity football squad...aka Team 8. While at ND, DeHaven had become friendly with Brother Paul, who was a popular administrator on campus and helped run the intramural athletics program. Team 8

DeHaven and Harless (via the U-M Bentley Library)

In South Bend they did have an IM sport which was something like football...but not really. Kryk described it this way: "A hundred boys to a side, all scrambling to get a round ball over the opponent's fence by any means. Kick it, toss it; slap it – whatever. If you want to get technical it was part soccer and part rugby, but mostly it was pure pandemonium."

Michigan didn't play many actual games against opponents back in those days, but they had an appointment for a Thanksgiving Day trip to Chicago to face against Northwestern (FWIW before the game NW would cancel; U-M ended up playing a Chicago-area prep school). In mid-October DeHaven wrote to Connors, shared a few details about this awesome new game and let him know they'd be heading his direction in late November. The missive caught the attention of the sports-loving Brother Paul. Kryk explains what happened next:

Brother Paul wrote back to his friend at Michigan and asked if DeHaven and Harless could convince the Wolverines to make a stop at Notre Dame, on their way to Chicago, and teach some seniors this rugby brand of football. DeHaven said he'd try, and this morsel of hope thrilled the Notre Dame campus.

"If matters can be properly adjusted," the student newspaper, The Scholastic, announced on Oct. 29, "a match game of football will take place on the senior campus about the 27th of next month... The Ann Arbor boys hold the championship of the West, and are such fine players that they will probably contend with the leading Eastern teams next spring for the college championship of the United States. However, there is good material here for a fine team, and the boys will undoubtedly give the Michigan players a hard 'tussle.'

Eventually a date was set for a meeting and a game. Brother Paul snagged a copy of a football rule book a shared it with a group of seniors who tried, for the most part unsuccessfully, to get a handle on the new sport. Making a stop on their way to Chicago, Michigan arrived at Notre Dame on Wednesday November 23rd at around 9am. After a 2-hour campus tour the Michigan men tossed on their lily-white uniforms and readied for battle. Here's what happened next, as described in Natural Enemies:

At about 11 o'clock the elevens trotted onto the slop, which we can only assume was somehow marked to proper proportions. Before the players were set to have at it, Brother Paul informed DeHaven that the Notre Dame boys – several of them former classmates of DeHaven's and Harless's – had had trouble playing by the book. Brother Paul then suggested the teams at first be mixed for a brief period of hands-on instruction. The Wolverines agreed.

"So, we played gently with them that day," DeHaven recalled, "...and carefully taught Notre Dame how to play modern football."

When the Notre Dame players learned just how physical this brand was, they took to it with reckless abandon. Too reckless, actually. One student in attendance recalled DeHaven and company having to caution their eager pupils against playing too violently.

After this brief tutorial, the players segregated into their proper squads and played a 30-minute game. When both sides finished slipping, rolling, and tumbling in the mud, Michigan tallied two touchdowns (worth four points each) to win 8-0. It was said the Notre Dame players, as well as the students in attendance, appreciated the fact the Wolverines did not try to run it up on their disadvantaged hosts.

So, there you have it. Want this and more? Put Natural Enemies on your shelf.

Now, go impress your friends at your respective tailgates / viewing parties on Saturday night.

Chapter 4 ND Football – The No Coach Years

Year	Coach	Record
1887	No coach	0–1
1888	No coach	1–2
1889	No coach	1–0
1890	No team	
1891	No team	
1892	No coach	1–0–1
1893	No coach	4–1

Circa 1890 Notre Dame Football Team

1887: As noted in Chapter 3, Notre Dame's football program began in 1887 with an unofficial match against Michigan, a reasonably close team by geography. The ND team was guided by the older players as there was no coach.

Michigan is credited with coming to Notre Dame for the purpose of teaching Notre Dame how to play football. It was a most gracious act; most appreciated by Notre Dame, and highly enjoyed by Michigan. Not unexpectedly Michigan prevailed in the 30-minute contest L (0-8). The scoring was much different than today.

From the moment that Michigan appeared on the field with their spanking new white, almost glistening uniforms, they looked every part the champs that they were that year.

A great source of information about Notre Dame is the Notre Dame Encyclopedia, 4th Edition by Michael Steele. The following charts which show Steele's top ND player picks from the beginning through 1950 are as follows:

1887-1910:

Pos	Player	Size
LE	John Farley	5'9", 160
LT	Pat Beacom	6'2", 220
LG	George Philbrook	6'3", 225
C	John Eggeman	6'4", 256
RG	Rosy Dolan	5'11", 210
RT	Ralph Dimmick	6'0", 225
RE	Frank Lonergan	5'10", 168
QB	Nate Silver	5'8", 150
LHB	Red Miller	6'0", 175
RHB	Dom Callicrate	5'11", 160
FB	Red Salmon	5'10", 175
K	Red Salmon	

1911-1930:

Pos	Player	Size
LE	Knute Rockne	5'8", 165
LT	Frank Coughlin	6'3", 215
LG	Hunk Anderson	5'11", 170
C	Adam Walsh	6'0", 187
RG	Clipper Smith	5'10", 160
RT	Buck Shaw	6'0", 185
RE	Eddie Anderson	5'10", 163
QB	Harry Stuhldreher	5'7", 151
LHB	George Gipp	6'0", 180
RHB	Don Miller	5'11", 160
FB	Ray Eichenlaub	6'0", 210
K	George Gipp	

1931-1940:

LE	Wayne Millner	6'0", 184
LT	Moose Krause	6'3", 217
LG	John Lautar	6'1", 184
C	Jack Robinson	6'3", 200
RG	Joe Kuharich	6'0", 193
RT	Joe Kurth	6'2", 204
RE	Johnny Kelly	6'2", 190
QB	Wally Fromhart	5'11", 180
LHB	Marchy Schwartz	5'11", 167
RHB	Ray Brancheau	5'11", 190
FB	George Melinkovich	6'0", 180
K	Marchy Schwartz	

1941-1950:

LE	Jim Martin	6'2", 205
LT	George Connor	6'3", 225
LG	Bill Fischer	6'2", 230
C	Bill Walsh	6'3", 205
RG	Marty Wendell	5'11", 198
RT	Ziggy Czarobski	6'0", 213
RE	Leon Hart	6'4", 245
QB	Johnny Lujack	6'0", 180
LHB	Terry Brennan	6'0", 175
RHB	Creighton Miller	6'0", 185
FB	Emil Sitko	5'8", 180
K	Johnny Lujack	

In addition to most of these players, this book has many more Notre Dame greats from 1950 onward for you to peruse.

In 1887, football as we know it was not completely defined. Association football, rugby, and even soccer were all having a major influence at the time on the college football rules and game play. For its first seven years, the "fighting Irish" football team had no formal coach. In fact, the whole idea of Notre Dame Football was so tentative that there were two years, 1890, and 1891, which would have been Notre Dame's fourth and fifth seasons. However, they were unable to field a team.

Surprisingly, we have the results of those seasons though not much is known about the prowess and the fortunes of the players in the early no-coach teams.

1887 (0-1-0)
Michigan 8 Notre Dame 0   11-23-1987

LE *Frank Fehr   RE *James Maloney
LT *Patrick Nelson   QB *George Cartier
LG *Edward Sawkins   LH *Joe Cusack
C *George Houck   RH *Henry Luhn (Captain)
RG *Frank Springer   FB *Harry Jewett
RT *Tom O'Regan

1888: Record 1-2; without a coach, Notre Dame sported its own brand new uniforms of brown and black. In muddy terrain, it was hard to tell the players from the ground. That season, the ND team of young men cheered: "Rah, Rah, Rah, Nostra Domina!" They finished the season with two more losses to Michigan L (6-26); L (4-10). The Michigan weekend was special. Michigan looked forward to coming to Notre Dame from how well they had been treated the year before. Notre Dame was a tough team and had just one year of football in them when Michigan came back.

Michigan had kept all of its opponents scoreless until ND scored a total of ten points in two days. The reports of the day say that it was a badly battered team that landed in the crowded Ann Arbor, Michigan train depot coming back from its weekend with Notre Dame. The team "received a proper razzing for breaking a four-year record" No Michigan football team returned to play at Notre Dame until 1942.

The 1988 squad follows:

```
1888
(fall game with Harvard Prep School)
LE - *John Meagher      RE - *Joe Hepburn
LT - *Gene Melady       QB - *Ed Coady, Tom Coady
LG - *Edward Sawkins    LH - *Joe Cusack
C  - *Frank Fehr        RH - *Harry Jewett
RG - *Frank Springer    FB - *Edward Prudhomme (Captain)
RT - *Francis Mattes
```

First Football Victory Ever for ND

On Dec. 6, 1888, the Harvard School of Chicago football team arrived on Notre Dame's campus. More than 500 students and many South Bend residents came out to watch the contest in just the university's second year of gridiron competition.

Notre Dame managed to win its first game ever against a Harvard School located in Chicago. The Harvard line was no match for Notre Dame's players, who outweighed their opponent by an average of 23 pounds.

Halfback Harry Jewett and captain fullback E.C. Prudhomme helped Notre Dame to a win W (20-0). It was the first football victory in school history. Little did anyone know at the time, that this was the beginning of a storied football program. Since that day in December 1888, Notre Dame has won more than 860 football games.

ND Football Great:
Halfback Harry Jewett Painting

—FOOTBALL:—The football game between the Harvard school eleven of Chicago, champions of Illinois, and the University team was won by the latter by a score of 20 to 0. The visitors were active and played well, but could do no effective work on account of the heavy rush line of our men. Donnelly was the best player on the visiting team, while Fehr played a strong game for Notre Dame. The boys scored on three touch-downs, two goal kicks and two safety touch-downs. A more extended notice of the game will be given next week. In the meantime, three cheers for our Rugby team!

E.C. Prudhomme was a member of Notre Dame's Yosemite crew team, while also playing fullback and captaining the football squad.

John B. Meagher was listed as a "rusher" (offensive lineman) on the 1888 Notre Dame roster. He was from Mankato, Minn. and earned a Bachelor of Law in 1889.

The Birth of the Rock

Irishlegends.com says that something else of major proportion was going on far from the football field. In Voss, Norway, Mr. and Mrs. Lars K. Rockne had a new baby named Knute. We Notre Dame fans well know that Notre Dame Stadium of today is the "House that Rockne Built." Well, the house building actually began in Norway. In about 25 more years later in 1913, the "Rock" would be playing football for ND under Coach Jesse Harper.

E. Coady (left above) quarterbacked Notre Dame to its first win, a 20-0 victory over Harvard Prep. Coady was part of the Yosemite boat, along with teammate E.C. Prudhomme. J. Mattes, (right above) was a "rusher" for the 1888 Notre Dame team and also rowed for the university's Evangeline boat.

1889: It was tough getting games in those first five years. With tongue in cheek, however, we can proudly state that in its third season of an infancy program, Notre Dame experienced its first undefeated and untied season. It was 1889. Notre Dame managed to schedule one game that year and won it W (9-0) against Northwestern. The squad follows:

1889

```
LE - *Charles Flynn       RE - *Joe Hepburn, *Steve Flemming
LT - *James Fitzgibbons   QB - *Ed Coady
LG - *Tom Coady           LH - *Sydny Dickerson
C  - *Frank Fehr          RH - *Edward Prudhomme (Captain)
RG - *Tom McKeon          FB - *Dezera Cartier, Ch. Sanford
RT - *Stafford Campbell
```

1890, 1891: During the following two years, 1890, and 1891, no games were scheduled and none were played. Shorter than even the first season and the third, these two years brought Notre Dame its two shortest seasons of all time. In 1892, the ND team was back.

1892: Notre Dame came back in 1892 with one victory, one loss, and no ties. The restarting team again had no coach and played just two games. The scores of its games included a victory W (56-0) over South Bend High School on October 19, 1892, and a loss L (12-14) to Hillsdale College on November 24, 1892. It was so hard to get games with other colleges that ND would play high schools. Athletic clubs, and seemingly any group large enough to give them a game.

1892
```
LE - *Ed Linehan, John Cullen    RE - *Nicholas Dinkle,
*Pat Crawley
LT - *Fred Schillo               QB - *Pat Coady (Captain)
LG - *Ed Schaack, *Fr.Murphy     LH - *F. Keough, J.Henley
C  - *Charles Roby               RH - *Earl Brown,*J.Kearns
RG - *John Flannigan             FB - *M.Quinlan, McDermott
RT - *Ernest Du Brul
```

1893: Coach-less again, the 1893 Notre Dame football team played more games than ever. It was a successful season by any standard.

The 1892 team revived the game after a lapse of two years. Captain Pat Coady with the ball.

The team record was four wins and one loss (4-1). Moreover, Notre Dame had outscored its opponents in aggregate by 92 to 24.

The 1893 Fighting Irish, with almost double the number of players from 1892.
1893 Notre Dame Football Team Record 4-1

```
1893
LE - *John Cullen              RE - *Nicholas Dinkle
LT - *Fred Schillo             QB - *Charles Zeitler
LG - *Charles Roby, M.Kirby    LH - *Ernest Du Brul
C  - *John Flannigan           RH - *Fr. Keough Capt
                                    *John Barrett
RG - *Abraham (Abe) Chidester  FB - *Roger Sinnott,
                                    John Studebaker
RT - *Frank Hesse, Muessel
```

Its first four home victories were against Kalamazoo College W (34-0), Albion College W (8-6), DE LaSalle Institute W (28-0), and Hillsdale College (22-10). Then, on New Year's Day, 1894, Notre Dame traveled to Chicago. They played coach Amos Alonzo Stagg's Chicago Maroons. Stagg by the way was a member of the first All American team in 1899. The soon to be "Fighting Irish," lost this one to the Maroons, L (8–0). Hey, folks, it was Amos Alonzo Stagg's team!!!! Few teams in those days would come close to victory v Stagg's boys!

Chapter 7 ND Football – The Second Seven Years

Finally, ND had coaches and scheduled games

Year	Coach	Record
1894	J.L. Morison	3-1-1
1895	H.G. Hadden	3-1
1896	Frank E. Hering	4-3
1897	Frank E. Hering	4-1-1
1898	Frank E. Hering	4-2
1899	James McWeeney	6-3-1
1900	Pat O'Dea	6-3-1

An 1894 American Football Game

J. L. Morison ND Coach #1

Notre Dame was now established both within the institution and outside with other universities as an independent football school, ready to play a full season and ready to be successful.
The University upped the ante in 1894 by reaching into its finances to hire its first football coach.

 J. L. T. Morrison was hired in 1894 as the University of Notre Dame's first head football coach. He resigned at the end of the season to become coach of the Hillsdale College "Dales." Notice in the roster below that he was also a tackle on the team. More than likely, he was asked to donate more than his salary for the good of the institution. Just supposing!

Nonetheless, Notre Dame's 1894 football season was its first with a formal head coach. With Coach James L. Morison at the helm, the team record was a very respectable 3–1–1. Notre Dame had outscored its opponents by a total of 80 to 31. The team celebrated victories over Hillsdale College W (14-0), Wabash College W (30-0) and Rush Medical College W (18-6). The team also played two games against Albion College T (6-6). L (12-19) ending in one tie and one loss.

1894
```
LE- *Ed Brennan, John Murphy         RE- *Charles Zeitler,
                                          Jack Mullen
LT- *Jacob Rosy Rosenthal,J.Morison  QB- *Nicholas D. Morse
LG- *George Anson                    LH- *Clarence Corry,
                                          Oscar Schmidt
C - *Abraham (Abe) Chidester         RH- *Fr. Keough (Capt)
                                          John Barrett
RG- *Dan Casey                       FB- *John Dempsey,
                                          John Studebaker
RT- *Sidney Corby, Fred Schillo
```

1895 H.G. Hadden ND Coach # 2

1895
```
LE- *John Murphy, Jenaro Davila    RE- *Jack Mullen,
                                         Albert Galen
LT- *Will McCarthy, Frank Hesse    QB- *Bill Walsh
LG- *John Gallager,*Tom Cavanaugh  LH- *Lucian Wheeler
C-  *Jacob Rosy Rosenthal,Hadden   RH- *Bob Brown
RG- *Dan Casey Capt, R.Palmer      FB- *John Goeke
RT - *Ed Kelly, Charles Zeitler
```

In 1895, Coach H.G. Hadden took over from Coach Morison and handled the Notre Dame Football squad. Like Morison, Hadden lasted just one year. His team compiled a 3–1 record and overall did quite well, considering all the changes it was experiencing. ND outscored its opponents by 70 to 20. All games were at home in South Bend. The team played Northwestern Law School W (20-0); the Illinois Cycling Club W (18-2); and the Indianapolis Light

Artillery L (0-18), and the College of Physicians & Surgeons of Chicago W (32-0). The only loss was in the third game to the Indianapolis Light Artillery.

1896 Frank E. Hering ND Coach # 3

Finally, with the 1896 team, Notre Dame had found a coach who would stay more than just one year. To do this, the university promised the coaching job to Frank E. Hering, who was also a player (QB) on the team. But, he was a bona fide coach—even paid for coaching.

In 1896, he became the team's captain and coach. ND compiled a 4–3 record. In the process, it shut out four opponents, and outscored its opponents by a total of 182 to 50. All of its games were played on the campus of Notre Dame.

1896
```
LE- *John Murphy, Sidney Corby      RE- *Jack Mullen
LT- *F. Schillo, Charles Moritz     QB- *Fran Hering Capt
                                        James Taylor
LG- *Jacob (Rosy) Rosenthal         LH- *Bob Brown,
                                        Angus McDonald
C-  *Bill Fagan, George Lins        RH- *Mike Daly,
                                        R.Palmer, F.Lyon
RG- *Tom Cavanaugh                  FB- *Bill Kegler,
                                        Francis O'Hara
RT- *Frank Hanley, Frank Hesse
```

ND Football Team with names, 1896. .Reardon, Bill Monahan, Agnus McDonald, John Murphy, Francis Lyons, Francis O'Hara, Trainer Housler, Jack I. Mullen (at left on one knee), Frank Hanley, Tom Cavanaugh, Bill Fagan, Jacob (Rosy) Rosenthal, Charles H. Moritz, John C. Murphy, Mike Daly, Bill Kegler, Captain Frank Hering (center with ball), Bob Brown, Fred Schillo—Image from the University of Notre Dame Archives.

On the way to its successful season, the team beat South Bend Athletic Club W (46–0), Albion College W (24–0), W Highland Views (82–0), and Beloit College W (8–0). It also lost three games to the College of Physicians & Surgeons W (0–4), Chicago L (0–18), and Purdue L (22–28).

1897 Frank Hering

1897

```
LE- *John Farley, Waldo Healy      RE- *Jack Mullen
    (Captain), Edward Littig
LT- *Charles Niezer                QB- *Fred Waters,
                                        David Naughton
LG- *George Lins, Joe Murray       LH - *Mike Daly,
                                        John Fennessey,
C-  *John Eggeman, Sera. Bouwens
```

With former captain and Coach Frank E Hering again at the helm, the 1897 Notre Dame football team enjoyed its second season with Frank E. Hering as coach. The ND squad compiled a 4–1–1 record by shutting out four opponents, tying another and getting a real dousing from Chicago. The team did well in scoring. In fact, ND outscored all opponents by a combined total of 165 to 40.

ND defeated DePauw University W (4–0), Chicago Dental Infirmary W (62–0), St. Viator College W (60–0), and Michigan Agricultural College W (34–6). Notre Dame also tied Rush Medical College T (0–0), and lost handily to the University of Chicago L (5–34). Every year it seemed at least one team would appear on the schedule that made it difficult for ND to finish the season undefeated.

1898 Frank Hering

In 1898, for the third year in a row, Coach Frank E Hering took the Notre Dame team to a successful season. His team compiled a 4–2 record. In so doing the squad shut out four opponents, and outscored all opponents by a whopping total of 155 to 34.

The teams defeated included Illinois W (5–0), DePauw W (32–0), Michigan Agricultural W (53–0), and Albion W (60–0). Notre Dame was again playing Michigan and did not fare too bad in a 0–23 loss. ND also was defeated by Indiana L (5–11). In many ways, we see the beginning of the Big Ten teams playing Notre Dame. It had been some time since Notre Dame had played Michigan but things were about to change.

1898
```
LE- *John Farley, Art Hayes     RE- *Jack Mullen (Captain)
LT- *Mike McNulty,John Donahue  QB- *Charles Fleming,
                                    *Angus McDonald
LG- *Anson Bennett              LH - *George Kuppler
C-   *John Eggeman,*Frank Winter RH - *George Lins,
                                     Peter Lennon
RG- *Joe Murray                 FB - *Bill Monahan
RT- *Al Fortin
```

Great Player: John Eggeman, C, 1897-1899

One of the finest centers in ND football was John Eggeman. He played varsity for three years from 1897 through 1899 and was one heck of a tough center. Eggeman is on a lot of pundit's all-time best teams. He was unusually large for the times at 6'4" tall and 256 pounds. He was a force with which to be reckoned and bolstered the ND teams of the day.

1899 James McWeeney ND Coach # 4

Frank Hering coached ND for the first five games of **1899** when the Notre Dame Football team turned over to Coach James McWeeney for the rest of the season. McWeeney was known as being abrasive and it may have had its effect on the morale of the team.

He did fine but stayed just half of one year as coach. His team along with the games coached by Hering compiled a 6–3–1 record. This was the most wins ever for Notre Dame and the most games played by a Notre Dame squad to that point. Football surely had become for real at Notre Dame.

1899
```
LE - *John Farley, 5-9, 160
LT - *Earl Wagner, 5-9, 185; *Al Fortin, 5-11, 180
LG - *Mike McNulty, 6-0, 195
C  - *John Eggeman, 6-4, 256; *Frank Winter, 5-9, 210
RG - *Dom O'Malley, 5-11, 185
RT - *Frank Hanley, 5-8, 178; J.S. Schneider, 6-0, 180
RE - *Jack Mullen, 5-8, 155 (Captain)
QB - *Angus McDonald, 5-11, 170; Charles Fleming, 5-9, 145;
     Charles Daly, 5-7, 140
LH - *Art Hayes, 6-0, 164; *George Kuppler, 5-8, 160
RH - *Ralph Glynn, 5-10, 155; George Lins, 5-10, 178
FB - *Ernest Duncan, 5-10, 160; *Bill Monahan, 5-8, 150
```

In 1899, Notre Dame shut out five opponents, and outscored all opponents by a combined total of 169 to 55. They defeated Englewood High School, W (29-5), Lake Forest, W (38-0), Michigan Agricultural W (40–0), Indiana W (17–0), Rush W (17-0) and Northwestern W (12–0). They tied Purdue T (10–10), and lost to Amos Alonzo Stag's Chicago team L (6-23), Michigan L (0–12), and also the Chicago Physicians and Surgeons by L (0-5). The Michigan losses were by fewer and fewer scores. Soon Notre Dame was due to win a game from Michigan.

1900 Pat O'Dea ND Coach # 5

The 1900 Notre Dame football team was coached by first-year coach Pat O'Dea. McWeeney had signed up as assistant but his abrasive nature did not sit well with O'Dea and he did not last the full 1900 season. In its first season with Pat O'Dea as coach, ND compiled a 6–3–1 record. The squad shut out six opponents, and it outscored all opponents by a total of 261 to 73. The victories included Cincinnati W (58–0), Rush Medical College W (5–0), College of Physicians & Surgeons W (5–0).

1900
```
LE - *George Lins, 5-10, 178
LT - *Jim Faragher, 5-10, 190
LG - *Charles Gillen, 5-10, 170
C  - *Frank Winter, 5-9, 210; *John Pick, 6-0, 170
RG - *Clement Staudt, 5-11, 175; *Dom O'Malley, 5-11, 185
RT - *Al Fortin, 5-11, 180; Joe (Jepers) Cullinan, 5-10, 175
RE - *Art Hayes, 6-0, 164
QB - *Clarence Diebold, 5-8, 155; *H.(Fuzzy) McGlew, 5-7, 155
LH - *Louis (Red) Salmon, 5-10, 165
RH - *George Kuppler, 5-8, 160
FB - *John Farley, 5-9, 160 (Captain); *R. Glynn, 5-10, 155
```

Additionally, the Fighting Irish tied Beloit T (6–6), and lost to Indiana L (0–6), Wisconsin L (0–54), and Michigan L (0–7). The Michigan victories were closer and closer to becoming wins for Notre Dame.

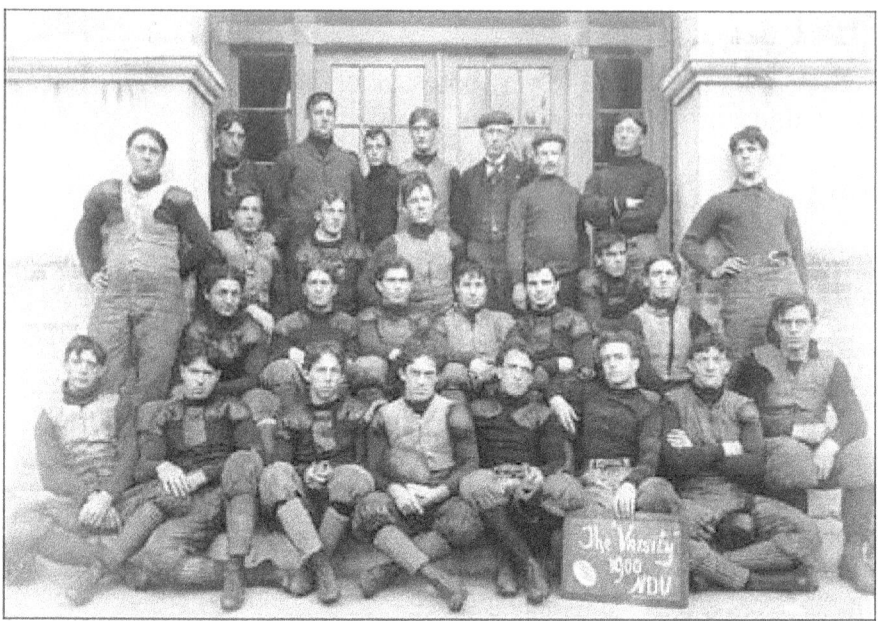
Notre Dame 1900 Football Team

John Pop Farley, CSC (Priest) ND Team Captain 1900

Great Player: John "Pop" Farley, FB, 1897-1900

John "Pop" Farley arrived to Notre Dame in the fall of 1897. He came to study for the priesthood, but also had a penchant for athletics. He won nine varsity monogram letters in football, baseball, and track, and was heralded as one of the great Notre Dame athletes for years to come. For over thirty years after his graduation, Farley became a beloved fixture among Notre Dame students as he served as a rector for three dorms.

In August of 1899, Farley wrote to University President Rev. Andrew Morrissey, CSC, with a dilemma — return to Notre Dame and continue his studies toward becoming a priest or attend Seton Hall, which was closer to home so he could better care for his mother and family [UPEL 75/11]. Morrissey's response does not exist in the University Archives, but Farley decided to return and ended up spending most of the rest of his life at Notre Dame.

Chapter 8 First Twelve ND Football Seasons of the 20th Century

1901	Pat O'Dea	8-1-1
1902	James Farragher	6-2-1
1903	James Farragher	8-0-1
1904	Louis Salmon	5-3
1905	Henry J. McGlew	5-4
1906	Thomas Barry	6-1
1907	Thomas Barry	6-0-1
1908	Victor M. Place	8-1
1909	Frank Longman	7-0-1
1910	Frank Longman	4-1-1
1911	John L. Marks	6-0-2
1912	John L. Marks	7-0

1903 Notre Dame football team- The Shutout Season

1901 – A Championship Season for Sure

Coach Pat O'Dea's Notre Dame Team was even stronger in his second year as coach. The 1901 Football season was a real championship season for the ND team. Notre Dame compiled an 8-1-1 record while shutting out six opponents. The team outscored all opponents by a total of 145 to 19. Highlights of the season included a victory over Purdue W (12-6), Indiana W (18-5), and College of

Physicians & Surgeons W (34–0). The team also tied the South Bend Athletic Club Y (0–0), and lost to Northwestern L (0–2).

1901

```
LE - *George Lins, 5-10, 175; Frank (Shag) Shaughnessy, 6-0,
175
LT - *Jim Faragher, 5-10, 190; Joe  (Jepers) Cullinan, 5-10,
175
LG - *Ed Piel, 5-10, 180; Charles Gillen, 5-10, 185
C  - *John Pick, 6-0, 170
RG - *Frank Winter, 5-9, 220
RT - *Al Fortin, 5-11, 180 (Captain)
RE - *Frank (Happy) Lonergan, 5-10, 168;
QB - *Henry (Fuzzy) McGlew, 5-7, 155; *George Nyere, 5-10,
165
LH - *Jim Doar, 5-11, 180; Harold Davitt
RH - *Harley Kirby, 5-11, 185; Charles Coleman, 5-8, 161
FB - *Louis (Red) Salmon, 5-10, 165; Francis Brent
```

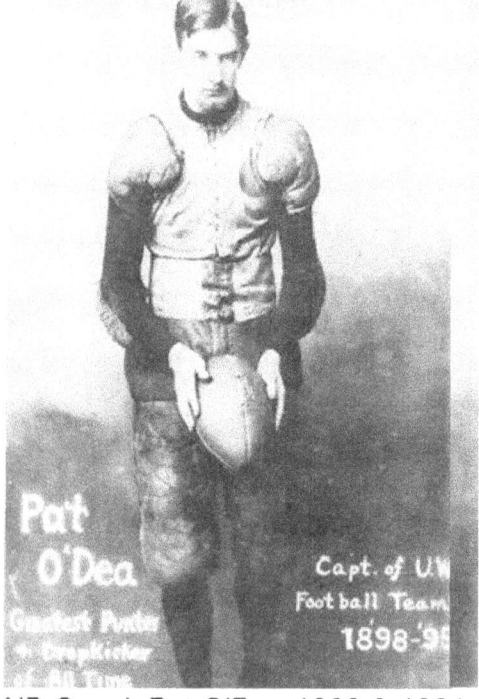

ND Coach Pat O'Dea 1900 & 1901

Though this was not a national championship as this honor would not come until the 1924 season, it was the year (1901) for the most significant Fighting Irish team honor to this point. With an earlier win over Purdue, the Irish clinched the Indiana State Crown with an 18-5 impressive victory against the Hoosiers.

This was a real big deal for the team and the history of Notre Dame Football. In 1901, the Scholastic a great publication of and by Students at Notre Dame began to take a deep interest in football and their reporting over time has been excellent. Please enjoy the following excerpt, written by J. Patrick O'Reilly. It was originally published in the Nov. 23, 1901 issue of Scholastic, the Notre Dame University student magazine.

"Nine rahs for Coach O'Dea, Captain Fortin, and the moleskin heroes who struggled so nobly for the Gold and Blue; and on last Saturday won for us the championship of Indiana. For the first time in years, the much-mooted question of supremacy among the Indiana colleges has been satisfactorily settled, Notre Dame winning a clear title by defeating both Purdue and Indiana. The "Big Three" fight aroused great enthusiasm, and the race for the title was closely followed by every football enthusiast in the State.

"Despite the drizzling rain which had fallen all morning, the field was in the best of shape. The two elevens were in splendid condition; about equally matched in weight, and both determined to win. The crowd was one of the largest and most enthusiastic of the year, and the rooting was of a high order. All in all, every requisite for a good game was present.

"The game was one of the fiercest and cleanest ever seen on Cartier Field. There was no unnecessary roughness, and although every inch of ground was desperately contested, the officials were obliged to inflict penalties but twice. On the defensive, the State representatives displayed a stubborn resistance, but they were unable to impede the progress of our speedy backs, and their offensive tactics availed nothing against our impregnable line and alert ends, never retaining the ball longer than two or three downs. Their only touchdown was in the nature of a fluke, Foster securing the ball on a fumble during a scrimmage, and sprinting thirty yards to Notre Dame's goal while our men were extricating themselves from the heap. In marked contrast to Indiana's poor work was the brilliant defense and offense of our men. The linemen charged well and several times broke through and stopped plays behind the line. Sammon, Doran, Kirby and McGlew were irresistible on the offensive.

"Sammon won new laurels by his sensational fifty-five-yard run through a crowded field. His line-bucking and punting were very much in evidence all through the game, and he established himself as a hero with the rooters, but he was not the only one. Pick's fearless tackling and work at center; McGlew's clever interfering and accurate passing, and the superb defense of the linemen. Gillen, Farragher, Winter and Capt. Fortin made the hearts of the rooters dance with joy. Doran and Kriby crashed and plunged through and round Indiana's line, making five and ten yards on every attempt, while their work on interference was the best of the season. Lins, Lonergan and Nyere, at the ends, were down the field on every punt and generally nailed the main in his tracks. Foster, Clevenger and Elfers were Indiana's stars. Clevenger and Foster tackled well and were in every play and under every rush."

1902 & 1903 James Farragher Coach # 6

First year Coach James Farragher took over the coaching duties for the 1902 Notre Dame football season. In his first season, Farragher's team went 6–2–1 and outscored all opponents by a total of 203 to 51. In compiling its 6-2-1 record, the team defeated Michigan Agricultural W (33–0), Indiana W (11–5), and DePauw W (22–0), and it enjoyed three other victories. Notre Dame tied Purdue (6–6), and lost to Michigan L (0–23) and Knox L (5–12).

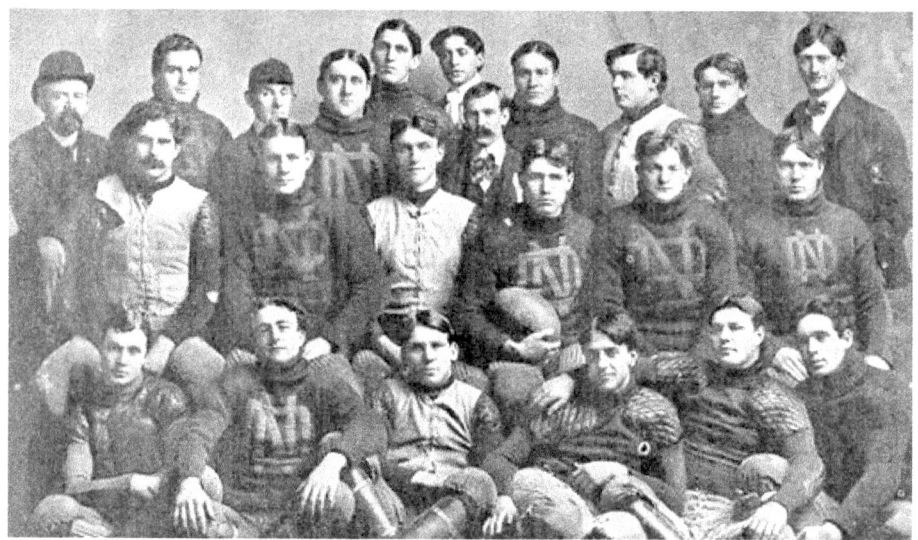

1902 ND Football Team

1902
```
LE - *Frank (Shag) Shaughnessy, 6-0, 178
LT - *Joe (Jepers) Cullinan, 5-10, 177; *Mike Fansler, 6-1,
175
LG - *Charles Gillen, 5-10, 185; Dan O'Connor, 5-11, 165
C  - *Art Steiner, 5-8, 175
RG - *Don O'Malley, 5-11, 185; *Nick Furlong, 5-9, 160
RT - *Bill Desmond, 5-11, 165
RE - *Frank (Happy) Lonergan, 5-10, 168
QB - *Henry (Fuzzy) McGlew, 5-8, 160; *Nate Silver, 5-8, 150
LH - *Jim Doar, 5-11, 185; *George Nyere, 5-10, 165; Harley
Kirby, 5-11, 185
RH - *Ed McDermott, 5-10, 170; Art Funk, 5-9, 170
FB - *Louis (Red) Salmon, 5-10, 175 (Captain)
```

1903 Fighting Irish

In his second year as coach, Farragher's 1903 Notre Dame Football team had a great year with an 8–0–1 record. The Fighting Irish were at their best and they shut out every opponent, and outscored all opponents by a combined total of 291 to 0. Along the way, the team defeated Michigan State W (12-0), Lake Forest W (28-0), DePauw W (56-0), American Medical W (52-0), Chicago Physicians & Surgeons, W (46-0), Missouri Osteopaths W (28-0) Ohio Medical University W (35-0), and Wabash W (34-0).

Notre Dame also played Northwestern to a scoreless tie T (0-0). The defense was obviously at its best the whole season. The offense was led by Louis "Red" Salmon and Frank Shaughnessy with a massive 291 points scored. The following year "Red" Salmon would take over as coach for just one year

1903

```
LE - *Henry (Fuzzy) McGlew, 5-8, 160; *Larry McNerny, 5-10,
170
LT - *Joe (Jepers) Cullinan, 5-10, 177;  Mike Fansler, 6-1,
175
LG - *Pat Beacom, 6-2, 215; *Dick (Smoush) Donovan, 6-0, 185
C  - *Clarence Sheehan, 5-10, 180
RG - *Nick Furlong, 5-9, 160; *John O'Phelan, 6-0, 165
RT - *Art Steiner, 5-8, 175; Tom Healy, 5-10, 200
RE - *Frank (Shag) Shaughnessy, 6-0, 178
QB - *Nate Silver, 5-8, 150
LH - *George Nyere, 5-10, 165; Ed McDermott, 5-10, 170; Dan
Dillon
RH - *Frank (Happy) Lonergan, 5-10, 168; *Bill Draper, 6-1,
170
FB - *Louis (Red) Salmon, 6-3, 230 (Captain); Art Funk, 5-9,
170
```

Great Player Red Salmon, fullback 1901-1903.

Red Salmon predated both Rockne and Gipp, but started something by being Notre Dame's first All-American. Salmon was immense for his day at 6'3" and 230 pounds. But he was skilled as well and racked up 35 touchdowns during his Notre Dame career, a record which stood for 82 years before succumbing to Allen Pinkett in 1985.

"The alabaster skinned Salmon has been described as both a smasher and a slasher who would run right over you if he could not run around you."
Platoon football was an idea whose time had not yet come.

Red Salmon played both ways. Salmon was a mauler on the defensive front and in '03, as in 1903, he also keyed the defense for the 8-0-1 Irish who allowed only 10 points the entire season.

He was ND's first All-American making the Walter Camp first team in 1903.
Salmon was inducted into the College Football Hall of Fame in 1971. He began to coach at Notre Dame the following year.

1904 Louis "Red" Salmon Coach # 7

In his first and only year as Notre Dame coach, Louis "Red" Salmon took the 1904 Notre Dame football team to a 5–3 record.

Louis J. Salmon

It was not one of the best seasons for Notre Dame and their new coach.

They were outscored by opponents by a combined total of 127 to 94. They had some good moments during the season when the team defeated Wabash W (12–4), Ohio Medical W (17–5), and DePauw W (10–0). However, they lost to Wisconsin (0–58), Kansas (5–24), and Purdue (0–36).

1904
```
LE - *Larry McNerny, 5-10, 170; Walter Keefe, 5-9, 150
LT - *Art Funk, 5-8, 175; Eugene Clear; John O'Neil
LG - *Pat Beacom, 6-2, 220
C  - *Dan Murphy, 5-11, 175; Clarence Sheehan, 5-10, 180
RG - *Dick (Smoush) Donovan, 6-0, 190
RT - *Mike Fansler, 6-1, 175; Tom Healy, 5-10, 200
RE - *Frank (Shag) Shaughnessy, 6-0, 178 (Captain)
QB - *Nate Silver, 5-8, 150; Dick Coad, 5-7, 155
LH - *Rufus Waldorf, 5-11, 170; *Durant Church, 5-10, 165
RH - *Bob Braken, 6-1, 165; *Dave Guthrie, 6-0, 175
FB - *Bill Draper, 6-1, 175
```

Great Player: Frank Lonergan, RE, 1902-1904

End: Frank "Happy" Lonergan was a great end though for today at 5' 10", he would not have considered tall. He played on some great teams from 1902 through 1904 and was a mainstay of the ND Offense.

Great Player: Patrick A. Beacom, G, 1903-1905

Captain Patrick A. Beacom was a standout guard on this team. He ended his football career from 1903 to 1905 at Notre Dame after three years of brilliant work. He was a tower of strength on offense and defense; he was never-tired. He never took out time, played in every game since he has been here, and was always the same old Pat in the same old way.

He has been the mainstay of. the team for. three years, and the, hole that will be made: by his absence will-be the hardest one on the team to fill. To say that Captain Beacom is the best line man Notre Dame ever had; is saying much, but; with impunity—it may be said that Beacom is the best in his position that has ever been put there; and is one of the best linemen in the country.

1905 Henry J. McGlew Coach # 8

The 1905 Notre Dame Football team was coached by Henry J. McGlew. The team compiled a 5–4 record and despite its mediocre record, Notre Dame outscored its opponents by a combined total of 312 to 80. The Fighting Irish defeated Michigan Agricultural W (28–0), American Medical W (142–0), and DePauw W (71–0), but lost to Wisconsin L (0–21), Indiana L (5–22), and Purdue L (0–32).

1905
LE – *Dom Callicrate, 5-11, 158
LT – *Art Funk, 5-8, 175; Frank Munson, 6-0, 200
LG – *Pat Beacom, 6-2, 220 (Captain)
C – *Clarence Sheehan, 6-0, 190; Tom Healy, 5-10, 200
RG – *Dick (Smoush) Donovan, 6-0, 200
RT – *Morris Downs, 5-10, 185
RE – *Tom McAvoy, 5-10, 160
QB – *Nate Silver, 5-8, 150; *Larry McNerny, 5-10, 175
LH – *Bob Bracken, 5-11, 165; *Rufus Waldorf, 5-11, 170; Tom Joyce, 5-10, 180
RH – *Bill Draper, 6-1, 180; John Brogan, 5-9, 160
FB - *Bill Downs, 5-10, 190

The American Medical game was on Oct. 28, 1905. Notre Dame turned in its greatest offensive performance of all-time, defeating

American College of Medicine and Surgery of Chicago, 142-0. The Fighting Irish scored 27 touchdowns, and the game was called after 33 minutes of play, meaning the offense averaged 4.3 points per minute.

Great Player: Nate Silver, QB, 1903-1905. (No picture available)

Nathan Silver graduated from North Division High School in Chicago, Illinois. He holds the distinction of being the first player to hold the starting quarterback job at The University of Notre Dame for three consecutive years, from 1903-1905.

He was also one of the first Jewish athletes to compete at the traditionally Catholic university, and was described as having exceptionally quick feet and being "slippery".

Led by Silver, the Irish achieved their first-ever undefeated season with more than one game, in 1903, outscoring their opponents by a combined total of 292-0 for a final record of 8-0-1. The combined record over the next two seasons would be a more modest 10-7.

However, the 1905 season would include the most lopsided victory ever by a Notre Dame team: a 142-0 win over the American College of Medicine and Surgery, in which Silver's touchdowns included a 40-yard run and an 80-yard kickoff return. The margin likely would have been much larger had the game not been called after just thirty-three minutes of play. [Facts from Wikipedia]

1906-07 Thomas Barry Coach # 9

1906
```
LE - *Oscar Hutzell, 5-10, 180; *Ben Berve, 6-1, 190; Henry
     Burdick, 6-0, 185
LT - *Pat Beacom, 6-2, 220
LG - *Fred Eggeman, 6-1, 220; Nick Doyle, 6-2, 185;
      Bob (Smousherette) Donovan, 6-3, 235
C  - *Clarence Sheehan, 6-0, 190; Al Mertes, 5-10, 180
RG - *Frank Munson, 6-0, 200; Art Henning, 5-10, 180
RT - *Sam (Rosey) Dolan, 5-11, 210
```

```
RE  -  *Ray Scanlan, 5-11, 180; Mike Moriarity, 5-11, 175;
Leroy Keach, 5-10, 175
QB  -  *Bob Bracken, 5-11, 170 (Captain);Alan Dwan, 5-10,165
165; John (Doc) Berteling, 5-9, 155
LH  -  *Harry (Red) Miller, 6-0, 168; Walter Keefe, 5-11, 175;
       Bill Schmitt, 5-11, 165
RH  -  *Dom Callicrate, 5-11, 158; *Rufus Waldorf, 5-11, 170
FB  -  *John Diener, 5-10, 195; *Joe Lantry, 5-11, 195; Ed
O'Flynn, 5-10, 185
```

1907

```
LE  -  *Frank Munson, 6-0, 200; *Henry Burdick, 6-0, 185
LT  -  *Chet Freeze, 6-2, 195; John Burke
LG  -  *Ed Lynch, 5-10, 200; James Ditton, 5-10, 180
C   -  *Al Mertes, 5-10, 180; Art Henning, 5-10, 180
RG  -  *Bob Paine, 5-11, 200; Harry Hague, 5-10, 185
RT  -  *Sam (Rosey) Dolan, 5-11, 210; Bill Dugan, 5-11, 180
RE  -  *Fay Wood, 6-0, 180; John Diener, 5-10, 195
QB  -  *Billy Ryan, 5-9, 160; John (Doc) Berteling, 5-9, 155
LH  -  *Harry (Red) Miller, 6-0, 171; John Duffy, 6-0, 190;
       Clarence Cripe, 5-9, 160
RH  -  *Dom Callicrate, 5-11, 160; Bill Schmitt, 5-11, 165;
Jacob Young
FB  -  *Paul McDonald, 6-0, 180; James O'Leary, 6-0, 175
```

The 1906 Notre Dame football team was coached by another first-year coach, Thomas Barry. Barry coached the team to a 6-1 record with wins against Franklin W (26–0), Hillsdale W (17-0), Chicago Physicians & Surgeons W (28–0), Michigan Agricultural W (5–0), Purdue W (2-0), and Beloit W (29-0). Additionally, ND was defeated by Indiana L (0–12)

Great Player: Samuel "Rosey" Dolan, RG.

Samuel Rosey Dolan played football at Notre Dame from 1906 to 1909. While at Notre Dame, Dolan was a four-year starter a right guard. In his four seasons as a player, the Fighting Irish were 27–2–2.[1] Dolan also attended school at Oregon Agricultural College in 1909, however did not play football for OAC

Great Player: Dominic Callicrate RHB 1907

(from Scholastic – picture below)

CAPTAIN CALLICRATE.

On Thanksgiving Day, the football season of 1907 passed into Notre Dame football history as one of the many successful years on the gridiron. Early in the fall things looked bad for the Varsity, and the prospects for a good team were anything but bright. But Coach Barry and Captain Callicrate set to work with what, they had, and gradually a team was developed that Notre Dame may be proud of.

Little by little the team improved; game after game they played stronger, until the first game of the Indiana championship was -played in Indianapolis against Indiana. The most loyal Notre Dame rooter dared not do more than hope for victory; and when the Varsity played last year's champions to a standstill, holding Indiana to a nothing to nothing score, the hard work of Coach Barry and Captain Callicrate, received its reward.

The next big game came with Purdue, and for the first time in several years Notre Dame gave the Boilermakers a good clean trouncing, winning the game by the score of 17 to 0. The season ended with St. Vincent's College of Chicago, and Notre Dame finished the year without having lost one game, tying two and winning six, having scored a total of 137 points to 20.

A large amount of credit for the showing made by the team this season must go to Coach Barry, for, as was said before, the material on hand when the season opened was about the poorest Notre Dame ever offered a football coach. Not that the men individually were incapable, for taken separately the men were good; but instead of a division of weight, making a line and backfield possible, nearly every man on the squad was underweight for a lineman, and those who had the weight had had little or no experience.

For the backfield, there was a wealth of material, including such men as Captain Callicrate and Miller of last year's Varsity. Speaking of Miller reminds us of another display of Coach Barry's football sense. For when things were going from bad to worse about the middle of the season Barry took Miller from the backfield and put him in at center, a position he had never played in his life; in fact, he had never played any place but in the backfield.

By nearly every critic in the State, Miller was picked as an all-Indiana center, which must prove but one thing: that in Coach Barry lay the brains that made Notre Dame's winning team a possibility. Then, too, the many chances that the team underwent, especially in the line, displayed Barry's prowess.

Munson was used at every position in the line during the past season. Starting him at center, Barry was compelled to move him to guard when "Nick" Doyle left school. He went from there to tackle, and finally landed on end, and on defense backing up the line.

Passing, it might be well to mention that in every position Munson put up a good game and was one of the most valuable men on the team. The season, as a whole, was a grand success; it is to be regretted that the Indiana championship did not come to Notre Dame, but that it went to no one else is a consolation. Notre Dame has an equal claim to it with Indiana, arid is content to wait for another year that they may try again to land the championship at Notre Dame. Captain Callicrate proved to be worthy of the honor bestowed upon him when he was elected captain.

A harder worker Notre Dame never had, and a cleaner, better football player would be hard to find. The many duties connected with the captaincy of the team affected Callicrate's playing early in the season, but in the three big games he was back in form, and played the game that has made for him the reputation of the best half-back in the state of Indiana this season. Callicrate's work in the Purdue game was as-fine an exhibition of football playing as anyone might ask to see. With his teammates, his word was s law, and every member of the team will remember the man who captained Notre Dame's football team in 1907 as a hard worker, a brilliant and clean football player.

In commenting on the season. Coach, and Captain, let us not forget the scrubs. As the man behind the gun is the soldier, so it is with the scrubs; for it is the scrubs behind the team that make a good team possible. Enough credit is never given the scrub, the man who day after day takes his bumps along with the regular, often-times taking more than the regular, for the star must be saved for the game.

With nothing to win individually, as a regular, who has a chance for a reputation and a name, the scrub plods along through the season filling in any place he is asked to go, working as hard, training as hard and remaining as lo3'al as the best man. on the team; to him every college man owes a debt, for without him no school can turn out a football team.

And so, we say to such men as Dugan, Beckman, Hague, Ditton, Diener, Duffy, Schmitt, Dionne, Murphy, Dillon, Boyle, Sprenger and Keefe, it is because of such as you that Notre Dame had a winning football team, and every student at Notre Dame returns to you, sincere thanks and gratitude.

Of this season's team, we will lose but two men, Capt. Callicrate and Munson. Both men graduate in June, and although both good men, whose loss will be keenly felt, the chances for next year's team are the brightest that we have had in years.

Such men as Dugan, Duffy, Schmitt, Dionne, Dillon, Boyle and a number of other men on the second team, will be Varsity caliber by next season, and Notre Dame should have one of the best teams in the history of the school.

Following is a complete list of games played this year:
Oct. 12—Notre Dame, 32 ; P. and S., 0.
Oct. 19—Notre Dame, 23 ; Franklin, 0.
Oct. 26—Notre Dame, 22 ; Olivet, 4.
Nov. 2—-Notre Dame, 0; Indiana, 0.
Nov. 9—Notre Dame, 22 ; Knox, 4.
Nov. 15—Notre Dame, 0; Alumni, 0.
Nov. 23—Notre Dame, 17 ; Purdue, 0.
Nov. 28—Notre Dame, 21 ; St. Vincent's, 12.

Written for Scholastic: R. L. Bracken,. '08.

This season was the first played under the authority of the IAAUS (now known as the NCAA) and the first in which the forward pass was permitted. There were no national champions declared. Though two teams that had won all nine of their games -- the Princeton Tigers and the Yale Bulldogs were looked upon as the best. The Tigers and Bulldogs played to a T (0-0) tie to end the season.

Thomas Barry again coached Notre Dame in the 1907 Notre Dame College football season. The team won six games again; had no losses and one tie. The wins were against Chicago Physicians & Surgeons W (32–0), Franklin W (23–0), Olivet, W (22–4), Knox W (22–4), Purdue W (17-0), St. Vincent's, W (21-12). The team also played a tie game against Indiana, T (0-0).

Deadly Injuries was of deep concern to the IAAUS. In 1907, the forward pass was used more extensively after being legalized the year before. Despite what some called "debrutalization" reforms, an unprecedented eleven players were killed (9 high school and 2 college). Ninety-Eight others were seriously injured. Yale had the best record that year (10-0-1). Again, no clear national champion was named.

There was already concern that every man was not good enough to start every football game for Notre Dame. And so, in the December 2006 Scholastic, this tribute was written:

T h e Scrubs.

T H E crowd cheers loud for the regulars,
>   Who have made the Varsity team,
For the men who have swept the football field
>   And stood in the limelight's gleam,
But little it knows of the silent men,
>   Of the lads who take the rubs,
Who work their best to advance the team—
>   Hurrah! for the Varsity scrubs!

The regular man feels well repaid,
>   When he hears the voices true
Of a thousand lusty college lads,
>   Who cheer for the Gold and Blue
But they show a love that is deep at heart,
>   The men who fight like cubs,
When there's no return. And it's ours to shout,
>   "Hurrah! for the Varsity scrubs."

T. E. B.

1908 Victor M. Place Coach # 10

Victor M. Place became coach of ND in 1908 and directed the team to an 8-1 highly successful football season. Notre dame secured victories against Hillsdale W (39-0), Franklin W (64-0), Chicago Physicians & Surgeons W (88-0), Ohio Northern W (58-4), Indiana W (11-0), Wabash W (8-4), St. Viator W (46-0), and Marquette W (6-0). Always having trouble with rival Michigan, Notre Dame lost the game L (6-12).

1908

```
LE - *Lee Matthews, 5-10, 170; *Jim Maloney, 5-9, 160; Henry
Burdick, 6-0, 190
LT - *Luke Kelly, 5-9, 185; *Howard (Cap) Edwards, 6-0, 195
LG - *Ed Lynch, 5-10, 200; George Philbrook, 6-3, 225; Bob
Paine, 5-11, 200
C  - *Al Mertes, 5-10, 180; *Tom Sullivan, 6-0, 205
RG - *Sam (Rosey) Dolan, 5-11, 210; *John Duffy, 6-0, 190;
     Chet Freeze, 6-2, 195
RT - *Ralph Dimmick, 6-0, 225; Jon Diener, 5-10, 195
RE - *Joe Collins, 6-0, 185; *Fay Wood, 6-0, 185; John
Murphy, 6-0, 170
QB - *Don Hamilton, 5-10, 175; *Pete Dwyer, 5-10, 170
LH - *Harry (Red) Miller, 6-0, 175 (Captain); *Paul McDonald,
6-0, 180
RH - *Ulric Ruell, 5-9, 170; Billy Ryan, 5-9, 160
FB - *Pete Vaughn, 6-0, 195; Bill Schmitt, 5-11, 165;
B.Clement, 5-8, 160
Reserves
E - Bert Daniel, John Kennedy, Mike Moriarity, Jesse Roth;
G - Art Henning; C - Garunde;
QB - Frank Binz, Lawrence Reynolds; HB - Walter Clinnen,
Louis Dionne
```

The Penn Quakers and the Harvard Crimson both finished the season unbeaten, each with a tie. The LSU Tigers went unbeaten and untied against weaker opposition. Nonetheless all three teams were declared national champions retroactively by various organizations. Only Pennsylvania's Quakers officially claims a true national championship for the 1908 season.

Great Player Harry "Red" Miller, Left Halfback

Red was the Irish's 1908 team captain. Four of his relatives also played at Notre Dame, including Don Miller, one of the fabled Four Horsemen, and Ray T. Miller, who later became mayor of Cleveland.

CAPTAIN MILLER.

CAPTAIN MILLER (Half-Back) proved to be a worthy successor of Callicrate, the 1907 Captain, not only as captain but as a valuable man in the backfield where he appeared most of the season. He put up a star game at center in the Michigan game, but was shifted to his old position at left-half in the remaining contests, and continued to display the form that won him a place on the All Indiana team last in 1907.

He was seen at his best in the Indiana game, his thrilling end-runs and all-around ' work bringing frequent rounds of applause "from the stands, and this despite the fact that he was frequently laid out with injuries. He also did the bulk of the punting, and his kicks were always consistent and for good distance. His toe work against the wind in the first half of the Marquette game put our goal out of danger time after time, and prevented the Wisconsinites from scoring. His brilliant playing again won him a berth on the All-Indiana team

----

In December, 1908, Notre Dame had been playing football for twenty-two years. The first mention of football in the Scholastic was in 1901, eight years prior. Nobody had taken the time to capture the full story of how football not only got its beginning with the kindness of the Michigan "lads," but also to how the sport had grown in prestige to the 1908 season. Joseph T. Lantry made up for that oversight in this wonderful short piece.

Note from President Theodore Roosevelt in ND Scholastic:
Athletic sports, if followed properly, and not elevated into a fetish, are admirable for developing character, besides bestowing upon the participants an invaluable fund of health and strength.
Theodore Roosevelt. North American Review, August, 1890.

1909 Frank Longman Coach # 11

Frank Longman

In 1909 Frank Longman took the coaching reins and directed Notre Dame to a 7-0-1 season. The Fighting Irish football team's wins were against the following teams: Olivet W (58-0), Rose Poly W (60-11), Michigan Agricultural W (17-0), Pittsburgh W (6-0), Michigan W (11-3), Miami of Ohio W (46-0) and Wabash, W (38-0). Notre dame also played Marquette at the end of the season to a 0-0 tie, spoiling the opportunity for a perfect untied, unbeaten season.

1909

```
LE - *Lee Mathews, 5-10, 170; *Jim Maloney, 5-9, 160
LT - *Howard (Cap) Edwards, 6-0, 195 (Captain)
LG - *George Philbrook, 6-3, 225; Ed (Cupid) Glynn, 5-11, 210
C  - *Ed Lynch, 5-10, 200; Joe Brenan, 6-0, 190
RG - *Sam (Rosey) Dolan, 5-11, 210; *Luke Kelly, 5-9, 185
RT - *Ralph Dimmick, 6-0, 225
RE - *Joe Collins, 6-0, 185; John Duffy, 6-0, 190
QB - *Don Hamilton, 5-10, 175; *Pete Dwyer, 5-10, 170
LH - *Harry (Red) Miller, 6-0, 175; *A.(Red) Kelly, 5-11, 170
RH - *Bill Schmitt, 5-11, 165; *Billy Ryan, 5-9, 160;
     Mike Moriarity, 5-11, 175
```
FB - *Pete Vaughan, 6-0, 195

Football Game Scene above page- ND vs. Wabash, 1909/1120. Offensive play including Harry (Red) Miller, William Schmitt, Joe Collins, George Philbrook, Al (Red) Kelly, Luke Kelly, Don Hamilton, Sam "Rosey" Dolan, Howard (Cap) Edwards, Ed Lynch..Image from the University of Notre Dame Archives.

During this 1909 IAAUS football season, the first 3-point field goal was kicked. They had previously been worth four points. Football deaths continued despite attempts to make the game safer.

1909 was one of the most dangerous seasons in the history of college football. Ten players were killed and 38 seriously injured in 1909. This was up from six fatalities and 14 "maimings," in 1909. Schools in the Midwest competed in the Western Conference became known as the Big Ten.

Notre Dame did not join. The teams at the time included Illinois, Indiana, Iowa, Minnesota, Northwestern, Purdue, Wisconsin and Chicago.

1910 Frank Longman Coach # 11

In 1910, Frank Longman continued as Notre Dame coach as the fighting Irish played a somewhat reduced schedule. Their record was 4-1-1 which included home victories at Olivet W (48-0), Buchtel W (51-0), and Ohio Northern W (47-0). The Irish also defeated Rose Poly W (41-3) in Terre Haute, IN, lost to Michigan Agricultural at East Lansing, MI L (0-17), and tied Marquette in Milwaukee W (5-5). In 1910, the association became known as the NCAA and again, there was no clear-cut champion in Division I football.

From the Notre Dame Scholastic Magazine, December 1910

The [1910] Season and the Men.
By ARTHUR HUGHES, II. {Athletic Editor, Scholastic).

> *The football season for the year 1910 was not as propitious as was the season of 1909... Last year Notre Dame closed the season Champions of the West. This year she failed in this respect. There were six games played. Out of this number were four victories, one tie game and one defeat. The defeat was suffered at the-hands of the Michigan Aggies. Marquette played us to a 5-5 tie on Thanksgiving Day and we vanquished Olivet, Buchtell, Rose Poly and Ohio Northern. Not a great amount of honor was won through our victories, for the teams defeated were vastly our inferiors in every way as the large*

scores indicate. In the Michigan Aggies' game at Lansing the team for some reason failed to play up to its standard, and as a result the M. A. C. men pla3'^ed havoc with ever}'- department of the Notre Dame representation. Michigan's cancellation of the Notre Dame game made it impossible for the team to show its strength and ability when playing in its usual form, for there is no doubt whatever but our men would have put forth a far better struggle than they did the week previous at Lansing. The men felt the sting which was administered by the Aggies, and they put in the following week working like demons in order to show their real strength at Ann Arbor. The game with Marquette brought out the ability and power of the team, for in that game ever)'- man in the line-up gave an exhibition which astonished the local fans and spectators at Milwaukee.

Last year the material for a championship team was a great deal more in evidence than was the case this season. While the men got out and fought hard for positions there were not the number of heavy, experienced men in the squad; and it is this that makes teams which get into the first page with their accomplishments. In addition to this, the absence of Billy Ryan and Don Hamilton proved a big factor in weakening the team. Had not Ryan's bad knee and Hamilton's being declared ineligible kept these men out of the game there might have been a different story to relate after the Michigan Aggies' contest. With the end came the close of the football careers of six men on the team: Joe Collins, Ralph Dimmick, George Philbrook, Lee Matthews, Luke Kelley, and John Duffy. The first five of these men were players on last year's team, and they have bade farewell to a branch of athletic sports in which they stood among the best.

Great Player: Ralph Dimmick, T, 1910

(Captain, Tackle). Ralph played throughout the season the same sure dependable game. The number of tackles in the country who can use their hands in offense in the manner of this giant player are few indeed. He was a sure man for a gain when given the ball, and his line plunges and tackle-around plays have brought him the reputation of being one of the greatest tackles in the collegiate world of sport.

Winners of Monograms, 1910

RALPH C. DIMICK
Captain and Tackle

Great Player: George Philbrook LG 1910.

George Philbrook was one of the finest ND players of all time. He played football and was a weight thrower at Notre Dame, and later for the [Cleveland AC]. He later became a football coach at Nevada-Reno from 1929-31. He competed at the 1912 Summer Olympics, where he failed to complete in his decathlon program, and finished fifth in the shot put and seventh in the discus throw.

1911-12 John L Marks Coach # 12

The 1911 Notre Dame coach was John L. Marks 6–0–2, who would last just two years. The eight-game 1911 schedule featured little glamor but the Fighting Irish were happy to play. In 1911, the games were against Ohio Northern at home, W (32-6), At St. Viator W (43-0), At Butler W (27-0) , Loyola (Chicago) W (80-0), at Pittsburgh T (0-0) and St. Bonaventure at home W (34-0), at Wabash, 6-3, at Marquette T (0-0). Notre Dame out-scored them 216-6. The Big Ten biggies decided to stay away from Notre Dame as they did not want to get beat by such an "inferior team."

Chapter 9 The Jessee Harper Coaching Era   73

John L. Marks

According to Murray Sperber, author of the 1993 book, "Shake Down the Thunder: The Creation of Notre Dame Football," the football program netted a loss of $2,367 dollars, and the total deficit in the athletic department that academic year was $6,472. Notre Dame had little money but an awful lot of heart. Would athletics last at Notre Dame was the question of the day.

In 1912, Notre Dame's John L. Marks in his second season delivering an undefeated and untied 7-0 season... the first. But, there was little room for a major celebration. With the apparent boycott from Big Ten teams that did not want to get beaten by teeny Notre Dame, this 1912 season was less appealing than 1911. The best that ND could do with such a low budget and the disdain of the Midwestern Universities was to add a few local schools such as Adrian and Morris Harvey. But, the ND team played well and won anyway.

The games included St. Viator at Cartier Field W (116–7), at Adrian W (74–7), at Morris Harvey W (39–0), Wabash at home W (41–6), at Pittsburgh W (3–0), at St. Louis W (47–7), at Marquette W 69–0).

Fitting tribute to the team of 1912 as written in the Scholastic:
The Season Just Closed. by
William E. Cotter 'Class of 12, (Manager of Athletics).

> *Success is intoxicating. And to one intimately associated with those responsible for the successes of the past football season, a review is apt to contain indications of intoxicating influences. Success of the highest grade came to the Notre Dame team of 1912. If the following record of the team's work appears to abound in superlatives, the excusing cause is that nothing less than superlatives can adequately express the conquests of the season. Hailed*

> *Hailed as one of the two or three teams possessing any logical claim to the Western Championship in football; with a record of seven games and seven*

victories. during the season; • with a total of 389 points scored on opposing elevens against 27 points tallied by opponents; with the championship of Indiana conceded even by prejudiced observers; with our captain recognized as one of the best since the days of Eckersall, Coy, Heston, and Steffen, and our fullback the almost unanimous choice of football experts of the West for the All-Western team; with five Notre Dame men nominated for the All-Indiana team and almost as many picked for second All-Western elevens by a number of different authorities—with all this as the result of the 1912 season, is there any reason why we should not feel triumphant over the work of our football warriors?

With the- exception of the- championship year of 1909, Notre Dame has never had reason to feel so proud over the gridiron efforts of her sons, as during the past season. In many respects, the 1912 season has been more successful than that of 1909. Recognition, long withheld, has been granted in a manner that stamps Notre Dame as one of the football leaders of the West. A foundation has been established in public opinion upon which future teams may build high and strong, secure in the knowledge that 1912 affords the basis for the highest efforts.

...

Coach Marks is deserving of more than passing, mention. A Dartmouth player of the present generation, and hailed as one of the best backs in the country during his three years in the eastern school, Marks brought to Notre Dame all the football knowledge the East afforded. Interested solely in the welfare of the team, and sincerely earnest in his desire to develop an eleven worthy of the material at hand, the coach brought out all the strength of all the candidates. His unassuming earnestness won the good will of the players, and his confidence in their ability inspired performances worthy of any team in the land.

Assistant coaches Dunbar and Philbrook rendered splendid service in the drilling of the line, and their work in connection with the second team merits no small credit, because of the important part played by the "scrubs" in strengthening the Varsity.

The Marquette game at Chicago, Thanksgiving Day, provided a fitting end for the football year. Victories over the University of Pittsburg, St. Louis University, and Wabash College heralded a conquest in the closing contest, but not even the most sanguine Gold and Blue follower hoped for the decisive result that ended the three-year tie existing between Marquette and Notre Dame. In Chicago, St. Louis, and Pittsburg our alumni showed their loyalty to Notre Dame in a manner that will be long remembered by the members of the team. Not until • we leave the University can we truly appreciate the love borne by her sons for all associated with her advancement in any field.

Only two members of the 1912 team will be graduated-this year, and the nucleus of experienced players that promises to be here on the field in 1913 insures an eleven that is certain to repeat this year's successes. Crowley and Rockne are: the men who will go from us in June. • *Both have given their best to the "teams of the past three years, and both have -won high honors on the gridiron. All-Indiana nominations -were won by them last season, and this same honor this year, with the additional honor of selection for several All-Western second teams; brings recognition which will give life to the memory of two of the best ends ever developed at Notre Dame.*

All said, the year of 1912 will go down in Notre Dame football history as among the most successful ever recorded. We have been fighting against misinterpretation for the past four or five seasons, and so were denied an opportunity to meet our logical opponents. The brighter day that we have been looking for is about to dawn, we feel sure, and Notre Dame will soon come into her own.

1912 Notre Dame Football Team John L. Marks, Coach

Chapter 9 Coach Jesse Harper 1913-1917

Coach # 13

1913   Jesse Harper   7–0
1914   Jesse Harper   6–2
1915   Jesse Harper   7–1
1916   Jesse Harper   8–1
1917   Jesse Harper   6–1–1

A young Jesse Harper in his University of Chicago letter sweater. He was a star halfback for Stagg's excellent teams in the early part of the century.

No money; no football

Many of the facts in this section were derived from the following very informative online article. Check it out when you have the opportunity. http://www.und.com/sports/m-footbl/spec-rel/082913aad.html

Football had surely become a popular sport among the student body as well as the Holy Cross priests in Notre Dame's community. However, the Notre Dame program was going no place nationally and regionally. This brought the future of the team into question. ND Football was at a crossroads.

It was obvious to those who handled the money, the Holy Cross Fathers, the student body, and the folks in South Bend that Notre Dame had to either get out of football or make a full commitment. Eliminating football had become an unappealing if not unacceptable option so the choice was made by simply defining the choices.

Notre Dame President Rev. John W. Cavanaugh opted for the future of the program. He hired the 29-year-old Wabash head coach Jesse Clair Harper as the school's first athletics director.

Harper's secret ingredient for the CSC Fathers was that he had a strong background in business administration. With this background, Harper knew very well that Notre Dame "had to make football pay for itself."

As good as he was, and he was good—Harper always seemed to be overshadowed by somebody. He played halfback and quarterback at the University of Chicago, He played behind three-time Walter Camp All-American, Walter Eckersall (1904-06). During his senior year in 1905, Chicago was declared the "Big Ten" champion after the team snapped Michigan's 56-game unbeaten streak.

Stagg knew how good of a person and how great an athlete Harper was. When Jesse graduated in 1906, Stagg helped make sure he got the head coaching position for Harper, then 22 years old at Alma College in Michigan. He brought the Alma Scots to a winning season in his second year (5-1-1).

Notre Dame liked Harper's coaching abilities as they observed in the ND-Wabash game and they also liked the fact that he had a sharp mind and was an astute business man. ND Administration hired the 29-year old Harper as the school's first athletics director.

He made just $5000 with bonuses. His football record was (34-5-1). In basketball, it was (44-20) (.686); and baseball (61-28) for an overall 139-53-1 mark (.723). Not too shabby.

In 1913, with Jesse Clair Harper as the coach, Notre Dame Football was full of the good kind of pride that continues as its hallmark today. This young coach scheduled some powerhouse games and he directed Notre Dame to an undefeated and untied season (7-0).

Harper had a few great players on the team who would make All-American that year. One of the great players' name was Knute Rockne. Many would agree that even more important than the great season Harper delivered was the new Notre Dame schedule he had negotiated. Harper worked hard to assure Notre Dame got to play great teams so that its wins meant more.

Jesse Harper enjoyed his time with Notre Dame and he helped the University until he retired in 1917. During his tenure, the Irish stopped playing high schools and trade schools and began playing only intercollegiate games. His Fighting Irish record was admirable with a record of 34 wins, five losses, and one tie.

This period also marked the beginning of the rivalry with Army and the continuation of a rivalry with Michigan State. The objective for Harper of course was to gain respect for a regionally successful but small-time Midwestern football program.

The new AD / coach was able to schedule games in his first season with national powerhouses Texas, Penn State, and Army. How could Harper have pulled this off? He was smart. He had guts. And most of all, he had a lot of Notre Dame spirit. That is basically it. Jesse Harper did not know the word, "No!"

Two major factors combined to make the 1913 meeting with Army possible. Army had been stiffed by Yale. They were deemed not good enough to compete with Yale by Yale, a major Eastern superpower football team. Yale broke off its series with Army, which had been played for 20 consecutive years from 1893 through 1912. Army therefore had a "hole" in its schedule. Jesse Harper knew it was his job to fill that hole with a team named Notre Dame. He did.

Another reason besides Harper's determination was that Notre Dame was in the midst of its scheduling crisis. Once the ND team had finally upset Michigan in 1909, it made the "Catholics" more shunned by the Big Ten. The Big Ten had formed in 1896 and nobody in the BIG Ten wanted to be beat by a little team.

1913 ND v Army

Harper was a diplomat. Through his intelligence and persistence, he eventually broke the Big Ten ice. He added Wisconsin to the 1917 schedule, followed by Purdue in 1918. Indiana and Northwestern were added to the slate by 1920. While Notre Dame's cache of great teams to play was growing under Harper, the great AD and great coach Jesse Harper turned it all over to another great football man in 1918. It was an All-American man who played end for him on his best football team. His name was Knute Rockne.

Rockne got the reins and the keys in 1918 from his boss, Jesse Harper who was ready to move on in life. We'll get there but not right now.

1913 Notre Dame Football Season Coach Jesse Harper

Looking again at 1913, Notre Dame had one heck of a team. Harper led the lads to an undefeated and untied season with seven wins: Ohio Northern W (87-0), South Dakota W (20–7) Alma W (62–0), Army W (35–13) @ West Point, Penn State @ University Park, PA W (14–7), Christian Brothers in St. Louis, MO W (20–7), Texas at Clark Field in Austin W (30–7).

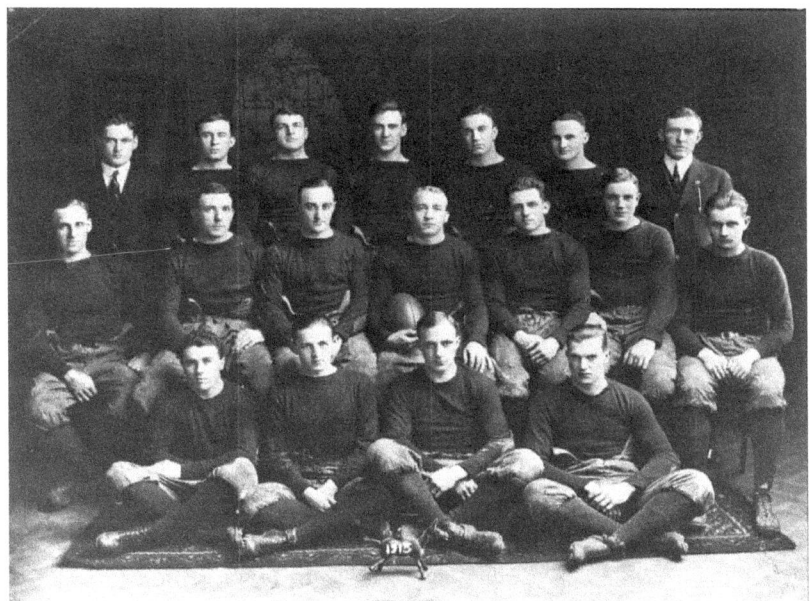

1913 ND Football Team w/ Coach Harper, Rockne & Dorais

By design, to get teams to play Notre Dame, Harper's Notre Dame team agreed to do a lot of traveling. By agreeing to this, ND was able to book games that otherwise, they would have been refused. Even at 7-0, there was little recognition in 2013 for this powerhouse team other than recognition that ND with Quarterback Dorais and Left End Rockne had perfected the forward pass.

Great Player Charlie "Gus" Dorais, QB 1913

The 1913 team was Led by quarterback Charlie "Gus" Dorais, another All-American and one of the Great Players noted in this book. With Rockne and Dorais, the Notre Dame team attacked the Army Cadets with an offense that featured both the expected powerful running game but also long and accurate downfield forward passes from Dorais to Rockne. This game was not the "invention" of the forward pass, but it was the first major contest in which a team used the forward pass regularly throughout the game.

Great Player Knute Rockne LE, 1910-1913

Knute Rockne was an All-American for Notre Dame as a player in 1913. Rockne joined the team in 1910 but had some problems because of size. He worked and worked and overcame the issue and became one of ND's greats at catching passes. In fact, Rockne helped to transform the collegiate game in a single contest. On November 1, 1913, the Notre Dame squad stunned the highly regarded Army team 35–13 in a game played at West Point.

Scholastic Athletic Notes

This is an excerpt of the athletic notes from the ND Scholastic for November 7, 1913, Jesse Harper's first year as coach. The Penn State Game was ND's closest game played in this year and so here are the game notes:

> *Penn State has been beaten by Washington and Jefferson, Harvard, and Penns3dvania this 3^ear, and b}' larger scores than the Varsity beat them, but all three of Penn's previous losses were sustained in the enemy's territory and to teams unwearied wearing travel. Besides this, Penn had determined to make good for its previous poor record in its first big game a t home. Furthermore, it was Penn Day—the big day - for their college. But notwithstanding all Penn's incentive to fight, the Varsity went in to win, and succeeded in doing so, the final count being 14 to 0.*

The game held particular interest because. Dorais, who is acknowledged to be the best quarterback in the West, was pitted against Miller, the Penn quarterback, who was mentioned by several critics last year for All-American. We would naturally be inclined to consider our own man the better, and although we have no doubt of Dorais' superiority, we choose to bring in a non-partisan critic to state our convictions. The following from the Philadelphia Evening Bulletin is our exact sentiment.

BILLY MORICE AT LEAST SEES OVER THE ALLEGHENIES

Billy Morice says that the best quarterback in America is Dorais, the Notre Dame pilot. Morice was a visitor at Franklin Field the other afternoon, and he boosted the little Notre Dame lad to the skies. 'He's the best quarterback in the country,' said Morice. 'I go all over the country officiating, and I will say that he is the king of them all this season. He can toss that pass like a baseball. He throws it, he flings it right at the man; he does not lob it so that while a fellow is waiting to get it, someone else comes along and nails him. He runs with the ball in front of him like Fred Geig, the Swarthmore coach did when he played. That enables him to shift it to either arm, and-use the other arm to straight-arm off a tackier. He is a great open field runner, and, above all other things, he is a great field general. There is nothing in the East as good as Dorais, and while a few of the critics will not see him play, and they may miss him in their selection, I'll take him as my selection.' — Philadelphia Evening, Bulletin.

Dorais was particularly brilliant in his open field running in the Penn game, returning punts from Tweit}" to thirty-five yards regularly, and once he caught the ball on the thirty-yard line and carried it the length of the field: —dodging practically every member of the Penn team— for a touchdown, only to be called back because he stepped out of bounds when catching the ball.

Penn State won the toss and kicked to Dorais who returned the ball fifteen yards. The ball see-sawed from one eleven to another, Penn gaining most of its yardage on fake end runs while line-smashing proved our forte. The Varsity grew dangerous toward the end of the quarter, but were unable to score.

The second quarter proved to be more exciting. Penn State worked the ball down to midfield only to lose it on downs. Miller punted to Dorais, and after a couple of plays Penn recovered a fumble within striking distance of our goal. Lamb dropped back ' for a field goal, but his trial was smeared by Lathrop who blocked his kick. When the Varsity recovered the ball, it uncorked a little of its old life, displaying the form that won victory for them at West Point. A well-executed forward pass from Dorais to Pliska was carried down the field forty yards. Dorais followed immediately with a thirty'-five yard end run, and another pass, Dorais to Rockne, put the ball the entire length of the field in three plays for a touchdown.

Even more exciting times were in store during the third period of play. Displaying their brilliant form, the Gold and Blue warriors received the ball from Penn on the kick-off and never lost possession of it until they had carried it all the way down the field for a second score. Line bucks, principally by Eichenlaub, but also some of very material assistance by Pliska and Finnegan, were responsible for three-fourths of the yardage on this wonderful incursion. Forward passes were almost invariably called back because of oft"-side plays, or were smeared by opposing interference. A few were successful, however, and these and end rims account for the rest of the distance. Dorais, whom we are beginning to believe infallible with his toe, kicked goal.

The Varsity received the kick again and worked, the ball past the middle of the field, but our backs began to tire and the ball was punted to Miller who was downed immediately. Then a series of fake end runs by Miller, interspersed by line bucks by Berryman and Tobin, brought the ball within fifteen yards of the Varsity's goal, when the only successful Penn forward pass put the home team across our goal for their only score of the da}'-, making the score 14 to 7, where it remained till the end of the game.

Knute Rockne, End & Gus Dorais, QB for Jesse Harper 1913

1914 Notre Dame Football Season Coach Jesse Harper

By1914, Harper had signed even more great teams to road games. Yale was # 1 in the national rankings at the time. ND played Yale at Yale in 1914 but lost L (28-0). Yale had a much better passing scheme than the Fighting Irish, a fact that did not go unnoticed by Harper, an astute coach like Rockne. Harper's team record was 6-2

Great Player: Ray Eichenlaub FB 1913-1914

Ray made second-team All-American as junior in 1913 on an All-American Team named by Walter Camp. That is phenomenal recognition. Camp favored Eastern Schools or so it seems.

As a Fullback, the 6'0 210 pound "bull" scored 12 touchdowns as senior in 1913. He finished ND with 176 career points. He was no slouch and would best be described as a workhorse. He put in four-years as the Irish starter at fullback. He gained his four monograms in football and when he did not want to play cards with the boys, he went ahead and won four more letters in track.

After college, Eichenlaub figured he would use his education so he went into the insurance business in Columbus, Ohio, but he loved the lure of the gridiron and spent 20 years as a Big Ten Conference football official. Like all of us, he loved ND University and its football program. He was elected president of University of Notre Dame Alumni Association in 1940. In 1972 Ray Eichenlaub was inducted into National Football Foundation Hall of Fame. He was quite a Notre Dame guy!

1915 Notre Dame Football Season Coach Jesse Harper

The 1915 team record was 7-2 with home wins over Alma W (32-0), Haskell W (134-0), and South Dakota W (6-0), The Irish won four away games at Army W (7-0), Creighton in Omaha W (41-0) Texas at Austin W (36-7) and Rice at Houston TX W (55-2).

The Irish also suffered one very close loss the first time the Irish met the Nebraska Cornhuskers at Nebraska Field in Lincoln, NE L (19-20).

1915 Notre Dame Football Season Coach Jesse Harper

1916 Notre Dame Football Season Coach Jesse Harper

The 1916 team record was 8-1 with home wins over Case W (48-0), Haskell W (25-0), Wabash W (60-0) and Alma South Dakota W (6-0), The Irish won four away games at Army W (7-0), Creighton in Omaha W (46-0). Away victories were Western Reserve at Cleveland W (48-0) South Dakota in Sioux Falls W (21-0), Michigan Agricultural in East Lansing W (14-0) Additionally ND picked up its first win on the road ever against the Nebraska Cornhuskers at Nebraska Field in Lincoln, NE W (20-0)

Unfortunately, the one loss in this 8-1 season came against the Black Knights of Army right in the middle of the season, game 5. On November 4, Notre Dame traveled to West Point and lost L (10-30) against Army.

1917 Notre Dame Football Season Coach Jesse Harper

The 1917 team record represented Jesse Clair Harper's last season with Notre Dame. The Fighting Irish were 6-1-1 with home wins against Kalamazoo W 55-0), South Dakota W (40-0), and Michigan Agricultural W (23-0).

The three away wins included Army W (7-2), Morningdale in Sioux City, IA W (13-0) and Washington & Jefferson in Washington, PA W (3-0). They had one loss, which was against the Nebraska Cornhuskers at Nebraska Field in Lincoln, NE L (0-7).

The Irish also tied Wisconsin at Camp Randall Stadium in Madison Wisconsin on October 13 T (0-0).

Jesse Harper; coach who hired Knute Rockne

Jesse Harper scheduled the 1918 season's games after he had hired Notre Dame's new Head Coach Knute Rockne, who had been his assistant. Rockne did well in his first year as coach after Jesse moved on.

Coach Jesse Harper & ND Player Knute Rockne

By the way, Frank Maggio in 2007 wrote a great book about Jesse Harper. Like me, Maggio is impressed with the historical Jesse Claire Harper. His book has a long title: *Notre Dame and the Game that Changed Football: How Jesse Harper Made the Forward Pass a Weapon and Knute Rockne a Legend.*

Jesse Harper waited until June, 2018 to turn in his resignation. It was not like today. ND was not worried about coaches / recruit signing days and such. Why did Harper wait so long to turn in his resignation as the ND head Football Coach?

The answer is simple. His job for the year was not finished. You may recall that Mr. Harper was not only the football coach; but also, the head basketball coach, and the head baseball coach of the University. Not only that but he was the Athletic Director. Today each of these positions has one or several people operating within the positions. Harper was heading back to the family farm in Kansas. Can it be said that after five years of holding four jobs, Harper was worn out and needed a break?

Chapter 10 Coach Knute Rockne 1918-30
Coach # 14

Three Consensus National Championships 1924, 1929, 1930; Five undefeated and untied seasons!

A Great Record

1918	Knute Rockne	3–1–2
1919	Knute Rockne	9–0
1920	Knute Rockne	9–0
1921	Knute Rockne	10–1
1922	Knute Rockne	8–1–1
1923	Knute Rockne	9–1
1924	Knute Rockne	10–0
1925	Knute Rockne	7–2–1
1926	Knute Rockne	9–1
1927	Knute Rockne	7–1–1
1928	Knute Rockne	5–4
1929	Knute Rockne	9–0
1930	Knute Rockne	10–0

Knute "Rock" Rockne Famed Notre Dame Coach

Please take some time to look at this record. Who could ever achieve such a record, anywhere—even High School?

This inserted piece introduces Knute Rockne to the reader. It was written by Dan Schofield, an analyst for Bleacher Report and the whole article can be found at http://bleacherreport.com/articles

The True Story of Knute Rockne, College Football's Most Renowned Coach

Rockne was also a great ND Player with his QB Gus Dorais.

By Dan Scofield, Analyst
Oct 2, 2009

This piece is a dedication to one of the founding fathers of college football, Knute Rockne. The University dedicated a handsome bronze statue to their legendary coach on Friday, October 2nd 2009 at Notre Dame Stadium.

> "The 'Swede'
>
> This story begins in a municipality of Voors, Norway, a quiet village surrounded by snow-cap mountains, cedar forests, and rivers flowing through valleys.
>
> It is here where a young boy, Knute Rockne, was brought into the world on the evening of March 4th, 1888.
>
> A mere five months later, the Rockne family made their way across seas to begin a new life in the bustling city of Chicago. Here, young Knute was introduced to the game of American Football on the neighborhood streets.
>
> Growing up, Knute had a variety of interests—chemistry being a large one.
>
> With his chemistry books and labs in hand, the Norwegian hopped on a train heading to South Bend, Ind. He would spend the next four years of his life at the University of Notre Dame.
>
> He found his way around campus and soon walked into the office of polymer chemist Julis Arthur Nieuwland. Trying to make his name in the world of chemistry, Rockne took the position of laboratory assistant to the famous chemist himself.
>
> At the time, Rockne attended the university, students were required to participate in a sport. With experience in the game from his high school days

at North West Division High, where he played end, it was an easy choice for the underclassman.

1910 marked one of the few times of failure during his life. He was cut from the team for being undersized.

It was one of the turning points in his life, as the man never gave up. He used this rejection as a form of motivation, and from 1911 to 1914, he played left-end for the Fighting Irish.

Rockne left the university w/ an undefeated playing record, 22-0-2.

The Legend Begins

A year after graduation marked the beginning of the greatest coaching career in the history of college football.

Jesse Harper, whom Rockne played for the previous season, hired him onto the staff as an assistant coach.

The two coaches were seemingly opposite of each other—Harper was more mild-mannered while Rockne had a different attitude than anyone before his time.

Warnings were not a word in his vocabulary book. He believed players would begin to think warnings did not mean much.

Instead, full punishment was given out on the first offense.

Off the field, Rockne became a favorite around campus. Players were soon coming to Rockne's office instead of Harper's with personal problems because of the close relationships the players had developed so quickly with their new "peer" coach.

After a 28-0 defeat, the first Irish loss in four seasons, Harper decided to make a change. He knew Rockne had a football mind like no other, and he used that to the team's advantage.

Before a 1916 game against Wabash, Rockne was asked to fill in for the ill coach. This marked the first time one of Rockne's famous, fiery pep talks echoed throughout the campus. He ended the emotional talk with, "Now go out there and crucify them!"

Notre Dame beat Wabash that day, 60-0.

1918-1930—The Legend Himself

At the end of 1917, Harper called "The Swede" into his office. He gave him the news that he wasn't going to be able to coach the team the next year, and named Knute as his successor.

At 30 years old, Knute Rockne stood on the sidelines of Notre Dame Stadium, clipboard in hand and dressed in full uniform, as the head football coach of the Fighting Irish.

On his first day on the job, he made his mindset known—and loud:

"Win or lose, I'm running this team. Nobody else has anything to say about it's make-up, it's plans, it's type of play. It's my show. If I flop, let 'em pan me. If we're a hit, let 'em say anything they want. I worked hard around here as an assistant for many years, and seldom saw my name in print. Well, all I want now is the truth".

From day one, the legend began his quest for truth and never looked back.

During his 13-year career, Rockne posted a record of 105 wins, 12 losses, and five ties. He lead the Irish to five seasons of undefeated football with zero ties.

Six of those victories won Notre Dame national championships.

His career record gives him the title as college football's all-time winning percentage leader at 88.1 percent.

The Coached Legends

Throughout his career, he coached players and turned some into legends themselves.

Despite no previous football experience, Rockne recruited George "The Gipper" Gipp to play for his team in 1916.

He finished his career with 83 touchdowns and never let a single pass be completed in his protective zone defense. During his four-year career for the Irish, he lifted the program to fame and notoriety.

Unfortunately, Gipp's career was cut short after contracting a serious strep infection in a game against Illinois. He died a few weeks later on December 19th, 1920.

In a game that seemed almost un-winnable for his injury-decimated team, Rockne delivered one of the most famous speeches in all of sports, "Win One for the Gipper."

Rockne told his team: "The day before he died George Gipp asked me to wait until the situation seemed hopeless—then ask a Notre Dame team to go out and beat Army for him. This is the day, and you are the team."

"One-Play-O'Brien's" scored the winning touchdown as the Irish defeated Army, W (12-6).

Other legends followed in the footsteps of The Gipper.

Don Miller, Jim Crowley, Elmer Layden, and Harry Stuhldreher possibly made the greatest mark during Rockne's time at Notre Dame.

After the "Four Horsemen" led a 13-7 upset win over an elite Army team, Grantland Rice put pen to paper and published some of the most famous journalism lines in college football history:

"Outlined against a blue-gray October sky, the Four Horsemen rode again. In dramatic lore their names are Death, Destruction, Pestilence, and Famine. But those are aliases. Their real names are: Stuhldreher, Crowley, Miller and Layden. They formed the crest of the South Bend cyclone before which another fighting Army team was swept over the precipice at the Polo Grounds this afternoon as 55,000 spectators peered down upon the bewildering panorama spread out upon the green plain below."

1918 Notre Dame Football Season Coach Knute Rockne

Jesse Harper scheduled the 1918 games after he had hired Notre Dame's new coach Knute Rockne. Rockne's first team won its first game against Case in Cleveland Ohio W (26-6). It won its second game against Wabash in Crafordsville, Indiana W (67-7). In the third game against Great Lakes Navy, ND managed a tie T 7-7).

Following this game Rockne suffered his first loss as coach of Notre Dame, L (7-13) against Michigan Agricultural. The team bounced back for its third win against Purdue in West Lafayette, IN W (26-6), Coach Rockne's first team finished the 1918 season with a tie against Nebraska in Nebraska Field, Lincoln, Nebraska. The Knute Rockne legacy was only beginning to begin.

Coach Rockne and ND Players

Here is a perspective from the December 1918 edition of the ND Student Newspaper, Scholastic. This was Rockne's inaugural season and things were not so good but he had the abilities of a great coach, trained by Jesse Harper with his own God-given talents, and he persevered and made it all OK:

1919 Notre Dame Football Season Coach Knute Rockne

This team was recognized retroactively as a co-national champion by the National Championship Foundation and Parke H. Davis. It helps to know that there were no championships for years after college football got is start.

Rockne's (9 wins, 0 losses) first undefeated and untied team won its first 1919 game W (14-0) against Kalamazoo at home followed by another home win against Mount Union (60-7). The team then went off to Nebraska and came back with a W (14-9) win.

The Fighting Irish then played Western State at home W (53-0) and followed this up with a road trip to Indiana W (16-3). Army was next at West Point W (12-9) followed by Michigan Agricultural at home W (13-0). From there, the Irish went to Indiana to play Purdue W (33-13) and then to Sioux City IA to play Morningside W (14-6) to finish the season undefeated and untied.

1920 Notre Dame Football Season Coach Knute Rockne

The 1920 team with Knute Rockne at the helm brought Notre Dame its second undefeated and untied season in a row (9 wins, 0 losses). The team again was selected retroactively as the 1920 national champion by the Billingsley Report and as a co-national champion by Parke H. Davis. Knute Rockne sure knew how to coach a football team and his great players responded.

Great Player: George "Gipper" Gipp HB 1920

The George Gipp story in Notre Dame history goes hand in hand with the Knute Rockne story. Therefore, the Gipp / Rockne story deserves its own spot as we plow through Knute Rockne's thirteen seasons as ND coach.

Gipp was as good as it gets and he was the first Notre Dame player ever to be declared a Walter Camp All-Americana. He is just Notre Dame's second consensus All-American (of 79). Gus Dorais, class of '14 the QB on the throwing end of Rockne's receptions, was the first. Gipp could play many different positions, but he was used most notably a halfback, quarterback, and punter.

Today, he is considered one of the most versatile athletes to play the game of football. For Notre Dame fans that do not know all of Notre Dame's storied history, who have not seen the movie, Knute

Rockne is thought of as the Gipper. Gipp in fact was the subject of Rockne's famous "Win just one for the Gipper" speech. He died at the young age of 25 of a streptococcal throat infection, days after leading Notre Dame to a win over Northwestern in his senior season. May he rest in peace.

Gipp was simply a good athlete, entering Notre Dame to play baseball for the Fighting Irish. He was literally spotted by Coach Rockne during an Irish practice session and the Coach recruited him for the football team. Gipp had never played organized football. The story goes a punt landed out of bounds and a passer-by (Gipp) kicked the ball back onto the field so hard, so high, and so long that Rockne inquired "who was that that did that?"

In his three years of play with Notre Dame under Knute Rockne, Gipp was the leading Irish rusher and passer (1918, 1919 and 1920). His career mark of 2,341 rushing yards lasted for more than more than 50 years until Jerome Heavens broke it in 1978. Gipp's baseball style athleticism made him an ideal receiver for the forward pass.

He not only could catch, he could throw. He threw for 1,789 yards and he scored 21 career touchdowns. He averaged 38 yards a punt. He snagged five interceptions. And he even returned punts with an average of 14 yards per punt return and 22 yards per kick return. Gipp still holds the ND record for average yards per rush for a season (8.1), career average yards per play of total offense (9.37), and career average yards per game of total offense (128.4). What a guy!

In 2002, looking back at the best of the best in football, the NCAA published "NCAA Football's Finest," Gipp was a top entry on the list.

Two weeks after being elected Notre Dame's first All-American by Walter Camp and second consensus All-American overall, George Gipp died of a disease that is totally curable today. As medicine was not as perfected in the US as it is today for diseases such as Staph, the speculation is that after the season Gipp contracted strep throat and pneumonia while giving punting lessons. Since antibiotics were not available in the 1920s, treatment options for such infections were limited and they could be fatal even to young, healthy individuals. What a shame.

Thank God that this will never happen again. I am sure that George Gipp would offer his thanks, and I bet Ronald Reagan, who played George Gipp in the memorable Rockne movie would offer his thanks to God for giving the human race the ability to combat so many one-time fatal diseases.

Next time any of us are in the right place at the right time, let's remember we can always ask anybody to "Win one for the Gipper!" Who could ask for anything more?

Great Player: Maurice "Clipper" Smith, G, 1920

The name of "Smith" is not foreign to the gridiron greats of Notre Dame football history. Years ago, this player was the first stellar midget of the line. He was none other than Maurice Francis Smith, also known today as "Original Clipper" Smith. He played with the great Rockne teams of '18, '19, '20. Known as the "lightest big-time guard in the United States," his grit and fight gained recognition in all the best selections of All-Westerns and won for himself a lasting place in Notre Dame's hall of famous athletes. He became a well-known coach at Santa Clara University but this Clipper Smith is still remembered as the great guard of the undefeated 1920 Irish, team which boasted George Gipp as its star performer.

1921 Notre Dame Football Season Coach Knute Rockne

The 1921 Notre Dame Fighting with fourth year football coach Knute Rockne at the helm, compiled an impressive 10-1 record with the only loss coming by a score of L (7-10) at Iowa. John Mohardt was the team's leading offensive player with 781 rushing yards, 995 passing yards, 12 rushing touchdowns, and nine passing touchdowns.

At the time, Grantland Rice wrote that "Mohardt could throw the ball to within a foot or two of any given space." Rice noted that the 1921 Notre Dame team "was the first team we know of to build its attack around a forward passing game, rather than use a forward passing game as a mere aid to the running game." Coach Rockne's strategy created some fine victories.

Notre Dame was becoming more and more accepted by big name college teams, many of whom would break tradition and come to Notre Dame to play their football games.

Great Player: Heartley "Hunk" Anderson LG 1919-1922

HUNK ANDERSON
GUARD 1922, COACH 1931-33

"Hunk" Anderson was a great football player and later was the coach picked to replace Knute Rockne when he was killed in an airline crash in 1931.

For all of his work in football, Anderson was a 1974 inductee into National Football Foundation Hall of Fame. He was a first-team All-American as senior in 1921 on teams named by International News Service (INS) and Football World Magazine.

He was a four-year starter at left guard for the Fighting Irish. He played on Knute Rockne's first team and he did a good share of the blocking for George Gipp. He also blocked two punts when placed in a defensive role and he recovered both for scores as a senior in the Purdue game.

He helped Irish to a great four-year mark of 31-2-2. Later, he served as Irish assistant coach under Rockne while also playing professional football for the Chicago Bears from 1922-26. His first coaching run was at the University of St. Louis in 1927-28. He then returned to Rockne's staff in 1930.

He was named Irish head coach from 1931-33 following Rockne's death, and his three-season record of 16-9-2 was not too shabby. The guy who succeeded Rockne was going to have a tough time being anybody but the Rock.

Anderson was brought in as head coach at North Carolina State from 1934-36, then, he coached at Michigan in '37 and Cincinnati in '38. After leaving the college ranks, the "Hunk" spent 11 seasons as an assistant coach with Chicago Bears. Heartley "Hunk" Anderson retired from football in 1951.

Great Player: Buck Shaw RT 1921

Lawrence T. "Buck" Shaw played for Notre Dame during the Rockne and Gipp Years and later he served as a head coach for Santa Clara University, the University of California, Berkeley, the San Francisco 49ers, the United States Air Force Academy, and the Philadelphia Eagles.

It was Notre Dame's track program, not its football program that attracted Shaw o Notre Dame. He enrolled and went out for the track team. However, Knute Rockne spotted him and the rest is history. Shaw became one of the greatest tackles and placekickers in Notre Dame history.

At 185 pounds, he was a starter for Rockne from 1919 to 1921, first at left tackle and then in 1920 and 1921 as right tackle opening holes for George Gipp. He finished his playing career being selected an All-American by Football World Magazine. Shaw also set a record by converting 38 of 39 extra points during his varsity career, a mark that stood until 1976, more than 50 years after he graduated. Shaw is a member of the all-time "Fighting Irish" football team. He b

He was a star player on Knute Rockne's first unbeaten team. He started his coaching career with one year as head coach at North Carolina State and four years as a line coach at the University of Nevada.

As a coach at Santa Clara, he compiled an impressive 47–10–4 record. In 1937 and 1938, his teams posted back-to-back Sugar Bowl wins over LSU. After war-time service, he served in 1945 as the head football coach at the University of California, where he compiled a 4–5–1 record. Shaw was the San Francisco 49ers' first head coach in the old All-America Football Conference and continued in that position from 1950 through 1954, when they entered the National Football League. After two seasons (1956–1957) as the first Air Force Academy Varsity head coach he returned to the NFL

Great Player: Eddie Anderson, RE, 1920-21

Anderson was a consensus All-America pick in 1921. As a top off to a nice career, he was elected to National Football Foundation Hall of Fame in 1971.

Anderson was great right from the start. He had the special gifts. He was Rockne's captain for the 1921 Notre Dame team. He led the Irish in pass receptions in both 1920 and 1921. He has the distinction of catching a rare pass from the immortal George Gipp to beat Army 12-9 in 1919. He loved football and coached for 39 years (at Loras, DePaul, Holy Cross and Iowa), while he was a practicing physician. FYI, only the great Amos Alonzo Stagg, Pop Warner and Jess Neely coached more years at the major-college level. Along with many other coaching and playing honors, Anderson was selected coach of the year in 1939 at Iowa by the American Football Coaches Association.

1922 Notre Dame Football Season Coach Knute Rockne

The 1922 Notre Dame Fighting with fifth year football coach Knute Rockne at the helm, compiled another impressive 8-1-1 record with a T (0-0) tie coming on November 11, 1922 at West Point against Army.

Great Player: Harry Stuhldreher, QB 1921-22

Harry Stuhldreher was quite a guy. At 5-7, 151-pounds, a native of Massillon, Ohio, he was so self-assured a leader that by his chutzpah and his talent, he convinced Knute Rockne to have him play QB on some great Notre Dame teams.

He could not only throw accurately but he also returned punts and proved to be a solid blocker. The quarterback was one component of the infamous Four Horsemen. He emerged as the starting signal-caller four games into his sophomore season in 1922. The self-assured leader went on to coach football at Wisconsin, as well as become the athletic director there. Stuhldreher was elected into the National Football Foundation Hall of Fame in 1958.

1923 Notre Dame Football Season Coach Knute Rockne

The 1923 Notre Dame Fighting Irish football team under Coach Knute Rockne had another great season. For the third year in a row, the team suffered just one loss. This time there were no ties. The loss came to Nebraska, a real nemesis to Notre Dame in the last several seasons.

Knute Rockne Having Fun with the Four Horsemen

The Cornhuskers won the game L (7-14) at memorial Stadium in Lincoln Nebraska on November 10.

1924 Notre Dame Football Season Coach Knute Rockne

The 1924 Notre Dame Fighting Irish football team was coached by Knute Rockne. The season started on October 4, 1924 at home against Lombard at Cartier Field. ND finished its season undefeated and untied.

Great Player: Adam Walsh Center, 1924

Adam Walsh made Second-team All-American as senior in 1924 on teams named by Newspaper Enterprise Association (NEA) and International News Service (INS). He was respected by Coach Rockne and served as the captain of Irish '24 national championship team.

Walsh was a two-year starter as Irish center and he played most of Army game in '24 with two broken hands, intercepting a pass and making a majority of the tackles. He was as tough as nails. He was a real athlete and earned monograms in basketball (one) and track (two).

Adam Walsh was a great track star—setting the indoor fieldhouse record at University of Wisconsin in 45-yard high hurdles. He became the head coach and athletic director at Santa Clara from 1925-28. He was the line coach at Yale from 1929-33, and moved to Harvard as line coach in 1934.

He served as head coach at Bowdoin from 1935-42, with a nice 34-16-6 record. He came back to Notre Dame in 1944 and served as an Irish Assistant. He then coached the Cleveland Rams in '45 to NFL title and was named pro coach of the year. He also coached the Los Angeles Rams and later returned as Bowdoin head coach from '47 through '58, winning four league titles.

He was also appointed by two different presidents as U.S. Marshal for district of Maine. Topping it off, Walsh was a 1968 inductee into National Football Foundation Hall of Fame.

Besides Adam Walsh, as you may already know by now, the 1924 Notre Dame team had four special people on the team. They were Harry Stuhldreher, Don Miller, Jim Crowley, and Elmer Layden. If their names sound familiar, it is because they played in the backfield on the 1924 Notre Dame undefeated and untied (10-0) season. Together these four great football players are known as the "Four Horsemen." The season topper was the victory over Stanford in the Rose Bowl.

The team was recognized as the consensus 1924 national champion, receiving retroactive national championship honors from the Berryman QPRS system, Billingsley Report, Boand System, Dickinson System, College Football Researchers Association, Helms Athletic Foundation, Houlgate System, National Championship Foundation, Polling System, and Jeff Sagarin.

The 1925 Rose Bowl was Notre Dame's last bowl appearance until the 1969 season. I think it is safe to say that anybody who was anybody in college football slotted the Notre Dame Fighting Irish as the number one football team of 1924 in all of the United States of America.

Notre Dame's Four Horsemen Hamming it UP!

Autographed Picture of the Four Horsemen of ND

Great Player: Don Miller RHB, 1922-24

Don Miller was a native of Defiance, Ohio. Notre Dame had been filled up with Millers for years. Don followed his three brothers to Notre Dame. At 5-11, 160 pounds, Miller proved to be the team's breakaway threat. According to Coach Rockne, Miller was the greatest open-field runner he ever coached. The halfback was a member of the famous Four Horsemen. Miller and his other three cohorts could have all made a career out of posing as one of the Four horsemen, but they all had a lot more to offer. Don Miller went on to coach at Georgia Tech for four years but then left to pursue a career in law.

Miller made it in law just as in life. This is his quick bio after passing on in the late 1970's

1925 Notre Dame Football Season Coach Knute Rockne

The 1925 Notre Dame Fighting Irish football team, coached by Knute Rockne felt the loss of key players (the Four Horsemen). Though showing a respectable record of 7 wins, two losses, and one tie, the team was rebuilding from their consensus national championship of 1924. T

After this two-loss season in 1925, Rockne quietly agreed to take the head coaching job at Columbia for $25,000 - $15,000 more than his Notre Dame salary. When the agreement went public, much to his embarrassment, he decided to stay at South Bend.

1926 Notre Dame Football Season Coach Knute Rockne

The 1926 9-1 Notre Dame Football Season under Coach Knute Rockne fought hard and did very well. There was an unexpected loss to Carnegie Tech in a game played at Pittsburgh. The Irish were held scoreless and Carnegie Tech prevailed (0-19). Let me tell you the whole story about that loss.

Knute Rockne was not only the greatest coach of all time, he made what was known as, "The greatest coaching blunders in history". Instead of coaching his team against Carnegie Tech, as he thought it was in the bag, he put an assistant in charge. Rockne traveled to Chicago while the Carnegie Tech game was being played for the Army-Navy game to "write newspaper articles about it, as well as select an All-American football team. Carnegie Tech used this toward their advantage and won the game 19-0. The loss likely cost the Irish a chance for the national title. They would have been undefeated.

1927 Notre Dame Football Season Coach Knute Rockne

Knute Rockne's 1927 Notre Dame Fighting Irish football team finished at 7-1-1. Based on the difficult caliber of play, it was looked upon as a fine season. T

1928 Notre Dame Football Season Coach Knute Rockne

The 1928 Notre Dame Fighting Irish football team was Newt Rockne's 11th season. It was the toughest, and least productive season since Rockne had become coach in 1918. At (5-4) the team was barely above 500 percent for the first time ever.

The Gipper Speech from the Movie

This 5-4 record in 1928 was clearly Coach Rockne's worst record ever. Nonetheless some history was made when the Coach delivered his famous "Gipper Speech." Rockne was trying to salvage something from his worst season as a coach at Notre Dame. To inspire the players, he told them the story of the tragic death of the greatest player ever at ND, George Gipp.

Rockne could really motivate the troops. After this speech, when the team came back to play, Notre Dame looked like a different team.

Here's how that one went down in history: On November 10, 1928, when Rockne's Notre Dame team was losing to Army 6-0 at the end of the half, Coach Rockne entered the locker room and he recounted the words that he heard from George Gipp's lips while on his deathbed in 1920:

Jack Chevigny of Notre Dame scores a touchdown in the third quarter to tie the game against Army at Yankee Stadium, New York, New York, November 10, 1928. Earlier, at halftime, Knute Rockne had given his famous, 'Win one for the Gipper" speech November 10, 1928

"I've got to go, Rock. It's all right. I'm not afraid. Some time, Rock, when the team is up against it, when things are going wrong and the breaks are beating the boys, tell them to go in there with all they've got and win just one for the Gipper. I don't know where I'll be then, Rock. But I'll know about it, and I'll be happy."

Rockne delivered this short speech as only he could. It fully inspired the team, which then went out and outscored Army in the second half and won the game 12-6. The phrase "Win one for the Gipper" was infused into the lexicon of American society and was later used as a political slogan by Ronald Reagan, who in 1940 portrayed Gipp in *Knute Rockne, All American.*

Rockne's Irish stormed onto the field in this famous game after the inspirational talk. However, it was Army that scored first in the second half to break the 0-0 tie. Jack Chevigny, who got Rockne's halftime message loud and clear then answered with a 1-yard plunge on fourth down, announcing "That's one for the Gipper!" as he plowed into the end zone. Or so legend has it!

Notre Dame rebounded the next season (1929) when Rockne was diagnosed with life-threatening phlebitis in his leg, missed some games and at times directed the team from a wheelchair or a cot. The team went 9-0, punctuated by a 13-12 victory over powerful USC, and won the national title. Notre Dame followed up with a 10-0 record and another national championship in 1930 as Rockne regained his health.

Great Player: Jack Chevegney RB, 1928

Picture to the left: Former Notre Dame Star Jack Chevigny, who scored the winning touchdown in the Irish's famous 1928 "Win one for the Gipper" game against Army, later became Texas' head football coach.

The Story of Cartier Field, Rockne, & Notre Dame Stadium

Every football team needs a place to play. Cartier Field was a stadium in Notre Dame, Indiana. When it was apparent that Notre Dame was keeping football, as played the American way, on its agenda, it adopted Cartier Field as its football spot.

This tradition-rich field hosted the University of Notre Dame Fighting Irish football team from 1900 to 1928. It held just about 30,000 people at its peak. Considering that there were games before 1930 played at Soldier Field, that had actual attendance records of 120,000, it was clear that a stadium that could just about hold 30,000 was appropriate for a team that was reaching for the stars if not the heavens.

Notre Dame always had a problem with finances and Jesse Clair Harper's five years helped Notre Dame's sports programs become self-sufficient.

However, even Jesse's financial acumen could not squeeze one more person into Cartier Field even when it was clear that twice to four times that number of tickets could be sold per home game.

Moreover, when Coach Rockne was hired by Harper and took over the team, he knew that for the ND program to grow, its stadium needed to grow. This became known as Rockne's dream. The coach worked very hard to achieve his dream. He loved and appreciated Cartier stadium and would not let it disappear while he was at Notre Dame.

The Cartier stands had to be torn down after the 1928 season to make room for Notre Dame Stadium, which opened in 1930. Notre Dame, while building its new stadium had to play its entire 1929 schedule away from campus. Chicago, ninety miles north of South Bend, promised to help.

And, so, all Notre Dame home games were played at Chicago's huge Soldier Field. Nonetheless the Rockne led team still went 9-0 and won the National Championship. At Coach Knute Rockne's insistence, Cartier Field's grass was transplanted into Notre Dame Stadium. Think about that.

For more than 30 years after the football team moved out, Cartier Field remained the home of Notre Dame's baseball and track and field teams. In 1962, as the University was growing and growing and it needed space, the original Cartier Field was replaced by a quadrangle adjoining the Memorial Library, which opened in 1963. Showing the sentimentality for the field, a new facility named Cartier Field was opened east of Notre Dame Stadium.

Since 2008, the Notre Dame Fighting Irish football team has held outdoor practices at the LaBar Football Practice Fields, and indoor practices at Meyo Field in the Loftus Center. Things change, mostly for the good.

> **By the way,** one of the most integral athletic buildings on campus today is the Loftus Center, which serves as an indoor practice facility for several Irish varsity sports (football, track and field, rowing, women's soccer, men's soccer, women's lacrosse, men's lacrosse, baseball and softball). It also hosts competition for the track and field teams and lacrosse teams. The Center also features Meyo Field, a 100-yard Field Turf field with end zones surrounded by a six-lane track one fifth of a mile long - making it as large as any indoor track in the nation

1929 Notre Dame Football Season Coach Knute Rockne

In 1929, the task of going undefeated was made even more complicated as construction was underway for Notre Dame Stadium. All of the Fighting Irish games in 1929 therefore had to be played on their opponents' home fields.

Knute Rockne's 1929 Notre Dame Fighting Irish football team made up for any losses from the prior year (5-4) and then some. During the season, Coach Knute Rockne fell ill, Tom Lieb, assistant coach in 1929, became in some respects the de facto head coach at times. Lieb helped Rockne's boys throughout the season to achieve their high success.

Rockne's Will Prevented him from Missing Games

The team at 9-0, was undefeated and untied and it was selected as the 1929 national champion by Billingsley Report, Boand System, Dickinson System, Dunkel System, College Football Researchers Association, Helms Athletic Foundation, National Championship Foundation, Poling System, and Jeff Sagarin's ELO-Chess system. It was not an undisputed all-consensus championship but it was just about as good as it gets. It should have been consensus but various organizations had their other favorites.

1930 Notre Dame Football Season Coach Knute Rockne

The 1930 Notre Dame Fighting Irish football team was coached for the 13th year by Knute Rockne. No coach prior to this had ever coached so many consecutive years. This would-be Coach Rockne's last season.

Everybody loved Knute Rockne and he could have coached at Notre Dame forever. This was another championship season as the Fighting Irish again were undefeated and untied and hailed a championship style 10-0 record. The Irish were consensus national champions.

Notre Dame was very excited and ecstatic about playing in the 1930 season because the team now had a stadium that looked as good as the revered stadiums of its most staunch foes. This was the first year that the Fighting Irish played its home games in Notre Dame Stadium, which quickly became nicknamed as *The House That Rock Built!*

ND National Championship Team Players 1930

Notre Dame's championship 1930 season included home wins in its new stadium (The House that Rockne Built!) against SMU W (20-14), Navy W (26-2), Carnegie Tech W (21-6), Indiana W (27-0), and Drake W (19-7).

It was a very close Army game that gave ND the Championship. Without the close 7-6 victory over Army, Notre Dame could not have won the national championship.

After season, Rock went off to be a movie star?

Early the next year in March, Knute Rockne received a lucrative offer to help in the production of a Hollywood movie, "The Spirit of Notre Dame." It would not take him away from coaching per se, and it would more than likely be good for the school. Traveling to

Los Angeles on March 31, Rockne was killed when his plane crashed in a pasture near Bazaar, Kansas. Knute Rockne was 43.

Knute Rockne's thirteen years of greatness at Notre Dame gave the University the idea that a guy like Rockne would always be available to the University of our Lady of the Lake. I like to call Rockne one of the first immortals because his first coaching boss, Jesse Harper would also be on that list along with Frank Leahy, Terry Brennan, Ara Parseghian, Lou Holtz, and now we're hoping, the real Coach Brian Kelly, not the writer of the great 2016 book about Notre Dame.

Every now and then God had to send a regular good or OK coach to Notre Dame so that the leaders of the University understand the gift from God when one of the real immortals or one of the immortals to-be began to show up for work on the campus fields every day.

REQUIESCAT IN PACEM: That is how the coach who survived the 1925 conversion to Catholicism would have heard our final tribute to him: RIP Rest in Peace.

Please Lord, give Coach Rockne a fine place with the stars as he has helped many of your people be stars on earth. And, so this chapter ends!

Chapter 11 Post Rockne: Coach Hunk Anderson 1931-1933

Coach # 15

Not too bad after 2 championships in a row

1931 Hunk Anderson   6–2–1
1932 Hunk Anderson   6–2–1
1933 Hunk Anderson   3–5–1

Hunk Anderson started off OK as ND coach.

Heartley "Hunk" Anderson Coach 1931-1933

1931 Notre Dame Football Season Coach Hunk Anderson

The 1931 Notre Dame Fighting Irish football team, coached by Hunk Anderson in his first year did reasonably well, but with a record of 6-2-1, it was clear that Anderson's team was either readjusting or rebuilding after two consecutive national championship seasons under Knute Rockne. Yet, Notre Dame finished with a rank of #11 in the country. Rockne had helped Notre Dame not only gain respect but gain the benefit of the doubt.

Great Player: Marchmont "Marchie" Schwartz, LHB 1929-1931

"Marchie" Schwartz was twenty years old when he began playing football for Notre Dame. He played from 1929 to 1931. His last year was with Hunk Anderson the year Knute Rockne was killed in a plane accident. Like many of Rockne's students, Schwartz later became a football coach.

Schwartz was a great player. He was a two-time All-American at halfback. Late, he served as the head football coach at Creighton University from 1935 to 1939 and at Stanford University from 1942 to 1950, compiling a career college football coaching record of 47–50–6; Stanford, like many other universities, suspended football during World War II. Another significant honor is that he was inducted into the College Football Hall of Fame as a player in 1974.

Schwartz was of Jewish heritage, and was a graduate of Saint Stanislaus College prep school in Bay St. Louis, Mississippi. He had three great years from 1929 to 1930, as he led Notre Dame, coached by Knute Rockne, to a 19–0 record and consecutive national championships. In a game against Carnegie Tech in 1931, he rushed for 188 yards, including touchdown runs of 58 and 60 yards.

Schwartz began his coaching career as an assistant football coach at Notre Dame from 1932 to 1933 under Heartley "Hunk" Anderson, and at the University of Chicago in 1934 under Clark Shaughnessy. In 1940, Shaughnessy hired Schwartz as Stanford's backfield coach. Marchie Schwartz helped coach the 1940 "Wow Boys" that recorded a perfect season and won the 1941 Rose Bowl.

1932 Notre Dame Football Season Coach Hunk Anderson

The 1932 Notre Dame Fighting Irish football team with second-year coach Hunk Anderson finished the season with seven wins and two losses (7-2). This was the second football season since the passing of Knute Rockne in a shocking accident and it brought Hunk's team the pride of being ranked # 4 in the Country.

Great Player: George Melinkovich HB, FB (1931-32, 34)

The 6'0" 180 pound George Melinkovich was worth every pound to all three ND coaches who shepherded his career at the university.

Yes, Melinkovich's career at Notre Dame spanned three coaching regimes.

He was recruited by Knute Rockne prior to his death and then he played for both "Hunk" Anderson and Elmer Layden. In his first varsity season, Melinkovich, from Tooele, Utah, quickly became the starting fullback position after starting halfback Nick Lukats broke his leg. It was Anderson's first year as well, and the two helped Notre Dame achieve a nice 6-2-1 record.

In 1932, Melinkovich stepped up even more and he led the team in rushing (88 carries for 503 yards} receiving (7 catches for 106 yards}, scoring (48 points}, and kickoff return average (41.0 yards}. He was named a first-team All-American by many organizations. He got sick and missed the entire 1933 season with a kidney ailment. He got well and was back on campus in 1934.

Elmer Layden, who took over the program in 1934, found himself a man short at the halfback position, so Melinkovich became his starting right halfback. The versatile backfield player with speed, power, and soft hands had another super great season. He led Notre Dame in rushing (73 carries for 324 yards} and scoring (36 points}, as Coach Layden kicked off his phenomenal coaching career with a 6-3 record.

Great Player: Joe Kurch, RT, 1930-1932

Joe Kurch was one of Knute Rockne's great ones on his 1930 Championship team. He was a three-year starter at right tackle from 1930-32. Lurch made first team All-American in 1931 and he was a unanimous selection in 1932. As noted he was a regular starter in his early career on Notre Dame's 1930 national championship squad in Knute Rockne's final season as coach. He also participated in the 1933 East-West Shrine game.

1933 Notre Dame Football Season Coach Hunk Anderson

The 1933 Notre Dame Fighting Irish football team with third year coach Hunk Anderson, finished the season with three wins, five losses, and one tie. It was Notre Dame's worst season ever and the fans were expecting a new coach for 1934. It goes without saying that this particular year's Fighting Irish were unranked.

Great Player: Ray Brancheau RHB, 1932-1933

Ray Brancheau was well respected by Coach Anderson and so once again, he gained the honor of captaining the 1933 Notre Dame team. Ray Brancheau it seemed to the pundits, was the most underrated back on the Irish team. Brancheau played a slashing, blocking, hard-tackling game at right halfback and it was felt that his play and his leadership would more than inspire the Notre Dame men to do as well as possible in what was a dismal season for the Fighting Irish.

RAYMOND BRANCHEAU
Right Halfback

Though listed as halfback, like all great players of the time, Brancheau was called on for duty on both sides of the ball. In fact, some might argue that he, just one man, actually was half of the defense.

In ND's Scholastic Football overview, the writer had a very favorable opinion of Brancheau and wrote this about the star athlete when he was on the field for the defense:

"She [Notre Dame] has one fair back, Brancheau, left from last year. Lukats is another, but when Brancheau comes out half the team's defense comes out with him." It is a tricky read, I admit but the writer implied that nobody else on the team was coming out, just

Brancheau, and that meant ND would play with half of its capability even with the new sub for Brancheau.

The ND victories included wins at Indiana W (12-2), at Northwestern W (7-0), and at Army played in Yankee Stadium in the Bronx W (13-12). The losses included Home Games against Pittsburgh L (0-14), Purdue L (0-19), USC L (0-19). Away losses included Navy L (0-7), and Carnegie Tech L (0-7). The Fighting Irish played Kansas to a tie at Notre Dame Stadium T (0-0) to begin the season. It was a dismal year for Coach Anderson. Few fans and few alumni, and few administrators at Notre Dame expected Coach Anderson to be given another opportunity.

Scholastic Magazine, run by ND Students always had something insightful to say about what is / was happening at Notre Dame when it is / was happening. They do not like writing anything negative. Hunk Anderson as all ND coaches was not a bad guy at all. He may even have been a good coach if there were somebody to help him out just a bit. But, he did not measure up to his promises. He had one really bad season. As we will see as we move forward in time. Ara Parseghian will define the whole rationale of being a successful coach at ND. He will reduce it to one word: *WIN!* I added the exclamation mark.

Summary of the "Hunk" Anderson Years:

There is a notion that when a person is looking for a top job, such as CEO, they can leverage their opportunity for success by coming after (meaning after in time) somebody who has done a poor job; was incompetent, miserable, could not get along with people, and that most people in the company would be tickled if the old guy had left lots sooner.

The worst scenario for success is when the old guy is terrific; has great business acumen, great results, a great personality, and everybody loves the guy and are sorry to see him gone. Though everybody from new coaching prospects, alumni, the CSC Fathers, and the Notre Dame faithful knew that nobody would be able to replace Rockne and succeed, somebody still had to gain the appointment for the job.

'HUNK' ANDERSON IS OUT AT NOTRE DAME

SOUTH BEND, Ind., Dec. 8 —(P)— Elmer Layden, one of the famous "Four Horsemen," will replace Heartly "Hunk" Anderson as head football coach at Notre Dame next fall as a result of a drastic shake-up of the University's athletic staff.

Jess Harper will also retire as athletic director. Harper's successor will probably be named within the next two weeks.

The most persistent rumor, however, was that Layden would hold both the director's and coaching jobs. He is now coach at Duquesne University.

In the 13 Rockne years, Notre Dame had been taken from a school in which most of its coaches lasted no more than three years to a university in which the last coach not only lasted thirteen years, he was at the top of his game for almost every one of those years. Not only that but he had three recognized national championships and five unbeaten and untied seasons including one in his last time out.

The notion that "Success breeds success" may not be the proper analogy but a derivative of that does apply: "Success breeds the demand for success." At Notre Dame, post Rockne, there was little room for failure and there was no apparent hesitation to oust unsuccessful Rockne successors. It can be called the downside of a winning culture.

As discussed, there was nobody who was unaware that following Rockne as coach would be a nearly impossible task. Almost immediately after the coach's death, university president Father Hugh O'Donnell put the squeeze on Jesse Harper to return to South Bend to help out. Harper loved Notre Dame but agreed only to take on the role of Athletics Director. He had no interest in being the predecessor and successor to Rockne. He knew of the major pressures and there were many. Despite the risks being well known, there were several candidates who nonetheless were confident enough to be interested in the job.

Heartley "Hunk" Anderson, Rockne's assistant was offered and accepted the job. He played and coached for Rockne and besides that, he was a five-sport letterman. Anderson was extremely athletic and very talented. While an assistant at Notre Dame, he was still playing pro ball for the Chicago Bears.

Anderson had no limit to his athletic aptitude and he could spot talent in others. He added the right amount of passion, commitment, love of football, and a drive to win to his overall package. He was without a doubt, a great paper choice to be head coach of Notre Dame. What he did not have, unfortunately for him, and it mattered in the end was Rockne's affable charm, but few do. Few could. The Rock was the whole deal.

Anderson had a knack of getting the most from his young players, but he did not have a style that helped him be successful when dealing with adults in high places. Rockne had a way of being able to control his inferiors and his superiors. The Rock was a great schmoozer.

Nobody can put a top US college team on the field without free tuition for many players. Rockne figured out how to get them what they wanted outside the bounds of the university's limited scholarship program. He would find various grants in aid and his relationships with wealthy boosters prompted financial help for student players.

When Anderson became coach. ND VP Father Michael Muclaire made clear that the new era would be different. The priests would subject the program to more oversight. Though Anderson had the same basic amount of scholarship packages from the school that Rockne had been given, that was it. Because Anderson was not Rockne, lots less students could get free rides to Notre Dame.

The "Hunk," failed to maintain the network of unofficial booster relationships to provide things such as off-campus jobs for ND players. That system had enabled Rockne to continually bring on more and better players. Additionally, Jesse Harper was the AD after Rockne. It was not Coach Anderson.

Rockne did everything and basically controlled everything, including the administration. He served as Notre Dame's athletic director, business manager, ticket distributor, track coach and equipment manager while concurrently being the Head Football Coach.

Anderson did not have the connections or the chutzpah to be like Rockne where interpersonal activity mattered and so the gravy-train dried up and nobody can field a great team without a shot at the best players.

"Hunk" was an aggressive task master as assistant and motivated players with his grit, not his charm. The ND head coaching job required both skills. Despite not having the structure to bring in more and more talent, there are analysts who have concluded that his teams did not lack talent. Rockne had recruited them and the Rockne deals were not taken away from students. There were three Rockne classes coming back the first year, then two, and then one, Anderson also had his own recruits but his seniors were Rockne's. The conclusion was that even in the early years when the team had few defeats, Notre Dame was too often out-coached in times that the team lost.

It got so bad that Jesse Harper, serving as Athletic Director had to explicitly address the situation. He told reporters that Anderson would be coaching at ND the following year: "The fact that he lost one game is no reason to fire him. We at Notre Dame feel he has done a fine job."

Hunk Anderson did not handle the press well and the press began their own private war against the coach.

Great Player Moose Krause, LT 1933

Moose Krause, who kept his real first name a secret even in the ND administrative files (just kidding), was as much Notre Dame as is Notre Dame. He passed away right before 1992, but was apparently in good health. We could have used him even longer at Notre Dame. He was one heck of a football player but his career at Notre Dame, was not of his prowess. Moose believed at the end that his life had a lot to do with making everybody else's career run smooth.

He was on a first-name basis with every Notre Dame athlete, coach and fan over the last 60 years while he was Mr. Notre Dame to many. When he passed away, the great thoughts came to writing:

"I think the true legend of Notre Dame has just died," said Gerry Faust, a wonderful man and a former football coach at the school. "They talk about Gipper, Rockne, the Four Horsemen, but I think he was the true legend."

Krause who was loved by everybody was able to survive at ND. I know that just today I sent an author's olive branch to the Sports Information Department and it did not come back. I did not even know I needed one. I think Moose Krause would have done whatever he could for anybody who writes well about Notre Dame University. Just saying.

At a school whose major athletic decisions, such as selecting the head football coach, are made by the university's president and executive vice president, athletic directors have not been all-powerful figures, but Krause emerged as both a wise and respected subaltern during his 31-year tenure. Bravo Moose Krause!

"He was a roving ambassador both for the university and the athletic department," said John Heisler, the director of sports information, who at his funeral described Mr. Krause as the best-known and best-loved Notre Dame figure of his era.

It was an era that began in 1930, when Edward W. Krause, a native of Chicago, was recruited by Rockne for what turned out to be Rockne's final season as coach.

A hulking tackle who came by his nickname honestly, Mr. "Big Moose" Krause lettered in football for three years, was named an all-American and played in the first college All-Star game, against the Chicago Bears in 1934.

But it was on the basketball court that the 6-foot-3-inch, 230-pounder, who also competed in track and baseball, truly excelled. Krause was an athlete and from the Rock's time, Notre Dame has loved athletes and scholars, not just football players.

A dominating center and three-year all-American who led the Irish to a combined 54-12 record, he was so invincible under the basket that the three-second rule, which limits the time a player can remain near the basket, was devised in his honor. Nobody could move the Moose!

Chapter 12 Post Rockne: Coach Elmer Layden 1934-1940

Coach # 16

Elmer Layden, New ND Coach

1934	Elmer Layden	6–3
1935	Elmer Layden	7–1–1
1936	Elmer Layden	6–2–1
1937	Elmer Layden	6–2–1
1938	Elmer Layden	8–1
1939	Elmer Layden	7–2
1940	Elmer Layden	7–2

Head coach Elmer Layden (left) had a sterling .770 winning percentage but left after seven seasons when no national title was produced.

Look at Elmer Layden's record. Remember, he was one of Rockne's Four Horsemen. What a fine record!

1934 Notre Dame Football Season Coach Elmer Layden

With Elmer Layden, the fullback in the famous 1924 Four Horsemen ND backfield, as the head coach of the 1934 Notre Dame Fighting Irish football team, Notre Dame was able to pick itself up, dust itself off and come back roaring and fighting for excellence. Having gone through a miserable 3-5-1 prior season, the Irish were ready to win some football games. But, the good feelings would not be back after the first game. Layden's ND finished at 6-3.

Great Player: Jack Robinson—C, 1932-1934

Jack Robinson was a serious athlete and great player for Notre Dame in this three-year career. He was the Irish starting center in 1932 and '34 and a consensus All-America pick in '34. Robinson had serious eye problems which kept him from competing during 1933 season. But he came back big in 1934. He went both ways Offense and linebacker and had five pass interceptions in 1934 as senior. Robinson was a major contributor.

1935 Notre Dame Football Season Coach Elmer Layden

The 1935 Notre Dame Fighting Irish football team was coached by Elmer Layden. The Irish finished the season at 7-1-1. Things started really nice for Elmer Layden's boys as the Irish won their first six games starting at home.

•

Great Player: Wally Fromhart, QB, 1935-36

WALLACE L. FROMHART

Wally Fromhart played football for the Notre Dame Fighting Irish football under coach Elmer Layden (of the famed Four Horsemen). Layden ran an offensive scheme in which the quarterback had a limited role in the passing game. Fromhart's primary responsibilities on offense were as a blocker for the halfback, Bill Shakespeare (who actually received the bulk of the snaps and passed the ball most often),. Fromhart was also a key receiver, a place kicker and a punt returner.

On defense, he played the safety position. When ND played arch-rival USC, in 1935, Wally returned an interception for 82 yards, a statistic that for years appeared in the annual Notre Dame Football Media Guide).

As a point of historical interest for college football aficionados, Fromhart made history as the starting quarterback for Notre Dame in the 18-13 victory against undefeated Ohio State in 1935.

He was a great player and a team player. He was good enough to be drafted by the Green Bay Packers in 1936. Instead, he chose to remain an additional year at Notre Dame to obtain teaching certification, during which time he also served as graduate assistant coach of the Fighting Irish freshman football team.

When Fromhart graduated from Notre Dame, he accepted a position as head football coach for Mt. Carmel High School in Chicago (1937–46), posting a 56-17-10 record, a Catholic League title and two city championships. During his coaching tenure at Mt. Carmel, Fromhart was called to serve in the US Navy as an armed guard officer in the US Merchant Marine (1944–45) in the Atlantic Theater of World War II.

Great Player: Wayne Miller LE, 1933-1935
(No Picture Available)

Wayne Miller attended and played college football at the University of Notre Dame from 1933 through 1935.

While at Notre Dame, Miller was characterized by many as a great player. He sure was. He was involved in many notable plays over the years of his tenure/

In 1933, for example, Notre Dame was playing unbeaten Army and trailing 12-6 with one minute to play. Out of nowhere, Millner blocked an Army punt and recovered it for a touchdown and Notre Dame won the game 13-12. So, Milner was a difference maker.

In 1935, both Notre Dame and Ohio State University were unbeaten. Notre Dame was trailing 13-0, but then was able to score two late touchdowns. Miller was johnny on the spot. He then caught a touchdown pass from Bill Shakespeare in the closing seconds to beat Ohio State, 18-13 and ND stayed undefeated.

As a pro, Wayne Miller was not sought initially at the top of the list but nonetheless, he got a job as a football player for the Boston Redskins. He went in the eighth round. Of the 1936 NFL draft. Lots of other teams wish they had used their bid on miller when they saw him play on the field in the NFL.

Coach Ray Flaherty saw him as a major component to winning a league championship. After losing to the Green Bay Packers in the title game that year, the franchise moved to Washington, D.C. in 1937 and defeated the Chicago Bears 28-21 to win the title. As expected, Miller played a big role in the victory, catching touchdown passes of 55 and 78 yards from Sammy Baugh. Everybody has heard of Sammy Baugh.

Miller then entered the United States Navy during World War II and after three years away, returned to the Redskins for one final season in 1945 before retiring. During his seven seasons, he caught 124 passes for 1,578 yards, a 12.7 average, and 12 touchdowns. He was quite a Notre Dame player, ETC.

1936 Notre Dame Football Season Coach Elmer Layden

The 1936 Notre Dame Fighting Irish football team was coached by Elmer Layden in his third season. Notre Dame began the season very strong with three home wins at Notre Dame Stadium.

Great Player: John Lautar LG, 1936

Everybody's favorite Guard in the 1930's, John Lautar was one of Notre Dame's best.

At 6' 1" tall, and just 184 pounds, he was not the biggest but he was a great athlete and a fine player.

Notre Dame finished the 1936 season at 6-2-1 and earned a national rank in the AP of # 8.

1937 Notre Dame Football Season Coach Elmer Layden

The 1937 Notre Dame Fighting Irish football team, coached by Elmer Layden with Joe Zwers as captain compiled a record of 6-2-1 and for this effort, they were selected as the AP's #9 ranked team.

Great Player: Joe Kuharich, RG, 1935-1937

Joe Kuharich was destined for Notre Dame from birth. He was born April 14, 1917 in South Bend, Indiana. He played college football at the University of Notre Dame as starting right guard. He played for Coach Elmer Layden, who rated Kuharich as one of the best and smartest players he ever had. In his college career, Kuharich's greatest game was the stunning Fighting Irish comeback over Ohio State in 1935.

The Irish played four home games at Notre Dame Stadium in 1937 beginning with a W (21-0) win against Drake, followed by a W (9-7) win against Navy (9-7), a loss L (6-21) against #3 Pittsburgh, and a season ending win against USC W (13-6).

ND was on the road five times starting with a T (0-0) tie against Illinois, a loss L (7-9) against Carnegie Tech, a win W (7-6) at Minnesota, a win W (7-0) against Army at Yankee Stadium before 76,359 fans, followed by another win W (7-0) at Northwestern in Illinois. With the same record, as in 1936, the AP selected Notre Dame in the same # 9 spot in the national rankings.

1938 Notre Dame Football Season Coach Elmer Layden

In 1938 with Jim McGoldrick as its Captain and Elmer Layden at the Helm, the Notre Dame Fighting Irish football team looked like it was going to have an undefeated and untied season until the final game at the University of Southern California. The game was played in Los Angeles at the huge Coliseum.

The Irish were undefeated and untied going into the game. USC, always a spoiler and did it again. The Irish lost in this last game of the 1938 college football season L (0-13). For its great season, ND was ranked # 5 by the Associated Press (AP) when all was said and done.

1939 Notre Dame Football Season Coach Elmer Layden

Great Player: Johnny Kelly RE, 1937-1939
(No picture available)

Elmer Layden trusted Johnny Kelly to get the job done and he did. Kelly was captain of the 1939 Fighting Irish playing a tough position at Right End.

The 1939 Notre Dame Fighting Irish football team finished (7-2) but started off undefeated for its first six games. Captain Johnny Kelly led Elmer Layden's team and it looked for a while that this would be another championship season for ND before the Irish traveled to Iowa on November 16. Iowa's Hawkeyes beat the Irish in a close match L (6-7). Notre Dame played its season finale at home against rival nemesis USC, and the Trojans again defeated Notre Dame L (12-20).

1939 Notre Dame v Navy in Cleveland's Municipal Stadium

Navy team captain Alan Bergner leads the way for Navy's all-out effort against Notre Dame. The game ended in a close win for ND and a disappointing 14-7 loss for the Middies.

1940 Notre Dame Football Season Coach Elmer Layden

1940 ND captain Milt Piepul was the player charged with leading Elmer Layden's seventh and last Notre Dame Fighting Irish team in the 1940 season. The team had another fine season finishing 7 wins, 2 losses with no ties.

The Fighting Irish were ranked # 2 at mid-season but after a close game at Navy and losses in two games in a row, the 10-6 victory in Los Angeles against USC did not help in bringing Notre Dame into the national rankings.

Notre Dame chalked up seven wins but not enough.

Notes about Elmer Layden

Nobody was asking for Elmer Layden to resign. He looked pretty good even next to the immortal Rockne and those immortals to come, but his record was not 100% wins and he had no undefeated seasons. He was a great coach and he was a great person and that is why the NFL snatched him away from Notre Dame while the university was figuring what to do.

Because he did not succeed in the way Rockne succeeded, he was perceived as a "not-so-great" coach. Nonetheless, it was Layden himself who got to decide when he would leave Notre Dame. I think he would have kept getting better; would have brought in a championship or two but like most, he too would have tired out from all the pressure. Maybe he thought so too.

He would not have been fired because he succeeded an OK coach, Hunk Anderson, another coach who could have been great if given some time. Layden did not immediately succeed Knute Rockne, an outstanding coach. Either way, Layden was a fine coach.

Chapter 13 Coach Frank Leahy 1941-1953

Coach # 17

Four National Championships 1943, 1946-47, 1949

Welcome Frank Leahy

Year	Coach	Record	
1941	Frank Leahy	8–0–1	
1942	Frank Leahy	7–2–2	
1943	Frank Leahy	9–1	
1944	Edward McKeever	8–2	Coach # 18
1945	Hugh Devore	7–2–1	Coach # 19
1946	Frank Leahy	8–0–1	
1947	Frank Leahy	9–0	
1948	Frank Leahy	9–0–1	
1949	Frank Leahy	10–0	
1950	Frank Leahy	4–4–1	
1951	Frank Leahy	7–2–1	
1952	Frank Leahy	7–2–1	
1953	Frank Leahy	9–0–1	

From the Website, which hosts the tribute sculpture from 1997

Coach Frank Leahy

Frank Leahy came to Notre Dame to play football for Knute Rockne. After suffering an injury his senior year, he became a student of Rockne's and entered the coaching profession himself.

Coach of the Fighting Irish from 1941-43 and 1946-53, he led the Irish to six undefeated seasons, five National Championships, and an unbeaten streak of 39 games in the late 1940's.

Selected for the College Football Hall of Fame in 1970, this sculpture commemorates Coach Leahy, and was unveiled next to Notre Dame Stadium in 1997.

The only thing you can do alone in life is fail

Before Coach Leahy coached at Notre Dame, he graduated from Notre Dame. He attended the University of Notre Dame, where he played football as a tackle on Knute Rockne's last three teams (1928–1930). He graduated from the university in 1931. He learned the notion of success from both Notre Dame and Coach Rockne. He learned the notion of love from a loving family and the many friends who loved him, even though for most of his life, he was a workaholic.

Like Rockne, whose coach was Jesse Harper, and Frank Leahy, whose coach was Knute Rockne, successful people need lots of help and lots of love in their lives. Very often, these otherwise tough people are too busy to notice or to understand their own need. Harper, Rockne, and Leahy were great family men and they benefitted immensely from a lot of love. They were self-inspired and encouraged to do well in life by their life experiences for sure, but it was not all them! Yes, even self-made men can fail when they are alone and when there is no loving support system.

Frank Leahy was a great coach and a great man. He loved his family deeply. He was tough but fair. He was also kind and good, and though not sloppy or gushy, he was very loving. Men do not want to think of Frank Leahy as *the family man* but it was his family that gave him his strength. Most men wanted to look up to him as an iron-man coach!

The words immediately below are excerpts from Bill Dwyre a great columnist for the LA Times http://articles.latimes.com/2012/oct/19/sports/la-sp-dwyre-notre-dame-20121020.

Bill Dwyre's piece was titled: "Frank Leahy always had Notre Dame standing tall and up straight."

Dwyre was interviewing Fred Leahy, the coach's # 6 child of 8. In this part of the piece, Leahy's son, Fred creates a quick snapshot of the coach and his family in this excerpt:

> *"Fred's summary of life in the Leahy family is a classic of all-encompassing brevity.*
>
> *"Dad belonged to the world, and mom had eight kids," he says*
>
> *Fred says Frank Leahy never turned down an autograph request and drilled into his family the need to treat people equally and well.*
>
> *"He wore the famous bow tie all the time," Fred says, "and that wasn't for any image reason. He knew, when he was out eating dinner, somebody*

would come over to the table, he'd get up and reach across to shake their hand and his tie would fall into the soup.

"When we went out to dinner, he'd eat ahead of time. People wouldn't leave him alone to eat, and he'd never turn anybody down. When dinner ended, he'd disappear into the kitchen and shake the hands of all the helpers."

A writer, seeking to characterize the presumed terror of failure with which Leahy's players existed, once asked star quarterback Johnny Lujack what Leahy was like after a loss. Lujack pondered the question and said, "I don't remember ever losing."

1941 Notre Dame Football Season Coach Frank Leahy

In 1941, Frank Leahy coached the Notre Dame Fighting Irish football team for the first time. Like Elmer Layden and Knute Rockne, and Jesse Harper, Frank Leahy was a natural coach on strategy and on motivation. He made everybody around him want to do their best.

Whereas Knute Rockne had the Four Horsemen, even before Frank Leahy got to BC or Notre Dame, he was a famous coach. As a lineman, himself, he had been a line coach at Fordham. While at Fordham for five years, Leahy was an excellent line coach. His job was to develop the Fordham line.

He did, and then some. He developed a solid Fordham line that were so tough, they became known as the "**Seven Blocks of Granite**." One of those "Blocks of Granite" was an intense, studious, blocky, raven haired young man named Vince Lombardi. That's right, great coaches teach great coaches. Rockne taught Leahy; Leahy taught Lombardi.

In Leahy's first season, Notre Dame was at its best. Its record was (8-0-1). It could have been a National Championship but for the tie against Army. Notre Dame was proud to clock in with four home wins out of four tries.

1942 Notre Dame Football Season Coach Frank Leahy

The 1942 Fighting Irish football team was coached by Frank Leahy in his second season with the Irish. Leahy was already a successful

Notre Dame coach with his 1941 team. At # 6 in the AP rankings at the end of the season, the (7-2-2) 1942 team also received much acclaim. Leahy was a natural coach in the order of other Notre Dame greats. The 1942 Notre Dame football and those Leahy coached until 1953 responded well to his great coaching talents.

1943 Notre Dame Football Season Coach Frank Leahy

Coach Frank Leahy's 1943 Notre Dame Fighting Irish football team represented the University of Notre Dame in Leahy's third year of being the head coach. The team ended its season with 9 wins and 1 loss, winning the national championship. This was the fourth Irish team to win the national title and the first for Frank Leahy.

Led by Notre Dame's first **Heisman Trophy** winner, Angelo Bertelli, Notre Dame played and beat seven teams ranked in the top 13 and played seven of its ten games on the road. Despite a devastating season ending loss to Great Lakes, a recent powerhouse comprised mostly of military men, Notre Dame was awarded its first national title by the Associated Press.

The war years were special years. The service academies and the semi-pro teams from the military were at their best. Because of Notre Dame and Navy's cooperation to educate midshipmen, the 1943 Irish team included 14 Navy apprentice seamen.

Sophomore quarterback John Lujack was one of those players. Lujack would win the 1947 **Heisman Trophy** after helping steer the Irish to a third national title under coach Leahy. Other seamen on the Irish roster included powerful lineman / left tackle Jim White -- who finished 9th in the 1943 Heisman balloting, and other starters including left end Paul Limont, center Herb Coleman and his backup Frank Szymanski, plus fullback Jim Mello.

Great Player: Angelo Bertelli QB, 1941-1943

Angelo Bertelli was a great quarterback. He was Notre Dame's first Heisman winner. When Frank Leahy switched to the T-formation starting in 1942, it was perfect for Bertelli's style of play and it literally made a star of Bertelli. The big change helped Bertelli win the Heisman Trophy as a senior despite playing in only six of Notre Dame's 10 games. While having a banner year, Bertelli was called to do his part in the war effort and he served his country.

Bertelli's Irish career began as a single-wing tailback in 1941 as his 1,027 passing yards (and a .569 completion percentage that led the nation) propelled his team to a 9-0-1 record.

<<< Angelo Bertelli

As a junior, he switched to quarterback in the T and ended up throwing for another 1,039 yards and 10 touchdowns.

In a 27-10 win over Stanford that year, he threw four touchdown passes and completed a record 10 straight passes. Runner-up to Minnesota's Bruce Smith for the Heisman as a sophomore and sixth as a junior behind winner Frank Sinkwich of Georgia, Bertelli's play enabled Notre Dame to average 43.5 points in its first six games in '43 before the Marine Corps called him into service.

Still, he threw 10 scoring passes in those six contests and helped Notre Dame claim the national title despite a final-game loss to Great Lakes while Bertelli was in boot camp. He played three seasons with Los Angeles and Chicago in the All-America Football Conference before a knee injury ended his career. For a number of years, Bertelli ran a beverage distributorship in Clifton, N.J. He joined the National Football Foundation Hall of Fame in 1972. Angelo Bertelli died on June 6, 1999.

Great Player: Creighton Miller, RHB, !941-1943

Creighton Miller was a consensus All-American pick in 1943. He led the nation in rushing as a senior in 1943 with 911 yards, the second-best single-season figure in Notre Dame history at that time in ND history.

He finished fourth in the 1943 Heisman Trophy voting. He was an Irish starter at halfback in 1942 and 1943 for coach Frank Leahy. There were lots of great Millers who played football at Notre Dame. It was in the blood.

Creighton Miller is the nephew of Four Horseman Don Miller and that explains a lot. His 911 yards came on 151 carries in 1943, plus 13 touchdowns. He played in College All-Star game in 1944 and was a second-round pick by Brooklyn in the 1944 NFL draft. He was elected to the National Football Foundation Hall of Fame in 1976.

Notre Dame was proud to have 17 Marine privates, among them were future College Football Hall of Fame inductees Ziggy Czarobski at right tackle, All-American right end John Yonakor, starting left guard Pat Filley and, of course, 1943 **Heisman Trophy** winner Angelo Bertelli at quarterback.

The football game was very serious in 1943 as was the war effort. Notre Dame had players involved in both.

Bertelli Off to War

On Nov. 1 during the 1943 season, after leading Notre Dame to a 6-0 record, QB Angelo Bertelli got his military orders and he departed for officer's training school in Parris Island, S.C. Johnny Lujack filled in more than capably to finish the national title run.

Angelo Bertelli Heisman 1943 & Johnny Lujack Heisman 1947

There also was one NROTC man, Jack Zilly, who would later serve as an Irish assistant coach from 1956-58.

The 1943 National Championship Notre Dame team was like no other. It defeated the teams that finished No. 2 (Iowa Pre-Flight, a semi-pro World War II outfit), No. 3 (Michigan) and No. 4—none other than the Naval Academy located in Annapolis, Md.

There are only two college football teams in history to defeat the teams that were the final #s 2-3-4 in one season. They are the 1943 Notre Dame Fighting Irish and the 1971 Nebraska Cornhuskers.

Furthermore, the 1943 Irish overpowered the teams that finished #9 (Northwestern), #11 (Army) and #13 (Georgia Tech). Beating six teams that placed in the final AP Top 13 might never again be achieved in college football again.

It is difficult to believe that such a team could ever be beaten. Going into the game with a 9-0 record against the Great Lakes Blue Jackets, a great team loaded with outstanding military personnel who knew how to play the game of football.

The home of this great Navy team was different from what we know. Its home is the Blue Lakes Naval Station and that should say it all. In addition to the 1943 football team, it is still the home of the United States Navy's only boot camp, located near North Chicago, in Lake County, Illinois. Important tenant commands include the

Recruit Training Command, Training Support Center and Navy Recruiting District Chicago.

Naval Station Great Lakes is the second largest military installation in Illinois and the largest training station in the Navy. Nobody thought this game would be easy, but Notre Dame had a great team.

This 9-1 season ended with a defeat L (14-19) by the Great Lakes Bluejackets, on a "Hail Mary" touchdown pass. Notre Dame pundits like to ask if this were "the one way any school named after Our Lady should never lose -- with 33 seconds remaining." --A Hail Mary Pass--. Lujack was just a freshman and Bertelli was off fighting the war.

To emphasize the Bluejackets talent and skill, note that Notre Dame neither required nor gave any excuses for the defeat. ND had played a semi-pro operation during the war years comprised of seamen (hence Bluejackets) that included future 1946-49 Notre Dame leading rusher Emil "Six Yard" Sitko—another member of the College Football Hall of Fame.

The Coach, staff, & the team go to War

After the 1943 season, Notre Dame head coach Frank Leahy and his entire staff and players volunteered for active duty in the Navy for World War II. That is why Leahy was not the coach in 1944 or '45.

Picture Courtesy Notre Dame Archives Leahy, Right, takes Oath

1944 Notre Dame Football Season Coach Edward McKeever

Coach Edward McKeever ND 1944

Since Frank Leahy and a number of the coaching staff joined the Navy after the 1943 Championship Season, Notre Dame asked Edward McKeever to coach the 1944 Notre Dame Fighting Irish football team. McKeever had attended Notre Dame from 1930-1931 and transferred to Texas Tech, where he played football from 1932-1934. McKeever had been a very successful backfield coach in 1935 through 1938.

He was hired by Frank Leahy while Leahy was at Boston College from 1939-1940. He joined Notre Dame with Leahy in 1941 even though he had been offered head coaching job at BC.

McKeever guided the Irish to a very nice 8-2 season and a ninth-place finish in the AP final poll. The 1944 team won its first five games as follows: At Pittsburgh W (58-0), At home Tulane W (26-0), At Dartmouth in Fenway Park W (64-0), At home Wisconsin W (28-13), At Illinois (13-7). The Irish had moved to the top of the rankings by week 3.

The 1944 Army ND Game

It had been thirteen years since Army had beaten Notre Dame. Notre Dame went into the game 5–1 and ranked No. 5, coming off the 32–13 loss to Navy. The Army squad was being led by Glenn Davis and Doc Blanchard. They overwhelmed the Irish. By halftime, Army had a commanding 33–0 lead. When the game was over, Army had beaten Notre Dame 59–0, handing the Irish the worst loss in the program's history. The Irish would recover, winning their last three games to finish 8–2 and ranked No. 9 in the nation.

When asked by a reporter about the score, Army halfback Doc Blanchard said "If there was anyone to blame for the size of the margin, it was Notre Dame, which fired our desire to win with its long humiliation of Army teams."

1945 Notre Dame Football Season Coach Hugh Devore

Hugh Devore coached the 1945 Notre Dame Fighting Irish football team to a 7-2-1 record. It was his first season as interim coach while the Irish were awaiting the return of Lieutenant Frank Leahy from active duty. Devore would have a second interim stint replacing Joe Kuharich in the 1950's.

Devore had graduated from Notre Dame in 1934. He had played end and was Irish co-captain as a senior. He stayed at Notre Dame as freshman coach under Elmer Layden for one year before he moved on and held various coaching positions.

Devore, shown on left with his best buddy, came back to Notre Dame in 1943 as Frank Leahy's end coach and left after his interim head coaching assignment in 1946. He held numerous head coaching positions at highly rated schools and was assistant coach for the Green Bay Packers in 1953 and head coach for the Philadelphia Eagles. In 1958 he returned to Notre Dame as Terry Brennan's freshman coach and assistant athletic director and he remained on the staff when Joe Kuharich took over the following year.

1946 Notre Dame Football Season Coach Frank Leahy

Returning Navy Lieutenant Frank Leahy's 1946 Notre Dame Fighting Irish football team ended the football season with 8 wins and 1 tie, winning the national championship for the second time in Leahy's tenure as coach.

This was the fifth Irish team to win the national title and the second title for Leahy. The 1946 Irish is the first team/season in what is considered to be the Notre Dame Football dynasty, a stretch of games in which Notre Dame went 36-0-2 and won three national championships and two Heisman Trophies from 1946-1949.

The 1946 team was as good as it gets. But it also produced one of college football's "games of the century," the famous 0-0 tie with Army at Yankee Stadium.

1946 Army ND Game

The last two ND Army encounters at Yankee Stadium in 1944 and 1945 resulted in Army wins of (0-59) and (0-48). There was lots of drama in the 1946 Army game. Both the Irish and the battle-hardened Army team came to win; yet the defenses were so good that neither could score.

The Cadets were riding an 18–game winning streak and they still had Doc Blanchard and Glenn Davis. Clearly. Nobody could beat Army or so it seemed and Army Coach Red Blaik's squad would have to be beaten to lose its status as the No.1 team in the nation.

Well, not exactly!

Frank Leahy had coached Notre Dame to a national championship in 1943, then left South Bend for the Navy and spent his duty time in the South Pacific. He returned to Notre Dame in '46 and he had a great bunch of lettermen-turned soldiers who still had playing eligibility remaining. The Irish were loaded and determined to win. Leahy's Irish not only wanted to get back their No.1 ranking, but they were none too happy about the trouncing the team received in the prior two years. They were ready to avenge the 0-59 and 0-48 losses to Army in 1944 and '45.

For years of matchups from 1913 to 1946, no games had ever been played at Notre Dame Stadium. So, it was a given that the game would be at Army, which played its home games against Notre Dame at Yankee Stadium.

The wartime gravy train of talent was over for Army, and no significant new players contributed in 1946. After two national championships, in a row, however, the Army team was still great at 7–0 and Notre Dame was 5–0 when the two met on November 9. The #1 Cadets came in averaging 30 points a game while the No.2 Irish averaged 35. Final score: T (0–0).

> **By the way:** The 1941 ND / Army game in Frank Leahy's first year at ND, was also a 0-0 tie. The Irish finished 1941 at 8-0-1. It was the only blemish on the record and it prevented Notre Dame from winning a mythical national championship (MNC).

Army's 25–game winning streak was over but the Cadets were still unbeaten. They won their last two games, but had to struggle past Navy. Meanwhile, Notre Dame shut out Northwestern and Tulane and beat Southern Cal by 20.

A week later, the final AP poll gave the championship to the Irish. Nonetheless the end-of-season polling was not always 100% accepted and there was no BCS. Army still claims what is called an MNC for 1946, giving them a trifecta. The MNC stands for Mythical National Championship.

As several other games over the years, the Army-ND game of 1946 was labeled "Game of the Century." Never before was the hype so pervasive as much as this meeting of #1 Army and #2 Notre Dame. Before the ND players and coaches went to fight the war, Notre Dame had won the 1943 mythical national championship (MNC). Army won in 1944 and 1945 when Notre Dame was absent with leave. This 1946 special game featured some outstanding statistics:

> *3 Heisman Trophy winners, 3 Outland Trophy winners, and 10 Hall of Famers, not counting the Hall of Fame coaches on each side. Notre Dame claims MNCs for 1943, 1946, 1947, and 1949, and Army claims MNCs for 1944, 1945, and 1946. This was a true clash of the titans, an intersection of 2 of the greatest runs in college football history: Army going 27-0-1 1944-1946 and Notre Dame going 36-0-2 1946-1949.*

Let's talk a bit about this great game. The information is from http://tiptop25.com/champ1946.html.

Army remained #1 after the scoreless tie, but when they struggled to beat 1-8 Navy 21-18 in their finale, Notre Dame passed them up for #1 in the final AP poll. To make matters murkier in 1946, (11-0) Georgia also claims an MNC for 1946, based on finishing #1 in the Williamson math formula rating. That's a lame basis for the claim, but Georgia did win all of their games by more than a touchdown, and they are definitely a worthy contender for the 1946 MNC.

Pictured above is the defining play of 1946's "Game of the Century." Notre Dame's Bill Gompers turning the corner on 4th down and heading for Army's goal line. But alas, he didn't make it. He didn't even reach the 2-yard line for a first down, and this game saw no other serious scoring threats, ending in a 0-0 stalemate. I do not have the link for the required cite below.

...Fullback Doc Blanchard and halfback Glenn Davis were still consensus AA, for the third year in a row, and Davis also took home the Heisman Trophy this year, Blanchard having won it in 1945. End Hank Foldberg joined them as a consensus AA, and quarterback Arnold Tucker was a non-consensus AA.

Some other games of the ND 1946 Season

The football seasons were again able to begin on time as World War II ended the prior September (1945). And, so on September 28, the Irish played at Illinois W (26-6) before coming back to Notre Dame against Pittsburgh W (33-0) and Purdue W (49-6). From here, on

October 26, the Irish traveled to Iowa W (41-6) and then on to Memorial Stadium in Baltimore to play Navy W (28-0) before 63,909 fans. Continuing to play the service academies in consecutive weeks, Notre Dame took off for Yankee Stadium before 74,121 for its November 9 game against Army for a tie T (0-0) as discussed.

Jim Martin (38), Larry Coutre (24), Leon Hart (82) and Emil Sitko (14) arrived with the 1946 class. Up front is quarterback Bob Williams. Notre Dame.

When the Irish came back home the next week against Northwestern, they won again W (27-0). For the week before Thanksgiving, Notre Dame hit the road again and on November 23 played Tulane W (41-0) before 56,481 at Tulane Stadium in New Orleans. On November 30, USC was back on the ND schedule for a home win W (26-6).

1947 Notre Dame Football Season Coach Frank Leahy

The 1947 Notre Dame Fighting Irish football team was another leg of the Notre Dame dynasty coached in the second year of Frank Leahy's second stint since the War. The 1947 team ended the season with 9 wins and no losses. They were unbeaten and untied and for the second time in a row for Leahy and the sixth time in history, Notre Dame won the national championship.

Great Player: George Connor LT, 1946-1947

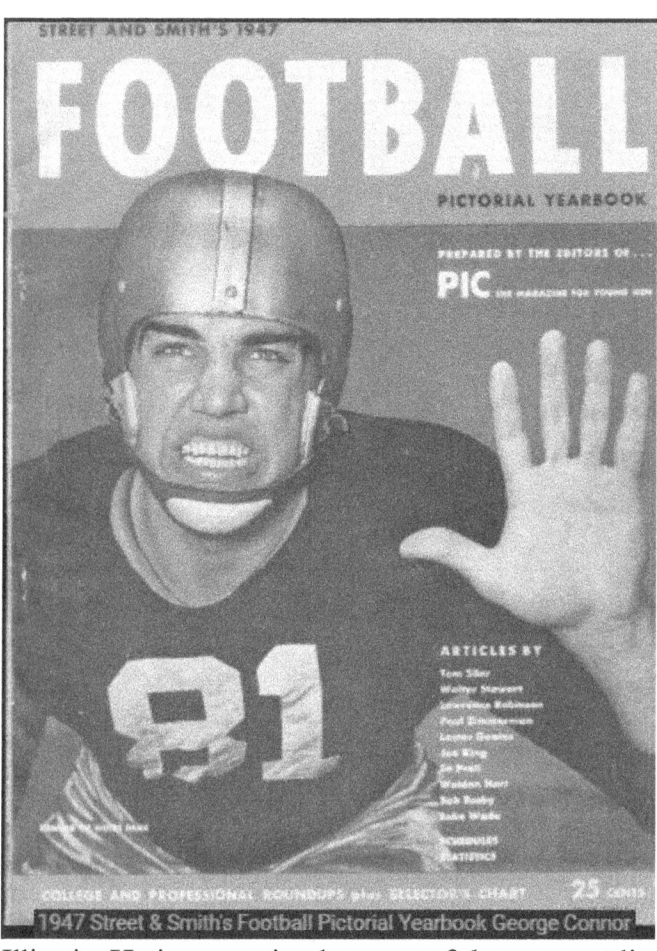

1947 Street & Smith's Football Pictorial Yearbook George Connor

George Connor was a pretty good football player and that is an understatement. He played for Frank Leahy's championship teams and Leahy liked him. That is a true statement. He had to be good. He was an All-American tackle and Captain of the Championship ND squads.

He came just a few miles south to Notre Dame from Chicago, Illinois. He is recognized as one of the greatest linemen ever to play college ball. With Moose Krause, he was known as the number two "Moose" in the Irish football administration.

George Connor said he would play pro ball only if given the right offer. Otherwise, he said he would go into business. He could not see himself as a coach. He had played a lot of football for Holy Cross before coming to ND as a Midshipman. He returned after discharge.

He has similarities to the one-time Notre Dame line and basketball coach, "Moose" Krause. Connor played high school ball at La LaSalle, tackle at Notre Dame and captain of the "Fighting Irish.". George also played an aggressive game of basketball for N.D. in his last season. When his bio was written, by ND students, he took a lot of heat. At the end, they said: 'Tis rumored the big Irishman has had many proposals of marriage . . . "'tis also rumored that that's the one field in which he is not interested at the present time."

After the war, Connor was drafted in the first round, fifth overall by the New York Giants in 1946, but instead transferred to the University of Notre Dame to be closer to his ill father. He was twice a consensus All-American as a tackle for the Notre Dame Fighting Irish football team, in 1946 and 1947.

He won the first Outland Trophy as the nation's best college interior lineman in 1946. Connor was a key component of Notre Dame's 1946 and 1947 national championship teams, and was the captain of the unbeaten 1947 team.

After graduating, Connor signed with the Chicago Bears in 1948 for $13,000 a year guaranteed for three years, a high salary at the time for a lineman. He played for the Bears from 1948 through 1955. In eight seasons, he was named a first-team All-Pro five times, and was an invitee to the first four Pro Bowls.

At first, he played exclusively as a tackle on defense. However, some things change. In a game in 1949, famous Bears head coach George Halas ordered Connor to stand upright outside the end in an attempt to thwart the running of Philadelphia Eagles halfback Steve Van Buren. The plan worked, as Connor held Van Buren in check and the Bears handed the Eagles their only loss of the season. "We always set high standards for George Connor and he exceeded them," said Halas. He became one of the first big, mobile linebackers in the NFL. Connor retired during training camp in 1956, still bothered by a knee injury sustained in 1954

Great Player: Ziggy Czarobski, RT 1942-43, 1946-47

Ziggy made the first-team All-American as senior in '47 on teams named by International News Service (INS) and Newspaper Enterprise Association (NEA). He began his playing as a starter for the Fighting Irish on the 1943 national championship team.

He spent two years in the military, then returned to play right tackle on '46 and '47 national title teams. He was a great player. As such, he was drafted in the seventh-round by the Chicago Cardinals in the 1947 NFL draft. He played two seasons with the Chicago Rockets and Hornets of All-America Football Conference, and then became administrative assistant to Illinois Secretary of State. In 1977 inductee into National Football Foundation Hall of Fame.

Lujack, 90, in the picture on the next page is considered one of the greatest players in Notre Dame history, leading the Fighting Irish to national championships in 1943, 1946 and 1947 in posting a 20-1-1 record as starting quarterback. He was named athlete of the year by The Associated Press in 1947, when he was a first-round draft pick of the Chicago Bears.

Legendary Johnny Lujack returns to Notre Dame Stadium

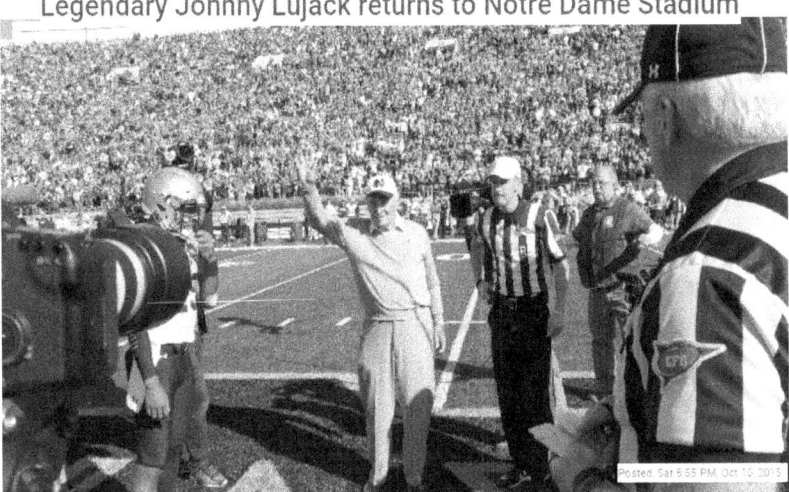

John Lujack, the 1947 **Heisman Trophy** winning quarterback who led Notre Dame to three national championships despite missing two seasons while serving in the Navy during World War II, went out with the Fighting Irish captains for the coin toss before the 2015 game against the Midshipmen.

Lujack, who battled health issues in 2015, appeared in great spirits giving a wave to the crowd after his name was announced and he received a big ovation from the Irish faithful.

My good friend, former Villanova QB Jack Lammers longed as a young man to be QB at Notre Dame. Hanging on his bedroom wall was a picture of Johnny Lujack. Jack and I have been sharing notes through the writing of this book. He recently sent me this note which says something about Johnny Lujack. It was a story that was related to him by his wonderful late wife Eileen:

> Brian, When I was playing at Villanova Eileen was already working in a surgical unit at St. Vincent's Hosp. in NYC. A man came in for minor surgery and Eileen struck up a conversation with him. In the course of the conversation she mentioned that I was a quarterback at Villanova and asked him if he played any football. He replied," A little". Johnny Lujack was a modest man.
> Jack

Great Player: Johnny Lujack, QB 1942-43, 1946-47

We do not attempt to identify the greatest player of all time in ND football but many who have done so, place Johnny Lujack at the top. Just saying! And, he played a long time ago. He is the oldest living Heisman Trophy winner.

Lujack was not supposed to start at QB in 1943. He took over at quarterback for Notre Dame as a sophomore when Angelo Bertelli joined the Marines. Bertelli by the way was one of ND's best also as he won the Heisman in 1943 though he played just six games.

Lujack then ended up helping the Irish to three national titles. He was the best or one of the best QB's in Notre Dame Football History. You make that call. There are a lot of greats who played QB and other positions at Notre Dame for sure.

He established a reputation as one of the great T-formation signal callers in college football history. In his initial start versus Army in 1943, he threw for two scores, ran for another and intercepted a pass in a 26-0 victory. He spent nearly three years of his own in the Navy but returned in time to earn consensus All-America honors as a junior and senior on Notre Dame teams in 1946 and 1947. Neither of these teams lost a single game.

Johnny Lujack attended Notre Dame, where he was given a scholarship by Coach Frank Leahy, from 1942 to 1943 and then from 1946 to 1947. Like a number of ND players, his career was interrupted for two years by World War II after his sophomore season. During the war, he served as an officer in the United States Navy. His time in the Navy was spent hunting German submarines in the English Channel as an ensign.

He was no slouch as runner also. He initially played halfback as a sophomore before taking over for Bertelli. He also punted -- and probably made his greatest individual play on defense.

On Oct 11, 1947, QB Johnny Lujack #32 of ND ran with the ball against Purdue at Ross Ade Stadium in Indiana. Lujack and the Irish beat the Boilermakers 22-7

He preserved a scoreless tie in 1946 between the second ranked Irish and top-ranked Army by making a touchdown-saving tackle of Cadet Fullback Doc Blanchard from his defensive back position. As a junior, he finished third in the Heisman voting behind Army's Glenn Davis.

As a senior, he earned the Associated Press male athlete of the year award. Lujack later played four years with the Chicago Bears, leading the team in scoring each year, tying a record with eight interceptions as a rookie, throwing for a record 468 yards in one game in '49 and playing in the NFL Pro Bowl his last two seasons.

He was an Irish backfield coach for two years following his retirement in '52, Lujack then ran an automobile dealership in Davenport, Iowa, until he retired from business in 1988. He was elected to the National Football Foundation Hall of Fame in 1960.

Lujack recently gave $200,000 to Notre Dame to establish an academic scholarship endowment.

Johnny Lujack played on both sides of the ball at ND but he is best known as a quarterback. In the most famous game of the century, you may recall as we just discussed above that it was Johnny Lujack whose shoestring tackle on Doc Blanchard prevented a touchdown and saved the day for the Irish. Well, quarterbacks are not typically on the field when the other team has the ball.

Johnny Lujack also starred at defensive back for the Bears in 1948. His 11 interceptions were third in the NFL that season, and he was named to the Chicago Herald-American's All-NFL team. The irony is that he was not supposed to be playing defense. He was drafted as a quarterback. The Bears had not drafted Lujack to play defense. So, how'd that happen?

"That first year up, Bobby Layne was the quarterback," Lujack recalled in an interview. "They got rid of Layne, thinking I was going to take over, which I did." Bobby Layne went on to have tremendous success and become a Pro Football Hall of, Lujack's accomplishments also stand out. After all, the Bears Famer kept him.

Johnny Lujack Running the Football for the Chicago Bears

Lujack was simply great and a great man besides. He was drafted in the first round by the Chicago Bears in 1948 after winning the

Heisman for ND. What his pro career will not tell you is that he had previously been drafted by Chicago as an ND Junior in 1946 after the war but the young man decided to finish his degree at Notre Dame and play football for the Irish. That was the year he won the Heisman.

In the final game of the 1949 Pro season, the 9-3 Bears defeated their hometown rivals, the Chicago Cardinal (6-5-1), by a score of 52-21 on December 11. In that game Lujack threw six touchdown passes and set an NFL record with 468 passing yards. The record was broken later by <u>Norm Van Brocklin</u>. In the same 1949 season, he was better than Bobby Layne and the rest of the league in passing yardage (2,658) and passing touchdowns (23).

This all-around Notre Dame graduate wasn't just a threat on defense or with his arm. The following year he set a league single-season record for rushing touchdowns with 11, and he averaged over 6 yards per carry. He played just four years as a pro until his contract was up. He never made more than $20,000 a season. He could have been the greatest pro football player ever but he had a sense of duty.

It was duty first when he joined the Navy after his standout football year of 1943. It was duty again when he was asked to return to Notre Dame to help Frank Leahy, his former coach. "I had the chance to become the quarterback coach at Notre Dame under [Head Coach Frank] Leahy's last two years, 1952 and 1953. I felt that was a good way to repay Notre Dame and Leahy for giving me a scholarship," Lujack states in the book: <u>The Game before the Money: Voices of the Men Who Built the NFL.</u>

1948 Notre Dame Football Season Coach Frank Leahy

The 1948 Notre Dame Fighting Irish football team was coached by Frank Leahy. Notre Dame won its first nine games and then at the end of the season, the Irish visited Southern California, a long-time rival and always a very good football team. Southern Cal tied the Irish T (14-14).

But for this one faux pas, Notre Dame may have had its fourth National Championship in a row. Instead the AP selected the

Fighting Irish as the #2 team in the country. The Michigan Wolverines were #1 based on strength of schedule.

Great Player: Bill Fischer LG, 1945-1948

Bill "Moose" Fischer was another one of the greats who played for Notre Dame University on its greatest football teams. He sure seems to be enjoying himself in this staged milk commercial from when he was playing pro ball with Chicago. Battered helmet, some blood on his forehead, a missing tooth and a glass of fresh milk is something everybody needs.

The war years were a funny time in college football. They say that Fischer made the short trek from Chicago and signed up at ND and the football program to play for coach Hugh Devore's 1945 team. At this time, you may recall, Coach Leahy, and all-time great player and others from ND were in the service, and Leon Hart was still making high school history in Turtle Creek, PA.

Fischer is known now as one of the few successful returnees when Notre Dame's team assembled its team for 1946. !945 was not a bad year per se, but 1946 was a wowser. No one, had ever brought in the degree and quantity of football talent into a program like Frank Leahy did in 1946.

Among many others who were great but may rarely be mentioned in history. Leahy brought in incoming freshmen such as Leon Hart and players like Lujack, Martin and many more who had been "in training" in the Pacific and European theatres in World War II. Fischer, with Hart, was one of the younger players, but in intensity, drive and performance he took no back seat to the returning veterans of America's Greatest Generation. He fit right in. And the team at ND in 1946 was grit tough.

Fischer was ready, and he never lost again through his senior season in '48. He was a key player on the dominant '46-'48 teams, football's greatest dynasty. At 6'2" 226 lbs., he was not the giant that Hart was, but was he could still be called massive for his era, the time when "watch-charm" guards were prized.

His size and physique prompted him to fall heir to the "Moose" nickname initially bestowed on fellow Chicagoan Edwin "Moose" Krause. Moose Krause, before he was elevated to become Athletic Director, was an Irish assistant for Frank Leahy and Moose Krause was coaching Moose Fischer.

With George Connor, Zygmont Carobski and Jim Martin, Fischer helped pave the way for Emil Sitko to earn the moniker "Six yard Sitko."

In 1946, the Irish gained over 3,000 rushing yards and allowed only 760. The Irish never stopped. The team averaged over 2,900 yards each year that Bill Fischer started.

Unlike his teammate, who some call the clown prince, Zygmont Czarobski, Bill Fischer was quiet, unassuming. Frank Leahy had played offensive tackle for Rockne. Leahy knew a great offensive lineman when he saw one, and he valued the quiet efficiency of a powerful craftsman like Fischer.

Bill Fischer was a consensus All-American in '47 and '48, a senior captain and outland Trophy winner in '48. Moose Fischer was inducted into the College Football Hall of Fame in 1983.

Great Player Bill Walsh, C 1945-1948

When former Irish center Bill Walsh was hired to be an assistant football coach at Notre Dame in 1955, the university summarized his play from 1945 through 1948 in a press release: "In four years at Notre Dame, Walsh established himself as one of football's real iron men. He played center in every one of the scheduled 38 games and started 27. The Irish went unbeaten three of Walsh's four seasons and won two national championships."

Walsh, a three-sport, nine-letter winner at Phillipsburg High in Phillipsburg, New Jersey, where he graduated in 1945, earned the starting center position at Notre Dame that fall. But circumstances changed in 1946, when several players returned from serving in World War II. George Strohmeyer won the regular position and became an All-American. Walsh persevered in practice. After the third game of 1947, he was elevated to the first team and Strohmeyer moved to the second squad.

The 6'2" 205-pound Walsh, who was strong, aggressive, and tough, held the starting position through the 1948 season, his senior year. Not chosen for any All-American teams, Walsh was still drafted number three by the Pittsburgh Steelers in 1949. He was also selected to play in the annual College All-Star game at Soldier Field in Chicago.

After three weeks of practice, the collegians were whipped by the National Football League Champion Philadelphia Eagles. But

Walsh went on to become the Steelers' regular center for six straight years and started in the first two Pro Bowls. A modest, quiet, and hard-working athlete who lived and breathed football, Walsh began a new career as an offensive line coach with Notre Dame in 1955.

He spent three seasons with the Irish, moved to Kansas State for a year, and launched his pro career with Hank Stram of the Dallas Texans of the American Football League in 1960. When he retired after the 1991 campaign, Walsh had coached for 32 seasons in the AFL and the NFL.

His experience included stints with the Texans, who became the Kansas City Chiefs in 1963, the Atlanta Falcons, the Houston Oilers, and the Philadelphia Eagles.

As a former star Phillipsburg High School football player, many in the Phillipsburg community see Walsh's phenomenal career as having put this New Jersey state border town in the Lehigh Valley on the map. They loved Bill Walsh and still do though he passed on recently. From high school, of course, Bill Walsh went on to play for the University of Notre Dame and the Pittsburgh Steelers. When he died on a Sunday morning in May 2012, he was 84 years old.

A 1945 graduate of Phillipsburg High School, he was a standout lineman for the Stateliners during the early 1940s before going on to be an All-American center at Notre Dame and an All-Pro for the Steelers in the NFL. His friends said the nicest things about him.

"He put Phillipsburg on the sports map," former New Jersey state Sen. and classmate Anthony Russo said of Walsh. "He was just a wonderful person."

Walsh, who was ranked No. 35 in the Express-Times 100 Greatest Athletes, also starred in baseball and basketball during his years at Phillipsburg.

"He was always very fond of the Phillipsburg area," Mike Walsh, his son, said. Bill Walsh was particularly proud of his 2006 induction into the Easton-Phillipsburg Football Hall of Fame, his son said.

The family returned north for the ceremony in the year of the 100th Easton-Phillipsburg Thanksgiving Day game.

In 1983, Bill Walsh was inducted into the Lehigh Valley chapter of the National Football Foundation and College Hall of Fame.

In four years at Notre Dame, Walsh played in all but one of 38 games, starting in 27 of them. He was part of three undefeated teams and two national championship teams when he played for the Fighting Irish.

"He was almost as proud of his time playing at Phillipsburg as he was of the Notre Dame and pro stuff," Mike Walsh, one of Bill Walsh's six children with Shirley Walsh, said. "He was a fantastic father, fantastic husband, fantastic friend and fantastic football coach.

"All of his players absolutely loved him. He had lot of influence on a lot of people."

Bob Stem, a star center at Phillipsburg who went on to become the Stateliners' winningest coach in football history, remembers the only time he met Walsh.

"When I was a senior in high school, he was coaching Notre Dame at the time and came to talk to me about playing there," Stem said. "I still remember sitting on the visitors' side of the field house with him."

"I told him I was more interested in Syracuse. He said, 'Well that's a great choice,'" Stem said.

Former Phillipsburg football coach Phil Rohm hardly knew Walsh but respects his accomplishments.

"I really didn't know him well," Rohm said. "I might have met him once. I'm not sure. He's one of the real legends of P'burg football. He really did a heck of a job for himself."

Great Player: Marty Wendell, RG, 1945-1948

Marty Wendell, another one of the Leahy bests who never learned how to lose a football game was four-year starting guard from 1945-48 and a Collier's magazine first-team All-American, He was a great offensive lineman. He credits Leahy with creating talent, not just using it:

MARTIN P. WENDELL

"A lot of people say that you got to have the ballplayers. But I think he made the ballplayers."

Among the ballplayers from Wendell's era – including the great '46 and '47 squads, 42 played professional football, a staggering number. Eight of them--Lujack, Hart, Connor, Fischer, Bill Walsh, George Ratterman, John Mastrangelo and Joe Signaigo--earned NFL all-pro honors.

Great Player: Terry Brennan LHB, 1945-1948

Terry Brennan played under Frank Leahy at Notre Dame graduating in 1949. He started for three seasons at halfback and led the Irish in receiving and scoring in '46 and '47 while also rushing for 1,269 career yards.

After winning three straight city championships at Mount Carmel High School as a coach in Chicago, he returned to Notre Dame in 1953 to coach the freshman squad under Leahy.

He succeeded Leahy as head coach in 1954 and his five-year 32-18 record included 9-1 and 8-2 records his first two seasons that ranked the Irish fourth and ninth, respectively, in the final Associated Press polls. In 1959 he became the player conditioning coach for the Cincinnati Reds in spring training and eventually joined a Chicago investment banking firm, gracefully making his exit from football. Terry Brennan would have been a great coach.

1949 Notre Dame Football Season Coach Frank Leahy

The 1949 Notre Dame Fighting Irish football team, coached by Frank Leahy for the seventh time, won the national championship for the third time in four years, The Irish, ended the season with 10 wins, and no losses. ND was undefeated and untied. This 1949 squad became the seventh Irish team to win the national title and to repeat, the third in four years.

The Fighting Irish were led by Heisman winner Leon Hart throughout this championship season as well as Jim Martin. Hart was a 6' 5" 260-pound end at time when they did not grow them that big. ND outscored its opponents 360-86.

Great Player Jim Martin LE, 1946-1949

Jim Martin was first-team All-American as a senior in 1949 on teams named by Associated Press, Newspaper Enterprise Association (NEA) and International News Service (INS). He played for the Irish during a four-year period in which they did not lose a game.

He was a four-year starter who played both ways in multiple position. His first three years at end and his senior season at tackle. He was co-captain of Frank Leahy's 1949 national championships team. He was a dynamo. He led the team in minutes played with 405.

Martin received many honors, including the George Gipp Award as top athlete on campus. He played in East-West Shrine and College All-Star Games. As a soldier defending our country, he won the Bronze Star in Marine Corps during World War II. He was a second-round pick of NFL Cleveland Browns in the 1950 draft.

James Martin played one season with Cleveland, then 11 more with the Detroit Lions (1951-61), earning all-pro honors in 1961 when he also led team in scoring with 15 field goals and 25 PATs. When he was finished with football, Martin became a court officer for the 48th Michigan District Court. He was inducted into the National Football Foundation Hall of Fame in 1995.

Great Player Leon Hart, RE, 1946-1949

Leon Hart won the Heisman Trophy in 1949. Hart and Larry Kelley of Yale (the '36 winner) rank as the only linemen ever to win the Heisman Trophy. Joining Irish teammate and tackle Jim Martin as the last of the two-way players with the advent of two-platoon football, Hart gained a reputation as an outstanding blocker and superb rusher on defense in addition to his estimable pass-catching skills.

A four-time letter-winner, Hart never played on the losing side during his years in a Notre Dame uniform as the Irish went 36-0-2 and claimed three national championships. He became a three-time first-team All-American and a consensus choice as a junior and senior.

In 1949 he was voted the Associated Press male athlete of the year, outpointing such famous names as Jackie Robinson and Sam Snead.

He also received the Maxwell Award as top collegiate player in 1949.

A mechanical engineering major, Hart called defensive signals and often played fullback as a senior to confuse defenses. He went on to play eight seasons with the Detroit Lions, helping the team to three NFL titles and earning all-pro honors on both offense and defense in 1951.

Now living in Birmingham, Mich., Hart heads up a variety of business enterprises, including the manufacture of tire-balancing equipment. He was elected to the National Football Foundation and Hall of Fame in 1973.

The 1949 team was the last Irish team to be considered part of the Notre Dame Football dynasty, a stretch of games in which Notre Dame were 36-0-2 and won three national championships and two Heisman Trophies.

Frank Leahy's teams after the war were the best of the best. But for the tie in USC against the Trojans in 1948, this would have been Notre Dame's fourth undefeated season in a row.

Hart and Martin Lead '49 Team
Leon Hart and James Martin, l to r... Hart was known as a 21-year-old "Monster" who had established himself as one of the great ends in Notre Dame history. This 245-pound

stripling, moved swiftly on offense, blocks and tackles sharply to earn fully his All-America rating. Martin moved to the tackle post from his old end position this season, Jungle Jim has carved a name for himself in the Irish forward wall. A senior, Jim at 27 years old was heavyweight boxing champ at Notre Dame in 1947.

1949 All American ND QB Bob Williams #14 tackled in end zone

The summary in the ND Scholastic Magazine on this game reads as follows:

> *Dallas, Texas, Dec. 3. —Mighty Notre Dame battled against Southern Methodist for its championship life today, and, like a champion, it won. Powering 56 yards on the ground to break a 20-all fourth period tie and then stand off a furious Mustang drive on their own four-yard line, the Irish defeated SMU, 27-20, in the biggest thriller of the 1949 season.*
>
> *The 75,428 who sat in the drizzling rain at the Cotton Bowl here expected Coach Frank Leahy's team to roll to an easy win. Instead, they saw Matty Bell's aroused Texans give Notre Dame its toughest contest in an unbeaten string that now stands at 38 games.*
>
> *Notre Dame has gone four consecutive seasons without losing and Coach Leahy's record stands at 60 wins, three losses and five ties.*

Great Player: Emil Sitko, FB, 1946-1949

Emil Sitko was what the Scholastic referred to as the little "Red" stick of dynamite that has sparked the Irish since 1946. He came from Fort Wayne, Ind. He was an all-around athlete at just 5' 8" and 180 pounds. Emil won four football, two basketball, and three track letters while in high school. He was an economics major. In college, he was not engaged but planned to marry Miss Dorie Anne Liddy of Fort Wayne in the near future

<<< Emil Sitko-- He always liked to pitch horseshoes and was quite a fisherman. He enjoyed all winter sports and was an excellent bridge player, and classical music is one of his favorite listening past-times pleases him.

Joe Osmanski, former Chicago Bear fullback and now coach at Holy Cross, rates Emil Sitko highest on his sports favorite list. Emil has won football monograms and the Hering Award as the most elusive back on the squad at Notre Dame. He was a great ND Football player.

Coach Leahy once said. "... But he was the fastest starting back I ever coached."

Emil Sitko spent time in the military during World War II and did not enter directly into college. When he came out of the service in World War II, he enrolled at Notre Dame as a 23-year-old freshman.

He started on the football team in ND's glory years from 1946 to 1949 at right half and one year at fullback. In those four years, the Notre Dame record was 36–0–2. Besides his nickname of "Red", he was known in football as "Six- Yard Sitko." He led his team in rushing all four years and his career average was 6.1 yards a try.

In 1949 he also led the team in kickoff returns, averaging 22 yards. He made the All-America teams of the Sporting News and the Football Writers Association of America in 1948 and was unanimous All-America in 1949.

Emil also finished eighth in the 1949 Heisman Trophy voting behind teammate Leon Hart. He also won the 1949 Walter Camp Award as outstanding college player. Sitko still stands seventh on Notre Dame's career rushing charts.

Sitko played three seasons in the NFL for the San Francisco After College, he took a shot at the Pros right and played three years for the San Francisco 49ers and then he played right up the road for the Chicago Cardinals before retiring and returning to his hometown to work in the auto sales business. He died in 1973, at age 50, after a heart attack. He was inducted into the College Football Hall of Fame in 1984.

1950 Notre Dame Football Season Coach Frank Leahy

The 1950 Notre Dame Fighting Irish football team, coached by Frank Leahy during his eighth year at Notre Dame, ended the season with 4 wins, 4 losses, and one tie. There were some sportswriters who blamed this season on a cutback by over ½ of player scholarships. Because Notre Dame as most colleges lives well from the munificence and beneficence of its alumni, the problem of the football team being short on scholarships would be self-correcting, regardless of the academic standards of the institution.

Besides a lack of scholarships to replace the greats who had moved on. The gravy train of servicemen who had come and who played football at Notre Dame had stopped.

1951 Notre Dame Football Season Coach Frank Leahy

Coach Leahy and Captain Jim Mutschweiller brought the Notre Dame Fighting Irish back from 4-4-1 to a respectable # 13 ranking and a 7-2-1 record in 1951.

1952 Notre Dame Football Season Coach Frank Leahy

The 1952 Notre Dame Fighting Irish football team, coached by Frank Leahy fought to a 7-2-1 season record. In the AP and the coaches poll Notre Dame was recognized as the #3 top team in the USA.

1953 Notre Dame Football Season Coach Frank Leahy

Let's begin our look at the 1953 season with a great introduction from the December 1953 edition of ND's Scholastic Magazine:

> *December 11, 1953 Notre Dame, Ind. To OUR READERS: When eleven members of Notre Dame's 1953 pigskin squad lined up for the first whistle down in Norman, Oklahoma, earlier this Fall, they were opening up the sixty-fifth season of Irish competition in intercollegiate football.*
>
> *And they were conscious of the fact too, that their predecessors—in the 64 seasons before them—had built a reputation for Notre Dame as one of the oldest and most consistently hard-to-beat football powers—in the nation. They carried quite a number of impressive laurels into that first game with them:*
>
> *Notre Dame teams had brought the National Championship back to South Bend seven different times—a feat no other school had equaled in the long history of collegiate football. Notre Dame teams had also won six Western Championship titles, and they had amassed a total of 17 undefeated seasons—ten of them, untied. They had established a record with modem college football's longest string of unbeaten games at 39.*
>
> *The Fighting Irish had also turned out more All-Americans than any other college or university in the nation. The prowess of Gipp, Crowley and Brown previewed the performances of the immortal four horsemen and their rampage that set the nation's gridirons afire in the early 1920s. Since then, the roster has grown with the names of men like Carideo, Brill, Connor, Lujack, Fischer and Hart.*
>
> *This year's team has done it again—in performances and personalities.*
>
> *They have plowed through a suicidal schedule with what we consider as a powerful precision that matches any previous team in Notre Dame's history. At times, when the odds were stacked, they produced the stuff that has earned for them the national recognition which they justly deserve. Although not every one of them got All-American honors, every one of them played like it.*

You've noticed, for example, that Notre Dame seldom shook one of its backs loose for long touchdown sprints this season; but they tore opposing teams to shreds with steady power plays and tricky tosses until they finally hit pay dirt. This is the story of teamwork ... the story that always ends well.

Looking back, we can truthfully say that it has been another great season. Most people say that this year's team will go down in the record books as one of our greatest. Only time will tell. One thing we do know, however, is that it was made up of the same stuff 64 teams before it had—the will to win.

We're again reminded of the words former Irish captain Jack Alessandrini once said at a pep rally before a game with Pittsburgh: "We can't be beat when we won't be beat." It's the same principle that wins National Championships and molds All Americans. As Knute Rockne put it: "I don't want a man to go in there to die gamely—I want a man to go in there fighting to live!"

Not -- Notre Dame plays so hard—not because she hates to lose, but because she loves to win.

Patrick Carrico
Editor, the Scholastic.

Great Player: Johnny Lattner, HB, 1951-1953

Coach Frank Leahy guided John Lattner to win the **Heisman Trophy**. It was Leahy's fourth player to win the Heisman. Lattner was an all-around great player. He did not lead the Irish in passing, rushing, receiving or scoring. However, Lattner held the Notre Dame record for all-purpose yards for twenty-six years until Vagas Ferguson broke it in 1979.

Lattner claimed the Heisman Trophy during his senior year. It was the second-closest Heisman balloting in history. It bears repeating that Lattner did not lead the Irish in rushing, passing, receiving or scoring. He was a jack of all trades who barely nosed out Minnesota's Paul Giel for the award, Lattner clearly benefitted from helping Leahy's final Notre Dame team to a 9-0-1 record and having the Irish win the national title recognition helped the balloting. Johnny received the Maxwell Award as the top collegiate player as both a junior and senior and finished fifth in the Heisman voting as a junior behind Oklahoma's Billy Vessels.

Johnny Lattner, ND Great Hauls One In

John Lattner #14 of UND Irish avoids being tackled circa 1952 at ND Stadium in S. Bend, Jan 01, 1952

In 1953, The Notre Dame Fighting Irish football team played its last season for Coach Frank Leahy who retired for health reasons. The Irish were undefeated again under Leahy with a record of 9-0-1, which got Notre Dame a #2 finish in the national standings.

Leahy Resigns at Notre Dame

Frank Leahy, the most successful college football coach of his time, resigned in 1953 from the University of Notre Dame.

Chapter 14 Coach Terry Brennan: 1954-1958

Coach # 20

Coach Terry Brennan Was Just a Kid

1954	Terry Brennan	9–1
1955	Terry Brennan	8–2
1956	Terry Brennan	2–8
1957	Terry Brennan	7–3
1958	Terry Brennan	6–4

Head coach Terry Brennan, and Heisman Winner Paul Hornung in his monogram sweater, with the Enterprise Football Medal.

Intro from Chicago Tribune continued

Brennan, who at 25 [was] the youngest of the Notre Dame corps, was the only one with extensive experience as a head coach. His Mount Carmel High School teams won the Chicago Championship three straight years – 1950, 1951, and 1952.

Coach Terence Patrick Brennan, who was born June 11, 1928, and was just 26 years old when appointed Notre Dame Head Football Coach in 1954, took over after Frank Leahy retired.

Notre Dame was beginning to believe in its own magic. Leahy worked sixteen hour plus days and (living 30miles away) never went home in order to bring winning seasons to Notre Dame. There was no magic in his results—just hard work. At 45 years of age, Frank Leahy had gotten old too, too quickly and he was feeling old when he retired.

Terry Brennan was a good man and always a good coach but Leahy, almost like Rockne before him, was so extra good that even today many expert analysts looking back consider him as a souped up coaching version of Knute Rockne. Notre Dame always has the highest expectations for all of its coaches. Rockne for thirteen and then Leahy for eleven spoiled Notre Dame into thinking wins came simply by being Notre Dame. Who, after Leahy could make anybody think that a loss or a tie was acceptable? Nobody!

When Leahy moved on, Notre Dame was so accustomed to winning that it had begun to take winning for granted in the appointment of Terry Brennan, a good man and a great coach but with just high school experience. Brennan took on the most major leadership collegiate football coaching role in the US at age 26. He did fine.

Some say Parseghian pulled a Leahy later on in ND history with all of his success. He helped the University again to take winning for granted. University officials again blindly trusted another great HS coach, Gerry Faust, a championship HS coach of the highest caliber, to bring in the bacon. Said differently, the University repeated the Terry Brennan mistake by bringing on a high school coach after Parseghian and Devine, even though they had been forced to fire Brennan, whose record was actually not bad at all.

As we will see in this chapter, Brennan got off to a fine start with a (9-1) campaign in 1954 with players that had been recruited and coached by Leahy. But, there were issues brewing.

ND Nation's reports were spot-on:

"In 1947 Notre Dame cut scholarships from 32 to 18 (Michigan and Ohio State had 45-50 scholarships to give) hobbling Leahy's great run and hastening his exit. [After Leahy's 4-4-1 1950 season, he got more scholarships and the team made a comeback]. That move was followed by questionable hires and rising academic standards. During Terry Brennan's era, Hunk Anderson said "You can't run this program with these numbers and I'll tell you what else, when the shit comes down, you guys will be the fall guys." Anderson actually organized a group of monogram winners to plead for more scholarships (Hesburgh turned him down.) To sum up quotes from "Talking Irish", and "Resurrection," Notre Dame's mediocrity seemed to come from a combination of poor coaching, low scholarships and a general lack of support.

When Ara came to Notre Dame, the Irish were far behind in the scholarship arms race. It started with the neutering of Leahy and Notre Dame didn't wake up until Ara. When Parseghian came in he convinced Hesburgh to increase scholarships from 24 to 34. Still far behind the land grant schools, but that move gave Notre Dame a chance to build a program and, importantly, signaled that Notre Dame was serious about competing again. Parseghian continued to push the administration along, earning concessions where Brennan and Kuharich failed."

What this meant was that Notre Dame had determined that either it could do well without scholarships or that it was OK if it did not do well so it could be recognized as more elite in academia.

The result for a fine coach such as Terry Brennan, was that he got stuck with an intolerable situation as without Leahy, nobody was fighting for the continued health of the football program. As a respectful young man, Brennan did what his elders and superiors told him to do and did not take them on as Leahy and as Parseghian a

1954 Notre Dame Football Season Coach Terry Brennan

First year coach Terry Brennan guided the 1954 Notre Dame Fighting Irish football team to a well-played 9-1 season and a #4 national ranking. Their one loss was against rival Purdue L (14-27) in the battle for the Shillelagh Trophy. The Irish beat Michigan State at home W (20-19) to claim the Megaphone trophy and they beat USC at home W (23-17) to snag the Jeweled Shillelagh.

1955 Notre Dame Football Season Coach Terry Brennan

Quarterback Paul Hornung #5 of the Notre Dame Fighting Irish stiff arms a player from the Navy Midshipmen during their game on October 29, 1955 at Notre Dame Stadium in South Bend, Indiana. The Fighting Irish defeated the Midshipmen. October 29

The 1955 Notre Dame Fighting Irish football team was coached by Terry Brennan. The 27-year old Brennan brought the Irish to an 8-2 season which gave them a # 9 ranking with AP and a #10 ranking in the Coaches poll. H

1956 Notre Dame Football Season Coach Terry Brennan

Terry Brennan coached the 1956 Notre Dame Fighting Irish football team to its worst record of all time (2-8) as Notre Dame remained unranked for the season.

Great Player: Paul Hornung, QB, HB, FB, 1954-56

It is an understatement to suggest that Paul Hornung was an outstanding all-around athlete who played quarterback, left halfback, fullback and safety and who remains the only player from a losing team (Notre Dame finished 2-8 in '56) ever to win the Heisman Trophy.

As a sophomore, Hornung served as the backup fullback and also averaged 6.1 points per contest while earning a basketball monogram. As a junior, he finished fourth nationally in total offense with 1,215 yards and fifth in the Heisman voting behind Ohio State's Hopalong Cassady.

Hornung ran for one score, threw for another and intercepted two passes in a victory over fourth-ranked Navy and then brought the Irish from behind against Iowa with a TD pass and game-winning field goal in the final minutes. In a loss to USC, he threw and ran for 354 yards, an NCAA high that year.

As a senior, he ranked second nationally in total offense (1,337 yards), accounted for more than half the Irish scoring-and converted 67 times on either third or fourth down as a junior and senior combined.

A bonus pick of the Green Bay Packers, he led the NFL in scoring in 1959, '60, and '61. He retired after the '66 season, as physical problems kept him from joining New Orleans as an expansion pick. Hornung joined the National Football Foundation Hall of Fame in 1985, and the Pro Football Hall of Fame in 1986. In addition to various business enterprises in Louisville, Hornung is involved in numerous television and radio broadcasts.

Hornung, who later had a great career with the Green Bay Packers was in his senior year in 1956. He carried the ball 94 times for 420 yards for an average of 4.5 yards per try. The versatile Hornung also completed 59 of 111 passes for a total offensive figure of 1,337 yards.

Hornung is the only Heisman winner to have ever played on a losing team. Hornung's path to the Heisman was filled with intrigue, surprise and adventure. Many pundits would suggest that his was the most controversial Heisman Trophy Award ever given, but nobody could deny his phenomenal athletic abilities.

Paul Horning Being Paul Hornung a great ND Heisman Winner --

Leahy had recruited Hurnung and beat Bear Bryant for his services. He took Hornung aside when he came to visit Notre Dame and calmly looked Hornung in the eye and told the young recruiting prospect that he thought "he could become the best football player in America if he came to Notre Dame." Hurnung signed up.

Hornung was the ideal football player. He was what they called "A triple threat." He could run, pass and KICK. When I was a kid I remember Hurnung also got a KICK out of life. "The lad" was a free spirit, very handsome, making it perfect for him to double as a playboy type with many off-field escapades well noted in what some call the sleepy hamlets of South Bend and Green Bay. Hornung had it all. He was personable and in fact dashing. He earned the nickname, the "Golden Boy!" Later in life he had some neck issues which limited his mobility.

Notre Dame's Press Agent, well-liked Charlie Callahan was continually lobbying for Hornung to be awarded the Heisman in his senior year. He was very convincing and very successful. The Golden Boy beat Johnny Majors by just 72 votes and he beat the great pass-catcher, Tommy McDonald, who came in a strong third.

Terry Brennan was Hornung's coach in his senior year, and surely Brennan claims Hornung as a product of his personal mentoring. However, for those who count things further back, Hornung counts as the fifth ND player to have been coached by Frank Leahy (freshman) to take away the Heisman. Leahy, I am convinced would have given this stat to Brennan but surely was not asked while in retirement.

1957 Notre Dame Football Season Coach Terry Brennan

The 1957 Notre Dame Fighting Irish football team coached by Terry Brennan had a much better year than in 1956. The team finished ranked # 9 in the coaches' poll and #10 in the AP with a 7-3 overall win/loss record.

The historical highlight of the season was on November 16. Terry Brennan's Fighting Irish marched into Oklahoma Memorial Stadium to play the proud Sooners, who were sporting a 47-game winning streak. At the time, this win streak was the record. Notre Dame's W (7–0) victory over Oklahoma snapped the Sooners' NCAA record 47-game winning streak. A lot of forgiveness was given by Notre Dame Fans for the 1956 season after this great triumph.

The win against Oklahoma was monumental. Victory was denied the Sooners that day by QB Bob Williams, Terry Brennan, and all of the Fighting Irish that afternoon at Owen Field.

Irish QB Bob Williams # 9 on ND's winning drive

"Great Player and great quarterback Bobby Williams, [my cousin from Wilkes-Barre PA] played superbly. "You could have quarterback meetings forever," Brennan said. "But the kid's gotta go out there and do it. And he did it." The Irish reached first-and-goal at the OU 8-yard line, then finally faced fourth-and-goal at the three. Williams called the play, a sweep for Lynch. A field goal never entered Brennan's mind. "We wanted a touchdown," he said. Lynch gave them one, with an easy trot around right end, and with 3:50 left in the game, OU trailed." They lost!

The 7-0 Irish victory at Oklahoma was the season highlight. The Irish finished off the season with a win against SMU at the Cotton Bowl in Texas (54-21)

In This Nov. 16, 1957 photo, Notre Dame head coach Terry Brennan is carried off Owen Field by Jim Just (44) and other players following their 7-0 win over Oklahoma in an NCAA college football game in Norman, Okla. Notre Dame's Ron Toth (43) and Jim Colosimo (41) also celebrate the final. That victory ended the Sooners' NCAA-record winning streak at 47 games and came just a season after the Sooners beat the Irish 40-0 in South Bend, still the most lopsided home loss in Notre Dame history.

1958 Notre Dame Football Season Coach Terry Brennan

For a Notre Dame fan, there is only one thing that is just a little worse than a (7-3) season. That of course is a (6-4) season. It's just a little worse. The 1958 Notre Dame Fighting Irish football team, coached by fifth-year coach Terry Brennan could not find that seventh win, and the Irish thus finished the season at 6-4. Notre Dame had just increased the number of scholarships but not in time for its 1958 season. Notre dame finished the season ranked # 18. Brennan had to take the fall. There would be no forgiveness.

After the end of this season, Terry Brennan and his whole coaching staff were fired and Joe Kuharich was appointed the new Notre Dame Head Coach. Coach Hugh Devore was eventually retained for Coach Kuharich as an assistant.

I did some checking on Brennan. I was expecting, at about a 100% level, to find that Mr. Brennan, a great ND player and a great ND coach had either become a successful head coach for another college football program or perhaps he had become a great pro football coach.

I did not know which to expect; but figured one or the other. I expected success for Brennan in football. Since he was before my time, I looked him up and I kept looking as what I expected to find in my research just was not showing up. I eventually tried the Notre Dame web site.

In his biography on http://www.und.com/sports/m-footbl/mtt/brennan_terry00.html, Notre Dame captured the fact that in 1959, Brennan ended his football coaching career and

"... became the player conditioning coach for the Cincinnati Reds in spring training. Eventually, he joined a Chicago investment banking firm."

That's all she wrote. Coaching at Notre Dame is like nothing else in the world. Terry Brennan stopped coaching for good after being fired by Notre Dame. It took me by surprise.

I would recommend a Sports Illustrated article by Leon Jaroff if you want a greater perspective on the Brennan era. http://www.si.com/vault/1959/01/05/668468/surrender-at-notre-dame

Chapter 15 Coach Joseph Kuharich: 1959-1963

Coach Kuharich # 21
Coach Devore # 19 (second time)

1959	Joe Kuharich	5–5
1960	Joe Kuharich	2–8
1961	Joe Kuharich	5–5
1962	Joe Kuharich	5–5
1963	Hugh Devore	2–7

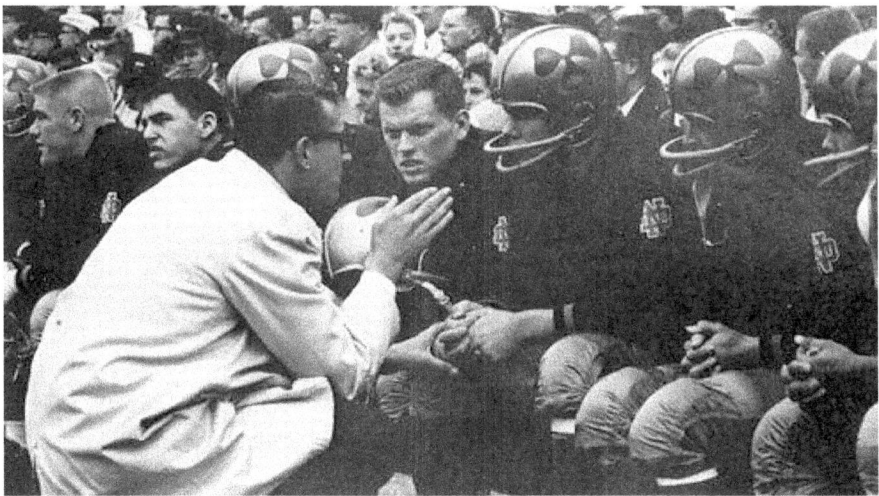

Coach Kuharich made his mark at Notre Dame with the addition of the green shamrock to the gold helmet. The Irish opened the '59 season with the standard all gold shell, facing off against North Carolina and Purdue in their first two games. When they took the field against Cal on October 10th, they unveiled the green shamrock design. However, the decal was placed upon each side of the helmet from a perspective that made it appear as if an airplane propeller was facing the observer, a most unique design! Some thought that the decal was placed upside down but it was merely an attempt by the Kuharich's staff to help jolt the program into a new era.

The Desert Sun Newspaper reported the following on Dec. 22, 1958
Joe Kuharich New Coach at Notre Dame
Succeeds Brennan, Fired by Irish, as Gridiron Mentor
December 22, 1958; **SOUTH BEND. Ind. (UPI)**

> "Joe Kuharich. head roach of the Washington Redskins of the National Football League and former Notre Dame guard, today was named football coach at Notre Dame, succeeding Terry Brennan. Kuharich's appointment was announced oy the Rev, Edmund P. Joyce, Notre Dame executive vice president, and chairman of the faculty Board in Control of Athletics. Release of Brennan, Notre Dame's coach for the past five years, was announced

Sunday by university officials. Father Joyce said that Kuharich has been given a four-year contract. Since 1954, Kuharich has been coach of the Washington Redskins. The new Notre Dame mentor, who is a native of South Bend, actually began his coaching career at Notre Dame in 1938, the year of his graduation, when he served as an assistant freshman coach while taking graduate studies."

1959 Notre Dame Football Season Coach Joe Kuharich

Joe Kuharich took over the Notre Dame Fighting Irish football team in 1959 from Terry Brennan when Brennan was able to achieve just six wins. It is always difficult for a new coach to come to a program and start with great results. In his first year, Kuharich's Fighting Irish finished 5-5. With a four-year contract in his possession. Coach Kuharich knew he would be able to eventually prove himself to Notre Dame fans.

1960 Notre Dame Football Season Coach Joe Kuharich

The 1960 Notre Dame Fighting Irish football team, coached by Joe Kuharich equaled the season and post-season misery index of Terry Brennan's 2-8 1956 team. Many fans think this poor record set the stage for Kuharich to be replaced.

The Irish started off their 1960 season sandwich with a nice slice of bread against California at home with a W (21-7) victory. Then, something went wrong. No matter how well Notre Dame played and no matter how close the games were, for eight straight games Notre Dame could not scrounge out one victory for luck or money. There were many close games in these eight and none went the luck of the Irish. The meat of the sandwich was the eight losses in a row.

Somehow, with all that pain behind them, the Fighting Irish (1-8) seemingly with all the fight kicked out of them, proudly went to California to play USC for the Jeweled Shillelagh. More than that, this game gave the Irish a chance to put a nice piece of bread on their poor tasting season sandwich.

Unexpectedly after such a dismal season, with USC always being such a tough major competitor, Kuharich's Fighting Irish found their fight; found their mettle; and they owned the game that brought them the Jeweled Shillelagh trophy W (17-0). This capped off; the season with a nice piece of bread on one of the ugliest season sandwiches in ND history.

Nobody can deny that without that last slice of California's finest bread, Coach Kuharich more than likely would not have been able to ever build another sandwich.

1961 Notre Dame Football Season Coach Joe Kuharich

The 1961 Notre Dame Fighting Irish football team were coached by Joe Kuharich in his third year as head coach. Coach Kuharich's team struggled in 1960 at 2-8 but came back in 1961 to a 5-5 record and like all ND coaches more would be expected in the future.

Kuharich had two fine co-captains, Norb Roy, and Nick Buoniconti, who had a major claim to fame for years in the NFL.

Daryle Lamonica set to pass

Many fans were talking about Terry Brennan having been ousted after a 6-4 season. How long would Joe Kuharich last if he did not turn around the team in his fourth year as coach? South Bend Tribune sports editor Joe Doyle in 1961, wrote of Kuharich's third year:

"It is hard to believe the same football team played the various parts of the schedule. One moment the Notre Dame team of 1961 seemed to be an eager, hustling squad that believed it could lick any opponent. At other times, it was indifferent, lethargic and unable to cope with anything out of the ordinary on offense or defense."

Great Player: Nick Buoniconti, LB, 1958-1961

Nick Buoniconti of the Notre Dame Fighting Irish was inducted into the Pro Football Hall of Fame in Canton, Ohio on Saturday August 4, 2001.

At just 5-foot-10, the 190-pound Buoniconti received a football scholarship to Notre Dame in 1958. He tells a story about feeling out of place everywhere in South Bend except when on the football field. He earned a starting spot at Notre Dame as a freshman when one of his teammates got injured. Buoniconti needed just one chance.

He dominated play at the collegiate level for Notre Dame. He then spent seven seasons in the AFL for the Boston Patriots and made six All-Star games. The Dolphins wanted him and he came to Miami in 1969. He was at the top of his game. He was quick and strong. He was a running back's nightmare. His speed would get him right to the hole and when the ball carrier got there, Buoniconti would be waiting for him.

At Notre Dame, it took a little time for Buoniconti to establish himself but the head coach when he was a freshman, Terry Brennan knew he had what it takes. Coach Brennan was the first to see the innate toughness and perseverance that would make Buoniconti special when Nick was a star at Cathedral High School in Springfield, Mass.

Brennan recruited him to come to Notre Dame as a lineman and linebacker, even though he was less than six feet tall and weighed barely 200 pounds. Terry Brennan left Notre Dame after Buoniconti's freshman year, and the pundits say Brennan's departure ushered in one of the worst eras in Irish football history under new leader Joe Kuharich.

Every team, good or bad, has a few bright lights. Nick Buoniconti was a huge bright light for three years for Joe Kuharich's Irish. Buoniconti admits they were his toughest football years.

In 1960, as a junior, Nick was second on the Fighting Irish in tackles (behind senior captain Myron Pottios) with 71. As a senior in 1961 he led the team with 74 tackles as the Irish co-captain and was rewarded with 2nd-team All-America selections from UPI, TSN, and the Football Coaches' Association. He was the only All-American on Notre Dame's 1961 team.

The Irish went 12-18 during the Buoniconti years and not Because of NB. That stretch had very few bright spots. Notre Dame managed to beat rival USC all three years and knocked off a highly-ranked Syracuse team with a dramatic last second field goal in 1961. Buoniconti made 212 tackles in his career, including 74 of them to lead the team in his senior season.

Nick Buoniconti said that playing on a losing team prepared him well to deal with the inevitable disappointments of medical research. On October 6, 1985, his son, Marc, a linebacker at The Citadel who played as tough and as fearless as did his dad, dislocated his neck between the third and fourth cervical vertebrae while making a tackle on third-and-short. "He was dying in the hospital in Johnson City," Buoniconti said. "He played East Tennessee State and made a tackle and before his arm hit the ground, he said, 'Dad, I knew I was paralyzed.'"

Marc Buoniconti, with NFL Hall of Fame dad Nick, played linebacker for the Citadel

There is a great article on Nick and Marc Buoniconti that you may like to read at http://notredame.247sports.com/Article/Former-Notre-Dame-All-American-fights-for-a-cure-for-paralysis-68056a.

Nick Buoniconti and his son Marc, have dedicated their lives to find a cure for paralysis. This is a much tougher mission than football. The team of Nick and Marc Buoniconti have helped to raise more than $350 million for spinal cord research. When many of us think of tough, we think of Notre Dame. Now, when we think of tough, we can think of Notre Dame's Nick Buoniconti and the Citadel's Marc Buoniconti who have played a tougher game than football, the game of life, and they are winning.

Feel free to help this great project that is determined to help those suffering catastrophic sports injuries. Please make a donation. http://www.themiamiproject.org/#sthash.wFrhzP6B.dpuf:

1962 Notre Dame Football Season Coach Joe Kuharich

The 1962 Notre Dame Fighting Irish football team again was coached by four-time head coach Joe Kuharich. Daryle Lamonica was Notre Dame's star quarterback but even with Lamonica, the record was another 5-5. Other eventual pro players such as Ed Hoerster and John Slafkosky also played their hearts out on the University of Notre Dame's 1962 college football team.

When Coach Parseghian and his staff from Northwestern arrived in 1964, they came with some first impressions of the ND players and their attitudes about playing top level football. They recall the impressions in words such as: "Geez, we never had personnel as talented as this at Northwestern" – even though the Wildcats were 4-0 against the Irish during the Kuharich years (1959-62).

Ara Parseghian as ND coach gave the Irish troops a pep talk early in his tenure before the 1964 season. He told the team that they were not a disciplined team – that when he was at Northwestern he could count on a lot of Notre Dame Penalties, and that those penalties would help shape the outcome of the game.

Joe Kuharich, a good guy for sure but not necessarily a good college football coach, knew he had not done the job for the University and he voluntarily stepped down after his third 5-5 season. He was succeeded with interim coach Hugh Devore in his second stint as an interim coach. (Leahy 1945).

The irony is that Joe Kuharich never achieved any of the fine season marks as Terry Brennan, including Brennan's last season at 6-4 record, which was "so bad," the young Brennan, barely thirty years of age with five-years head coaching experience at Notre Dame was fired. It was not predestination but fine, determined talented coaching that brings victories.

1963 Notre Dame Football Season Coach Hugh Devore (#2)

The Press was not as kind to Joe Kuharich as the administration of Notre Dame: From 1959 to 1962, Kuharich had become the first and only coach at Notre Dame to compile a losing career record. His 17 victories against 23 defeats are still a record. Kent Baer who filled in for Ty Willingham in 2004 for one game and lost it may technically have the worst record of 0-1, but he took the reins only as a substitute not even as interim. When Kuharich resigned, he was able to land on his feet in the NFL.

Games with Hugh Devore

Devore had put a lot of heart back into the Irish team during his one season at the helm. Although Notre Dame began the season by losing two games-- they played very tough teams bravely and with spirit and the scores were very close. For example, a powerful Wisconsin team beat Notre Dame in the home season opener, L (9-14), and then Purdue scored a victory L (6-7) at Purdue when an Irish two-point conversion try for the win, failed.

The Irish looked pretty good even in defeat. Then ND played two games at home in which they upset a tough Southern California team W (17-14) and then clobbered UCLA W (29-12). They looked so good, it was as if the Irish were back and Devore had the spirit of Rockne and Leahy helping him drive the team to victory.

At (2-2), the prospects of a good season seemed achievable for the remainder of the season. ND had devastated UCLA and beat their big nemesis Southern Cal. After just four games, it did not appear the season would be a failure. It was. ND finished 2-7.

Despite the 2–7 record for the year, Hugh Devore was still loved by all members of the Fighting Irish Community. He was their beloved, personable Devore, affectionately known as "Hughie."

The following year, after the permanent coach was hired, Hugh Devore was presented with a game ball after Notre Dame's victory over Stanford. The 1964 new head coach, Ara Parseghian praised

Devore for making his job that much easier. Hugh Devore was 9-9-1 as a head coach. His not-too shabby football record was well exceeded by his record as a human being.

Chapter 16   Coach Ara Parseghian: 1964-1974

Coach # 22
Two National Championships 1966 & 1973

Rockne, Leahy, Parseghian, All Time Greats— National Championships

1964	Ara Parseghian	9–1	
1965	Ara Parseghian	7–2–1	
1966	Ara Parseghian	9–0–1	*
1967	Ara Parseghian	8–2	
1968	Ara Parseghian	7–2–1	
1969	Ara Parseghian	8–2–1	
1970	Ara Parseghian	10–1	
1971	Ara Parseghian	8–2	
1972	Ara Parseghian	8–3	
1973	Ara Parseghian	11–0	*
1974	Ara Parseghian	10–2	

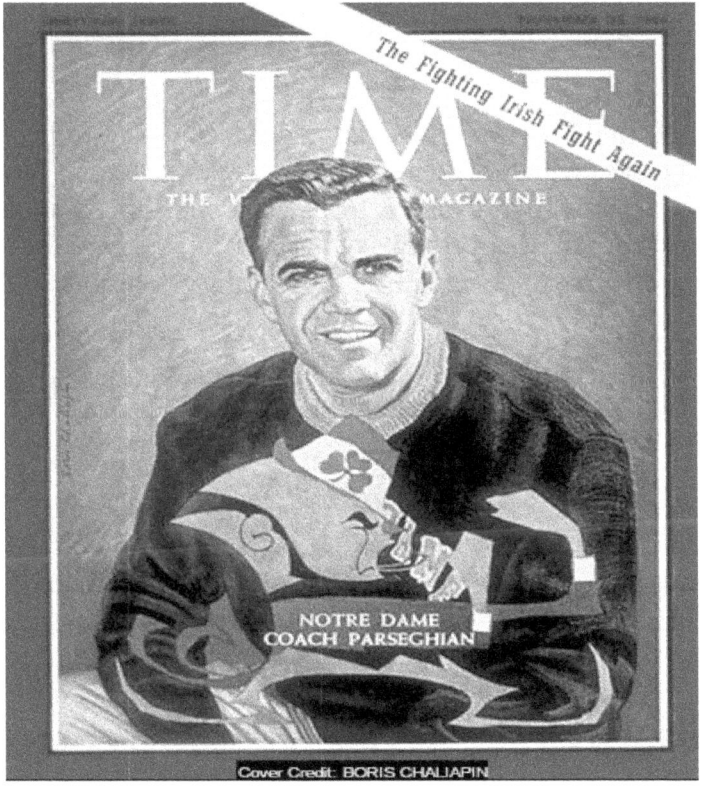

Cover Credit: BORIS CHALIAPIN

Introduction to the Ara Parseghian Era

Ara Parseghian, just like Frank Leahy and Knute Rockne before him was an inspirational person. The story goes that like these two "immortals," Parseghian could make it stop snowing or stop raining if he chose to do so. There were times many Irish fans chanted to stop the snow or stop the rain and magically, they got their wish. Ara Parseghian could take what would have been a lousy team if coached by anybody else and turn it into a dynasty. And, for many, he often did stop the rain and the snow. They'll swear to it!

I recall sitting with my dad on Saturdays as a sixteen-year old senior in High School in 1964 and later when I attended King's College, a Notre Dame founded school in Wilkes-Barre PA. We watched many a game together and we loved Ara Parseghian as the coach.

As Roman Catholics, we were surprised he got to be the coach but we were ever thankful for it. After all, he was one of God's creatures just like us. God surely shined his great light on Ara Parseghian and most of the light went right on through to the Notre Dame Football Team.

As we enter the Ara era in this book, I have collected some very nice historical pieces which relate the Ara Parseghian story at Notre Dame. Here is the first, which is from the Daily Illini, a student newspaper from the University of Illinois. They capture the essence of the negotiations to bring him on-board and the results:

THE DAILY ILLINI
The independent student newspaper at the University of Illinois since 1871

These pieces capture the essence of what happened in the negotiations between Notre Dame and Ara Parseghian, then coach of Northwestern. The Illini paper also got in some stuff about Alex Agase, Parseghian's replacement at Northwestern

From Daily Illini, 18 December 1963
Ara Named Irish Mentor
SOUTH BEND, Ind.

After nearly 36 hours of confusion and speculation, Ara Parseghian was named head football coach at the University of Notre Dame Tuesday and minutes later Alex Agase was appointed his successor at Northwestern University.

Parseghian's appointment was announced here by the Rev. Edmund P. Joyce, executive vice president of Notre Dame. Agase's appointment was announced in Evanston by Northwestern Athletic Director Stu Holcomb. Agase had been head line coach of the Wildcats under Parseghian.
The rapid-fire sequence began with a statement by Father Joyce that Parseghian was in as mentor of the Irish. Only Monday, the fiery, 40-year-old Parseghian had walked out of a meeting with Father Joyce concerning a four-year contract with the Irish. Since Parseghian's walkout, speculation ran rife as to the real reason for the apparent break between the Wildcat head coach and Notre Dame. There still is no immediate answer to the question.

There still was no immediate answer except that Notre Dame did see fit in the face of what could amount to national embarrassment, to keep the door open for Parseghian.
The following statement was released by Father Joyce:
The slight difficulty which arose Monday morning has been resolved. Ara Parseghian will immediately assume the position of head football coach at the University of Notre Dame and will be resident at the university following the East-West Shrine game in San Francisco.

As we said before, we are delighted to have Mr. Parseghian as our head football coach and we look forward to a successful football program under his direction. Simultaneously at his home in Wilmette, Ill., Parseghian made the same announcement given to the press by Father Joyce and said:

"I regret the embarrassment caused Notre Dame by the brief delay. I'm looking forward eagerly to directing football fortune of the Irish. He said: I will immediately assume the position of head football coach at Notre Dame and will be a resident of Notre Dame after the East-West Shrine game.

A native of Evanston, Agase began his athletic career as a guard at Evanston Junior High School. He slipped away from Northwestern and went on to All America fame at Illinois and also at Purdue, where he was a Marine trainee, in 1943, after serving as a lieutenant in the Pacific, where he was wounded in the Okinawa campaign and earned the Purple Heart and Bronze Star, Agase returned to Illinois to lead the Illini to the 1946 Big Ten championship and a 1947 Rose Bowl victory over UCLA.

Agase is one of five children. Two of his brothers also earned letters at Illinois, Lou Agase played football at Illinois and was on the 1946 Big Ten championship team.

Another brother, Herb Agase was a star left-handed pitcher for Illinois in the late 1940's. Alex Agase played with the Chicago Rockets in the defunct All-America Professional Conference, and with the Cleveland Browns for four years before ending his professional career with the Baltimore Colts in 1953. He entered the college coaching ranks as line coach at Iowa State in 1954. Two years later he came to Northwestern as line coach and No. 1 assistant under Parseghian.

We thank NDNATION for permission to use this article to help introduce Ara Parseghian. It is posted on their site: http://ndnation.com/archives/3930

Hardnose
by SEE

(The Rock Report) – Sports Illustrated described Parseghian thusly, "Ara is an impatient, determined man, convinced he can return Notre Dame to a position of dominance in college football, and this he undoubtedly will do one day – but not in 1964."

...

Nicknamed hardnose at Miami by none other than the legendary Paul Brown, Parseghian has lived his life with a passion and conviction that led him to stick his hard nose and square chin into tough situations and create change through force of will and stalwart determination.

Ara simply wouldn't accept mediocrity for himself or his teams and never let conventional thought dictate his success. In fact,

Ara Parseghian may never have become a legend at all at Notre Dame if he didn't take matters into his own hands.

Just to get into the running for the position, Ara had to overcome two hurdles. One, Ara didn't go to Notre Dame and to that point in time, Notre Dame had a history of only hiring Notre Dame Alums for the head coaching role. Two, Notre Dame had an unwritten rule that it did not "poach" coaches and Ara was the coach of Northwestern. [The third rule about having to be a Catholic with eight kids was just a rumor.]

Knowing this, Ara made the first move. He called Father Joyce, and inquired first to see if ND was looking for a new coach (that Hugh Devore was just an interim coach.) Father Joyce confirmed that he wasn't stealing another man's job, Ara made it clear to Father Joyce that he was not going back to Northwestern.

But the question about a non-alumnus, no less an Armenian-Protestant non-alumnus, coaching at Notre Dame wasn't answered clearly and Ara left the conversation doubting that Notre Dame would break tradition. Parseghian deemed the conversation, "a little chilly" to his wife and made plans to interview at Miami.

The Miami down south.

While on his way to Florida, at a layover in St. Louis, Ara called home to see if Notre Dame had returned his call.... they had and wanted to meet with him. Ara ditched the Hurricanes and jumped back on a plane, this one was headed to Chicago.

Still, the marriage almost didn't happen. Ara was eventually offered the job verbally, but he didn't feel comfortable with a verbal agreement that didn't have dollars attached to it and after flirting with Northwestern again, finally hammered out a deal with Father Joyce.

After that, things moved quickly.

When Ara spoke to the team, according to Resurrection, he held up his fist "Just look at my fist" he said, "When I make a fist, it's strong and you can't tear it apart. As long as there's unity, there's strength." He went on for over an hour mesmerizing a team that had stumbled through a decade of mediocrity.

By the time he was done, Tony Carey said he was ready to run through a brick wall for him.

And Ara returned the favor. Upon learning that Nick Rassas didn't have a scholarship, Ara called father Joyce and got him one. When he learned Carey might be eligible for medical-year, he picked up the phone and called father Joyce again, securing an extra year.

Ara could relate to the players, because he had it in his blood. One of his great disappointments was an injury that kept him on the sidelines in the pros for much of his "career."

His playing career over, he channeled that passion into Miami of Ohio, where he became head coach, and compiled a 39-6-1 record. Ara was in the crucible period at the cradle of coaches.

Then, on to Northwestern where after one magical season and many other "good for Northwestern seasons," Northwestern grew tired of Ara constantly pushing for more and told him his contract wouldn't be renewed. Tired of fighting a battle with scholarships tied behind his back, Ara was determined to move on.

When he arrived at Notre Dame he brought order quickly to a program that had fallen into disorder.

Parseghian immediately started fixing what was broken, bringing process and precision where previously there was dysfunction and indecision. He kicked players off the team for rules violations and enforced discipline while motivating players in a way they'd never seen before. In summing up his impact, Jim Dent noted that "more than anything, he was a master organizer" and that Notre Dame's staff operated like a "finely tuned military unit."

Ara brought that same precision to the roster. When Ara evaluated the team, he found players in the wrong positions all over the field. When at Northwestern, Ara befuddled Kuharich, whose "elephant backfield," made Notre Dame easy to defend. Parseghian, who'd had small and fast teams that passed all over the field (for the day) with Tommy Myers at Northwestern, promptly moved the entire elephant backfield to the defensive line at Notre Dame.

Perhaps his biggest position move was really a position elevation. John Huarte, 4th or 5th on the depth chart, threw gorgeous spirals all over the practice field and Ara was intrigued. But after years of what Huarte viewed as unfair treatment by prior coaches, he was stricken with confidence problems. Ara would mold him into a Heisman winner. [He brought back Huarte's confidence in himself.]

Huarte had gone through some rough times, but Ara shared his own experiences at Northwestern and noted how he battled through them. He turned to Huarte and said, "I think your time has come."

The same was true for Notre Dame.

Happy Birthday, Hardnose.

1964 Notre Dame Football Season Coach Ara Parseghian

After enduring a losing composite record after the Frank Leahy years, Notre Dame Head Coach Ara Parseghian, the new coach, immediately put fight back into the Irish and put the Fighting Irish back on the map. It was the beginning of the Parseghian Era in 1964, the coach's first season at the helm.

This 1964 Notre Dame Fighting Irish football team was nothing short of remarkable. Many sports pundits suggest that without some questionable officiating in their final game against Southern California, the Irish would have been undefeated and untied, and would have been the consensus National Champions in Ara's first year. All it takes is a will!

http://bluegraysky.blogspot.com/2005/05/call-him-hardnose.html

"The spirit might be willing, but it takes a powerful amount of flesh to make a football winner—and the most optimistic experts did not figure Notre Dame for much this year [1964]. The school hadn't had a winning season in five years; 22 out of 38 lettermen had graduated from the prior year's squad that lost seven of its nine games. Parseghian rebuilt the team as though he were running a fire sale."

Great Player: John Huarte QB, 1962-1964

What would have or might have is not the 1964 Notre Dame story. Parseghian would have his time to win championships for Notre Dame. The 1964 Notre Dame story is that Ara Parseghian, fresh from turning in a terrific job at Northwestern, came to Notre Dame and took a team that barely broke 500 and with mostly the same players, including quarterback John Huarte, turned them into a #3 consensus ranking team and clearly one of the best, if not the best in college football.

Inspirational stores such as these make Notre Dame watchers become Notre Dame lovers and Notre Dame faithful and fans.

During this season, a great player who benefitted from the one-on-one mentoring of a great coach and great person, John Huarte, a quarterback who re-learned the word "can" instead of "can't" from his new coach, became the sixth Notre Dame player to win the **Heisman Trophy**. Bravo Irish! Bravo John Huarte; Bravo Coach Parseghian. Huarte's talents had gone unrecognized by Joe Kuharich and Hugh Devore.

By season end, Huarte had become a household name in sports. He kept throwing touchdown passes to another ND great from California, Jack Snow, who incidentally had also been overlooked by the previous coaching regimes. With Parseghian, Notre Dame had become a football power again. John Huarte got his Heisman by being a great player. His Heisman Trophy victory, however, went down in history as one of the biggest upsets for the award.

Huarte missed much of his sophomore season due to injury and he had not played enough for Coach Kuharich as a junior to win a monogram (Letter). Yet, he was brilliant as a senior. The Passes between Huarte and Snow are legendary. (60 passes for 1,114 yards and a record nine touchdowns). Moreover, Snow was not Huarte's only receiver.

Ara Parseghian threw out the Joe Kuharich book on the team, its procedures and its players and John Huarte was the greatest beneficiary. Parseghian used his own cranium and took ND from a 2-7 team in '63 into a 9-1 squad with John Huarte leading the charge. Moreover, Parseghian and Huarte were within minutes of the national title.

Huarte threw for 270 yards in the '64 opening-game upset of Wisconsin -- including TD tosses of 61 and 42 yards to Snow -- and ended up finishing the year ranked third nationally in total offense (2,069 yards). He set 12 Irish records that year, and also earned back of the year and player of the year honors from United Press International. John Huarte capped off his senior year being picked in the second-round of the NFL draft by the New York Jets, He played in the NFL for eight years.

Parseghian took what arguably was Joe Kuharich's 5-5 team and made it work. It would be the first of many great seasons with a brand new fired-up great man and great coach, Ara Parseghian. Watching Notre Dame games with my dad became a lot more fun, when Notre Dame began to excel. Notre Dame all of a sudden believed it could win. And, Ara Parseghian helped John Huarte know that he too could win again.

Let's look at one of the games that stand out in this season and we shall use some great write-ups of the day to convey the spirit of the games and highlight some great players. The is Michigan State brought to us by bluegraysky and the next is the USC game, which is supplied as a link from uhnd.com. The full references are shown.

1964 ND v Michigan State at ND Stadium
Time Magazine Ara Parseghian
http://bluegraysky.blogspot.com/2005/05/call-him-hardnose.html

From Sports Illustrated. Author Unknown
Nov. 20, 1964

Toilet-paper streamers festooned the trees. Strings of firecrackers chattered like machine guns. Signs were everywhere. SONS OF ERIN, UNITE! They said. RUB THEIR NOSES IN THE IRISH SOD! Sturdy young men stopped strangers, flashed their "Hate State!" buttons and inquired politely: "You wouldn't be a State man, now, would you?" South Bend, Ind., was no place for the faint of heart last week. Notre Dame, the No. 1 college football team in the nation, was taking on Archrival Michigan State—and the Fighting Irish were in a fighting mood.

The Irish had not beaten State in ten years; inside the Notre Dame stadium, Athletic Director Edward ("Moose") Krause surveyed the sellout crowd of 59,265 and sighed: "We could have sold 250,000 tickets to this game." He could have sold a million—to all the Americans, the vast Subway Alumni, to whom Notre Dame is and always has been the one and only college football team. To the Bronx taxi driver who has never seen the inside of a college but lights a candle to Our Lady every Friday night. To the San Francisco dock walloper who hasn't the foggiest notion where South Bend is but knows every player on the Irish squad. To the nuns in convents, whose radio-side prayers on Saturday go something like this: "God's will be done . . . but please let Notre Dame win." And what about the two Indiana priests who walked into a polling booth last Nov. 3 and wrote in the name of Ara Parseghian for President?

On His Knees. Down beneath the stands, wearing his lucky brown trousers and a blue sweater with NOTRE DAME lettered across the front, the Subway Alumni's candidate stood in the middle of the noisy locker room. "Everybody stay where you are!" he yelled. Then, pounding his fist into his palm, Ara Raoul Parseghian, 41, began to talk. "Boys (bang), you read the newspapers (bang). The predictors (bang, bang) say Michigan State is going to beat us. But we (bang) are a better team than they are. We're going out there (bang) and prove it (BANG)!" Then, along with the rest of the Fighting Irish, Coach Parseghian, a French-Armenian Protestant, sank to his knees and bowed his head. "Hail Mary, full of grace . . ."

Sportswriters had billed it "the game of the year." It was that—for Notre Dame and for the 35 million fans watching on nationwide TV, the millions more clustered around radios in bars and stores and barbershops. A good game might have been enough; a narrow victory would have sent them into ecstasy. What they got was beyond their wildest dreams.

In the next two hours, a great team systematically took a good team apart. Michigan State did not get a first down until it was two touchdowns behind.

Only twice in the whole first half did a Notre Dame running play fail to gain. First it was Halfback Nick Eddy, spinning off tackle on the second play from scrimmage, racing 61 yds. For a TD—while Coach Parseghian matched him step for step, shouting "Go! Go! Go!" Then it was Fullback Joe Farrell, cracking the Spartan line on three straight plays for 15 yds. On the fourth play, he faked a line buck and zigzagged downfield to take a pass from Quarterback John Huarte. That put the ball on the Michigan State eight. Another Farrell fake, another Huarte pass—touchdown.

Ara Parseghian prowled the sideline, lips peeled back over his teeth. "Pursuit! Pursuit!" he screamed at the Notre Dame defense, and again Michigan State had to give up the ball. "More! More!" he yelled at the offense, and again the relentless Irish began to march. The massive (219 lbs. per man) Notre Dame line ripped gaping holes in the Spartan forward wall, gave Quarterback Huarte so much protection that he could have tied his shoe laces and still had time to pass. A screen to End Jack Snow gained 19 yds. A flare to Fullback Bob Merkle picked up 26. Then he turned Nick Eddy loose. In five carries, the 195-lb. halfback racked up 40 yds. And his second TD of the day. A pass to Snow was good for two extra points, and Notre Dame led at half time 20-0.

Anything & Everything. Back came the two teams, and the excitement leaped a notch. Desperate now, the Spartans tried anything—and for a while everything worked. They shifted from the T into a short punt formation and drew the Notre Dame line off side. They caught the Irish secondary napping, with a 51-yd. pass that cut the gap to 20-7. Luck helped a lot: two Notre Dame touchdowns were nullified. But now the aroused State defense was starting to harry Huarte. Somehow he still managed to get the ball away—sidearm, underhand, any way at all. And when he couldn't pass, he ran like a halfback—ripping out of the grasp of three tacklers for 21 yds. And a touchdown that made it 28-7. After that, the spectators stole the show. Twice, play was stopped while the sheriff's deputies chased fans around the field. That was enough to frighten even Parseghian. Off came the first team; in went the subs. Another Irish touchdown. Final score: Notre Dame 34, Michigan State 7.

The victory was doubly sweet because it was the sort of thing that wasn't supposed to happen in 1964—and did anyway. It was the season of surprises, the year the experts all guessed wrong. This was the year a Penn State squad that lost four out of its first five clobbered unbeaten Ohio State 27-0, the year Texas did not win the Southwest Conference championship, the year mighty Mississippi had to settle for a tie with weak little Vanderbilt. It was the year free substitution and the platoon system came back to college football—if the coaches were willing to take penalties to get their subs into the game. It was the year collegians outdrew the pros—when attendance in the Big Ten averaged 59,000 a game to 49,000 in the National Football League. And, most of all, this was Ara Parseghian's year, the year a restless vagabond from Ohio took over a demoralized Notre Dame team that had spent five years forgetting how to win—and taught them how again.

Notre Dame v USC – the only loss
http://www.uhnd.com/football/Irish-history/documentary-profiles-infamous-chapter-scnd-history/

Great Player: Jack Snow, WR, 1962-1964

This is a great story of a great player and a great man, Jack Snow. I extracted it from his football eulogy http://www.und.com/sports/m-footbl/spec-rel/011006aag.html. The web eulogy was written by Pete La Fleur.

Jack Snow will be remembered forever by Notre Dame fans for playing a lead role in the 1964 season that ushered in "The Era of Ara," the 11-year coaching tenure of the legendary Ara Parseghian that included two national championships and a 95-17-4 record during that 11-year span.

Snow combined with quarterback and fellow California native John Huarte (Heisman winner) to form the record-setting passing combination for the 1964 team that won its first nine games, rose to No. 1 in the national polls and came within minutes of completing a national-championship season before losing 20-17 at USC.

A lifelong Notre Dame fan who once remarked that it "took 20 seconds to decide whether to accept the scholarship offer," Snow brought plenty of tools to the receiver position. A powerful presence at 6-foot-2 and 215 pounds, the Long Beach, Calif., native owned many of Notre Dame's team weightlifting records while also boasting excellent speed, smooth moves, clever route-running and soft hands.

Notre Dame's aerial attack in Parseghian's first season helped produce 27 team and individual records, including five set by Snow: receptions (60), receiving yards (1,114) and touchdown catches (9) in a season; receiving yards in a game (217, vs. Wisconsin); and career receiving yards (1,242). He more than doubled the old record for receiving yards in a season and racked up 19 more receptions in one season than any previous Notre Dame player.

Huarte went on to earn the 1964 Heisman Trophy and Snow finished fifth in the balloting for the prestigious award, behind Huarte, Tulsa quarterback Jerry Rhome, Illinois linebacker Dick Butkus and Michigan quarterback Bob Timberlake. Both Notre Dame stars finished high in the voting, above the likes of Gale Sayers, Craig Morton, Roger Staubach and Joe Namath. The duo of Huarte and Snow helped Notre Dame more than double its total offensive yards from the 1963 (1,980) to '64 (4,014) seasons while producing more than triple the number of passing yards (654 to 2,105) and 41 total touchdowns, after the 1963 team had scored just 15.

Jack Snow's longtime connection with the L.A./St. Louis Rams included spending the past 14 seasons as the team's radio analyst.

Parseghian made several key position switches in 1964 - when two-platoon football returned to the college game - and one of those timely shifts was moving Snow out of the backfield, where he had been a starting flankerback in '63. Snow shed 15 pounds and emerged as a dangerous receiver who was set to burst onto the college football scene.

<<<< Snow entered his senior year on the heels of a dismal 1963 season that produced a 2-7 record and an unthinkable fifth straight season for the Irish without a winning record. The bar of expectations for 1964 was set low for traditional Notre Dame standards - "six-and-four in '64" became a common catchphrase among the ND alums - as the Irish took the field playing for their third head coach in as many seasons.

Huarte and Snow quickly served notice that the Irish were back by spearheading the 31-7 rout at Wisconsin that vaulted Notre Dame to No. 9 in the AP poll. Snow hauled in a 61-yard bomb to open the scoring in that game and later produced a 42-yard touchdown to cap his nine-catch day. The Irish then climbed to the 6th, 4th and No. 2 spots after wins over Purdue (34-15), at Air Force (34-7) and back at home vs. UCLA (24-0).

Two more wins over Stanford (28-6) and the Staubach-led Navy squad (40-0, in Philadelphia) preceded a 17-15 escape at Pittsburgh that pushed Notre Dame up to the No. 1 ranking for the first time in a decade. Snow latched onto eight Huarte passes in the win over Stanford and hauled in a 55-yard pass versus Navy, as the Irish knocked off a squad led by the 1963 Heisman Trophy winner.

John Huarte and Jack Snow combined to rewrite the Notre Dame record books during the 1964 season.

Snow - whose biggest claim to fame was that he "never got caught from behind" when he was playing for the Rams - ranks fifth in Rams history for career receiving yards (6,012) and touchdown catches (45), plus seventh in receptions (340). He played in 150 games during an NFL career that included a Pro Bowl season in 1967 (28 rec. for 735 yds, 8 TDs) while his best overall season came in 1970, when he finished fifth in the NFL with 51 receptions and ninth in receiving yardage (859, plus 7 TDs).

Snow's 11-year career with the Rams included a 1967 Pro Bowl season and a 1970 season in which he ranked fifth on the NFL receiving charts.

He had a brief acting career, appearing in the movie Heaven Can Wait starring Warren Beatty and in an episode of the television show Bewitched.

1965 Notre Dame Football Season Coach Ara Parseghian

The 1965 Notre Dame Fighting Irish football in the second year of the Parseghian Era were voted # 8 in the coach's poll and # 9 in the AP poll against every other college team in America. Notre Dame was clearly back on the map. When ND showed up or a team had to play in South Bend, they did not come ready to lose.

They played to win. They were aware of the Notre Dame tradition and its hall of fame coaches from the past. They had a sense that there was another Hall of Fame coach inspiring new National

Championship teams in a new era and they were ready to try their darndest to get a win against Notre Dame.

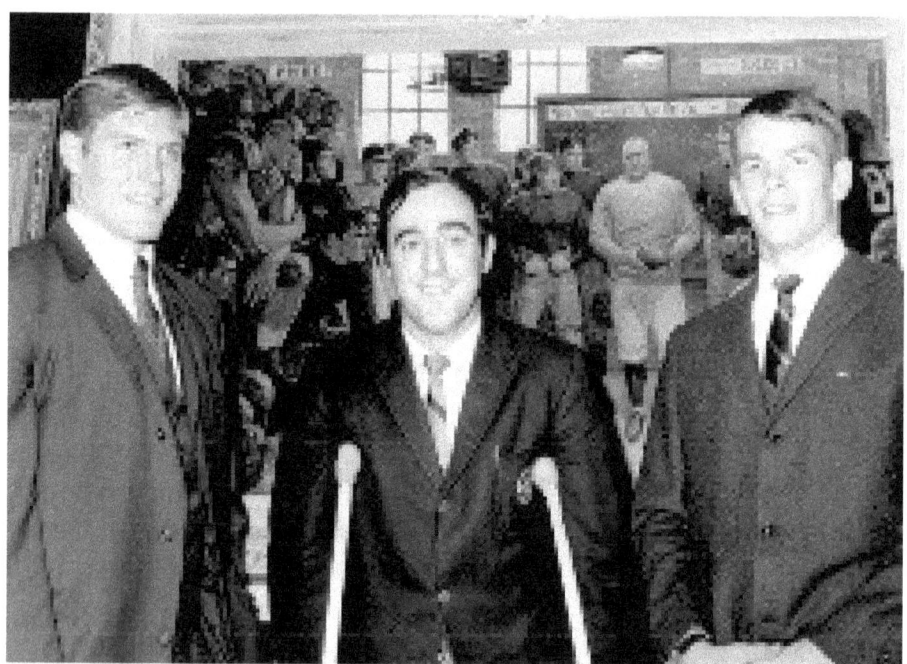

Left to right, tackle Georgie Kunz, quarterback Terry Hanratty and wide receiver Jim Seymour led the 1965 recruiting class

Consequently, the Fighting Irish needed all the fight it had to squeeze out wins against the best teams in America, who wanted more than anything to take a win from Notre Dame. Notre Dame finished with a season record of (7-2-1.) and a top ten finish in the rankings.

1966 Notre Dame Football Season Coach Ara Parseghian

In his third year as head coach of Notre Dame, Ara Parseghian brought a National Championship to Notre dame for the first time since Frank Leahy's teams in the 1940's. The 1966 Notre Dame Fighting Irish football team ended the 1966 season undefeated with nine wins and one tie away at Michigan State.

The Fighting Irish earned a consensus title after beating No. 10 Oklahoma W 38–0 in Norman, tying unbeaten and No. 2 Michigan State T 10–10, and ending the season defeating No. 10 USC, W (51–0), in the LA Coliseum. The 1966 squad became the eighth Irish team to win the national title and the first under Parseghian. The Irish outscored its opponents 362–38.

Great Player: Jim Seymour, WR, 1966-1968
Great Player: Terry Hanratty, WR, 1966-1968

Jim Seymour was a handsome, speedy, lanky, glue-fingered end who helped lead Notre Dame to a national championship in 1966 by catching perfect and not so perfect spirals from Terry Hanratty, Notre Dame's starting Quarterback.

Terry Hanratty's best playing days were at Notre Dame, and they were great. He was drafted by Pittsburgh and played eight years in the NFL off and on. Jim Seymour played three years for the Chicago Bears in the National Football League, but he too had made his name as an athlete in college.

At 6 feet 4 inches, weighing more than 200 pounds and able to run 100 yards in less than 10 seconds, Seymour was bigger and faster than virtually any other college receiver at the time, a physical type who set a standard for the position long before the likes of Keyshawn Johnson, Randy Moss and Terrell Owens ever caught a pass.

Seymour made all-American teams in each of his three seasons at Notre Dame, where he and quarterback Terry Hanratty helped transform a team known for its defense into an offensive powerhouse.

By the time, he graduated in 1969, Seymour was the career receiving leader at Notre Dame, with 138 catches for 2,113 yards — an average of more than 15 yards a catch — and 16 touchdowns.

In 1965, the Fighting Irish, coached by Ara Parseghian, had gone 7-2-1 and given up only 73 points, but without a solid passing attack they had ended the year scoring a total of 3 points in their last two games. Enter Seymour and Hanratty, who had been recruited by Parseghian in the hope of replacing a previous twosome, the

Heisman Trophy-winning quarterback John Huarte and the receiver Jack Snow, who had graduated in 1964.

Hanratty and Seymour were both sophomores in 1966 — at the time N.C.A.A. regulations barred freshmen from playing varsity football — and their presence made an immediate impact. In their first game, a victory against Purdue, Seymour caught 13 passes for 276 yards, which remains a Notre Dame record.

Throughout college football, passing games were exploding that year, so much so that in midseason Time magazine ran a story proclaiming a revolution in the game. On the cover was a painting of Hanratty and Seymour.

Seymour missed three games that season because of injury, but after a famous 10-10 tie against another undefeated team, Michigan State, a game in which Hanratty was hurt, Notre Dame clinched a national championship the next week by beating Southern California, 51-0, a game in which Seymour caught 11 passes for 150 yards and 2 touchdowns.

"We had a great team," recalling that the defense had future pro standouts in Jim Lynch, Pete Duranko, Kevin Hardy and Alan Page and a fine running back in Nick Eddy, all holdovers from the previous season. "The only two question marks were the two snot-nose sophomores."

<<< Left- Jim Seymour in a photo in August 1973, when he was a player for the Chicago Bears.

Hanratty said he and Seymour got to know each other by working out together in an old field house, a dirt-floor arena with a ceiling so low that any long pass had to be looped over the roof support beams.
Sports

"We got to know each other so well that I knew his every move, when he was going to cut inside, when he was going to cut outside," said Hanratty, who played eight years in the N.F.L. "Anyway, it was so different back then. Jim was 6-foot-4, 215, and ran like a deer; he was a hard cover for anyone. I mean, add 30 more pounds to him and he's a lineman. I've got a son going to Notre Dame this fall, and he's 6-5 and 300. I tell him he's bigger than anybody I ever played with in college or the pros."

Many who saw Seymour play at Notre Dame recall his extraordinary grace as a pass-catcher. As Time described him, "he could 'juke' his hips, dip his shoulder, toss his head, flutter his eyelashes, and leave a safety man twisted up like a pretzel as he cuts downfield for a pass."

The magazine continued: "He can then leap four feet straight up and pluck a football out of the sky — with such tenderness that one observer reported: 'You can stand right next to him and never hear the ball hit his hands.' "

On September 24, Purdue came into Notre Dame Stadium carrying the Shillelagh trophy to play #6 ranked Notre Dame. The Irish won back the trophy with a W (26-14) win. Playing the next week at Northwestern, the Irish came home with a victory W (35 7). The following week at home, they met rivalry Army in a rare South Bend appearance. Parseghian's Irish defeated Army W (35-0) and the following week, October 15, unranked North Carolina came to ND, who at the time were ranked #2 and lost W (32-0).

In all these games, except for the USC game, when Hanratty was injured, Terry Hanratty was the thrower and Jim Seymour was the catcher. Hanratty and Seymour formed a passing / receiving duo all season that led Notre Dame to the national championship. Hanratty, who went on to play for Pittsburgh in the NFL, would also be teammates and friends with halfback Rocky Bleier at Notre Dame before the two were teammates in Pittsburgh. After North Carolina, the next week number one ranked Notre Dame went to Oklahoma to play the # 10 ranked Sooners and the Irish won big W (38-0).

Then, it was off to Navy in Philadelphia for a win W (31-7). The next week on November 5, unranked Pittsburgh came to ND Stadium and were beaten solidly by the Irish W (40-0). After the tie with Michigan State, the Irish went to arch rival USC and soundly beat the Trojans W (51-0). Notre Dame was declared the consensus National Champion.

The Michigan State game had its controversies

For nearly 50 years, Parseghian has been defending his end-of-the-game strategy, which left many fans feeling disappointed at the game not having some sort of resolution. Both Michigan State fans and other Notre Dame detractors called Parseghian a coward, and college football expert Dan Jenkins, led off his article for Sports Illustrated by saying that Parseghian chose to "Tie one for the Gipper."

In that same article, Parseghian was quoted as saying, "We'd fought hard to come back and tie it up. After all that, I didn't want to risk giving it to them cheap. They get reckless and it could cost them the game. I wasn't going to do a jackass thing like that at this point."

The tie resulted in 9–0–1 seasons for both Michigan State and Notre Dame. The final AP and Coaches' polls put the Irish and Spartans at #1 and #2, ranking both teams above the undefeated, and two time defending national champion 11–0–0 Alabama. Both schools shared the MacArthur Bowl.

Nothing in football is ever easy

Notre Dame beat USC handily 51–0 the next week, completing an undefeated (but tied) regular season and solidifying its Number 1 claim.

Great Player: Alan Page, DE, 1964-1966

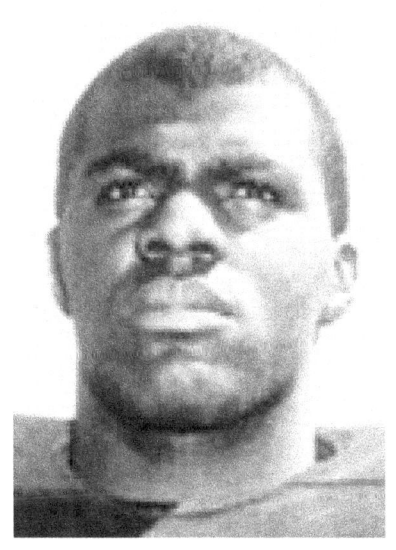

Defensive Lineman get some accolades every now and then but unless it is a sack or a hurry or a great game winning tackle, they just go ahead and do their jobs and when they get the ball back for the offense, the O team gets on the field as quickly as possible and there is very little time to gloat. Alan Page had a lot of opportunity to gloat but he too was a team player, and a great one.

The was a Consensus All-America pick in 1966 after starting three years as defensive right end from 1964-66. His stats prove how much he mattered to Notre Dame such as 63 tackles in 1966 while helping the Irish to the national title.

Alan Page was a great player all during his football career at all levels. At Notre Dame, he made 134 career tackles; recovered four fumbles; broke up two passes and he even scored a touchdown. Everybody says he is the greatest and his record shows it. In 1967, he participated in both honor games—the East-West Shrine game and College All-Star game. When he stopped tackling ND opponents, he was ready for his pro career.

He was a first-round choice of Minnesota in 1967 NFL draft as 15th overall selection. He also played with Chicago Bears. Alan Page got his big paws on runners in four Super Bowls with the Vikings and earned NFL MVP one year. He also received the NCAA Silver Anniversary award in 1992 and was elected to National Football Foundation Hall of Fame in 1993.

He was the recipient of the 2001 Dick Enberg Award given annually to a person whose actions and commitment have furthered the meaning and reach of the Verizon Academic All-America Programs and/or the student-athlete programs while promoting the values of education and academics.

Alan Page was also voted one of the top 100 Minnesotans of the century and 100 most important Minnesota sport figures in history. He became a lawyer and was elected to Minnesota Supreme Court in 1992. Thank you, Alan Page, for a great career and for putting the bad guys away.

1967 Notre Dame Football Season Coach Ara Parseghian

The 1967 Notre Dame Fighting Irish football team was coached by Ara Parseghian in his fourth year. The Irish finished 8-2 and were # 4 in the coaches' poll and # 5 in the AP poll. The season started a little rocky and after the first four games, the Irish were unranked with a record of 2-2.

Great Player: Rocky Bleier, RB, 1966, 1967

Rocky Bleier, who later played for the Pittsburgh Steelers four-time Super Bowl Champions, was picked by Coach Parseghian to be the 1967 ND team captain. Rocky graduated in 1968 with a degree in business management. During his junior season in 1966, the Fighting Irish won the national championship and he was a team captain as a senior in 1967. He was selected in the 16th round of the 1968 NFL/AFL Draft by the Pittsburgh Steelers, 417th overall.

Bleier was tougher than nails and was drafted into the Army for the Vietnam War after his first Pittsburgh Steelers season. In Vietnam, he was hit twice in the same battle and was told he would never play again. He was lucky to be alive. He lost part of his foot. Bleier was Notre Dame tough. He rejoined the Steelers in 1971.

Rocky Bleier 1967 ND Captain -- SuperBowl Star with Steelers

Upon his return, he couldn't walk without being in pain, and he weighed only 180 pounds. Bleier never said "never." He spent two years trying to regain a spot on the Pittsburgh active roster, and was waived on two occasions. But He never gave up, in 1976, it all paid off as both he and Franko Harris rushed for over 1,000 yards.

Bleier played very well in all four Pittsburgh Super Bowl victories. He caught the touchdown pass from ace Terry Bradshaw to give

Pittsburgh the lead in Super Bowl XIII. Rocky Bleier retired after the 1980 season with 3,865 rushing yards, 136 receptions for 1,294 yards, and 25 touchdowns. At the time of his retirement, he was the Steelers' fourth all-time leading rusher.

Rocky Bleier did not have the pounds to play as well as he did. But, he did play well because he was built Notre Dame tough. And that's that!

1968 Notre Dame Football Season Coach Ara Parseghian

The 1968 Notre Dame Fighting Irish football team under Coach Ara Parseghian had another fine year. Notre Dame consistently played the best teams in the nation and 1968 was no exception. The Irish record was (7-2-1).

1969 Notre Dame Football Season Coach Ara Parseghian

The 1969 Notre Dame Fighting Irish football team was coached by Ara Parseghian. The Fighting Irish finished the regular season with eight wins, one loss, and one tie.

Great Player: Joe Theismann, QB, 1968-1970

Joe Theismann was not known for being the biggest QB on the field. In fact, at 5'10 and less than 150 lbs., ND coaches upon meeting Theismann the first time were amazed at his small stature for a star football player. One of the assistant coaches remarked that he was looking at the team's new water boy rather than a quarterback. Theismann was on the bench until his sophomore year when Terry Hanratty was lost to an injury. It took Joe Theismann no time to make a difference. He led the Irish to two wins and a tie in his first three games.

As an ND 1971 graduate from the University of Notre Dame where he received All-America honors, Theismann takes pride in having led the Fighting Irish to consecutive Cotton Bowls and was runner-up to Jim Plunkett in the Heisman Trophy balloting. In 2003, Theismann was inducted into the College Football Hall of Fame. He was always a great player.

I could not find an ND outfit for Joe Theismann that made him look this nice. Sorry folks!

In 1969, as a junior, Theismann was unquestionably the starter. He led the Irish to a number five ranking, their first bowl appearance, and a near upset of national champion Texas. In 1970, the Irish had a 10-1 record, a number two ranking and gained their revenge win over top-ranked Texas.

Theismann was the runner-up in the Heisman voting and was recognized as a first-team All-America and as an Academic All-American. As a starting quarterback, he compiled a 20-3-2 record while throwing for 4,411 yards and 31 touchdowns. Theismann set school records for passing yards in a game (526), yards in a season (2,429), and touchdowns in a season (16).

A great athlete in all sports, Theismann began his professional career in 1971 with the Toronto Argonauts of the Canadian Football League, after being drafted by the Miami Dolphins and Major League Baseball's Minnesota Twins.

Today, Joe Theismann is a much sought after motivational speaker. He also oversees a popular Washington, DC restaurant that bears his name. He is also the author of The Complete Idiots Guide to Understanding Football Like a Pro.

Recently, Theismann was named the recipient of the 2013 Walter Camp Football Foundation "Distinguished American" Award.

Following his graduation, he had a 15-year professional career, 12 of which were spent with the Washington Redskins. In 1982, he led the Redskins to a Super Bowl victory. The next year he became the league's MVP. Upon retirement, he became a successful businessman and sports caster.

Joe Theismann may have been runner-up for the Heisman Trophy but all ND and Theismann fans know that if we take away the "T" in the beginning and the last "n," Joe always has been a tHeismanN plus. He sure played like it all the time. He is one of Notre Dame's finest gentlemen.

ND 1970 Cotton Bowl Game

For the first time since a Rose Bowl victory in 1925, after a 40-year self-imposed hiatus in which pundits believe ND would have been invited to at least 20 games, Notre Dame finally accepted a Bowl Game bid.

The January 1, 1970 Cotton Bowl played in Texas featured # 8 ranked Notre Dame v #1 ranked Texas Longhorns. In a great game, Texas outlasted Notre Dame L (17-21).

Great Player: Mike McCoy DT 1967-1969

Mike was a unanimous first-team All-American as a senior in 1969, after finishing sixth in 1969 Heisman Trophy voting. He was a two-year starter at left defensive tackle in 1968-69. He received the Lineman of the Week honor by Sports Illustrated after the defeat of Northwestern in 1969.

He was also named Lineman of the year by Associated Press in '69. His career tackles are an enviable 203, with two for losses. He even intercepted two passes.

McCoy was a 1970 participant in the College All-Star game and was chosen by Green Bay in the first round of 1970 NFL draft as second overall player selected. He went on to the NFL and played 11 years' total--six with Green Bay, two with Oakland, two with New York Giants and one with Detroit.

1970 Notre Dame Football Season Coach Ara Parseghian

The 1970 Notre Dame Fighting Irish football team was coached by Ara Parseghian. The squad played to a 10-1 record and finished # 5 in the coach's poll and # 2 in the AP poll. If you could take Purdue and USC off the ND schedule in the Parseghian years, the Irish would have had three or four more national championships.

Again in 1970, the only blemish on the Fighting Irish record was a season finale against unranked USC at USC in which the Irish lost L (28-38). Not having an especially good year with a 5-4 record, John McKay's 1970 Trojans were ready for the Fighting Irish and they played their hearts out to gain the victory.

The game started out with a Theismann completion for a touchdown followed by three straight first quarter scores which set the Irish back for sure. ND fought its way back to cut the lead but then, the Blue and Gold suffered two major miscues in a row in the end zone and USC scored touchdowns both times.

In his final Notre Dame game, 1970 Heisman runner-up Joe Theismann, # 7, threw for one touchdown and ran for two in a span of 9:30 to help end No. 1 Texas' 30-game winning streak.

This was enough to secure the margin of victory. Even with two late game Theismann passes for touchdowns, Notre Dame could not muster up enough points to overcome these major mistakes.

The Irish did get a second Cotton Bowl opportunity against the Texas Longhorns. This time the Irish would disappoint none of its fans as it conquered the Longhorns at Dallas, W (24-11) before 73,000 fans. The game was telecast on CBS TV.

The ND Alumnus Magazine offered its thoughts on the Cotton Bowl Victory:

This was a long-awaited rematch! ND vs Texas in the Cotton Bowl on the AstroTurf on a warm afternoon in Big "D." The pundits have had their say—The Irish came up with a magnificent team effort that dominated the talented Longhorns for most of the afternoon and earned a decisive 24-11 victory, and eventually a No. 2
National ranking.

It was a great collective effort and superb coaching which severed Texas' 30-game win streak and it undoubtedly brought back into the fold most of ND's fair-weather advocates of the "can't win the big one" theory. No matter!

1971 Notre Dame Football Season Coach Ara Parseghian

The 1971 Notre Dame Fighting Irish football team was coached for the eighth year by Ara Parseghian. Notre Dame finished the season with an 8-2 record and were #15 in the coaches' poll and # 13 in the AP. The season opener at home was Northwestern W (50-7) followed by a very close away game victory at Purdue. The Purdue game is one of the all-time great games for both Purdue and the Fighting Irish. Here is how it went down:

The famous "genuflect play"

Notre Dame was the preseason #1 in 1971 even without Joe Theismann, who led the Irish to No. 2 the previous year. Theismann was great but even the Sportscasters felt ND could win the championship with just regular talent at QB. In fact, Sports Illustrated wrote "even a cheerleader could quarterback this team" after the Irish's 50-7 opening game trouncing of a Northwestern team that would finish as the Big Ten runner-up.

But, even with Parseghian, ND had lost four straight at Purdue and trailed 7-0 with about four minutes left in the contest while driving down to the PU 5. QB Pat Steenberge then lost the ball on a fumble.

Steenberge said that when the ball was snapped, he could not find it and then found it in between his legs. Purdue recovered. Game over! Many left their TV sets as they felt Purdue had just grabbed its fifth win in a row from the Irish

Not exactly! At the rain-soaked Ross-Ade Stadium, Notre Dame pulled out a miracle win in the final seconds to defeat Purdue. The quarterback of the Irish that day, Pat Steenberge has a YouTube video describing what happened in the last three minutes. https://youtu.be/953ezjHy33U... It is a nice recap of an exciting game.

Here's the skinny. The ND Defense held Purdue after the recovery. The Boilermakers had to punt to protect their win. It was a sea of mud, and all anybody could see from the field was umbrellas in the stands—no eyeballs. A low long snap into the end zone and a bobble by the punter permitted ND cornerback Clarence Ellis to tear in from the left side and force the off-balance Purdue punter to fumble. End Fred Swendsen then pounced on the loose ball past the goal line for the ND Touchdown. ND was still down 6-7.

After all the crap Parseghian had taken for the championship season when he "tied one for the Gipper," the Irish Coach was determined to win the game or lose the game. He had a special play picked put.

In QB Steenberge's video he relates that Parseghian said "go get us two… run the play," rather than kick a tying extra point to knot the score at 7-7. The Irish had been practicing the "genuflect" play all week as a means of scoring 2.

On the two-point conversion, left end Mike Creaney went down on one knee (thus the genuflect). It looked like he was blocked, and so he was uncovered at the line of scrimmage. He then got up and snuck past the goal line. Steenberge was about to be tackled by Gary Hrivnak, who was not fooled by the QB's machinations on the play. "Steeny" just about got the pass away. He lofted the ball just over Hrivnak to Creaney for the score with 2:58 left for the W (8-7). ND was 2-0. Nice job Ara and Steeny and Creaney et al!

With just two losses, the Irish finished ranked # 15 in the Coaches' Poll and # 13 in the AP. Because ND did not play ranked teams other than LSU, there was no bowl game offer and thus the poor showing in the rankings.

1972 Notre Dame Football Season Coach Ara Parseghian

The 1972 Notre Dame Fighting Irish football team was coached by Ara Parseghian. Notre Dame finished the regular season with an 8-2 record and were #12 in the coaches' poll and # 14 in the AP. The Fighting Irish were invited to the Orange Bowl against Nebraska and the Irish had a tough time in defeat L (6-40)

1973 Notre Dame Football Season Coach Ara Parseghian

The 1973 Notre Dame Fighting Irish football team was the tenth season coached by Ara Parseghian. Parseghian's squad ended the season undefeated with 11 wins and no losses, winning the national championship. The Fighting Irish won the title the hard way. They earned it!

First of all, they defeated the previously unbeaten and No. 1 ranked Alabama Crimson Tide in the Sugar Bowl by a score of W (24–23).

The 1973 squad therefore became the ninth Irish team to win the national title and the second team under Parseghian to win this coveted recognition.

Stranger things have happened but despite Notre Dame finishing No. 1 in the AP Poll to claim the AP national title, they were not awarded the Coaches' title. The Coaches voted before the bowl season and selected Alabama as the # 1 team in the country.

Like most of Parseghian's teams in his ten years to that point, the 1973 Fighting Irish were hardened and tough. His second national title team was led by its relentless rushing attack. Fullback Wayne Bullock topped the list with 750 yards; followed by halfback Art Best, who gained 700 yards, halfback Eric Peneck with 586 yards and quarterback Tom Clements clocked in with his own 360 yards. This unit made up one of the fastest Irish backfields of all time. Peneck and Best both ran the 100-yard dash in under 10 seconds.

The Irish started the season strong, amassing large margins of victory over Northwestern W (44-0), Rice W (28-0) and Army W (62-3) to set up a highly-anticipated contest with No. 6 and unbeaten USC. USC always gave the Irish a tough time and were a perennial season spoiler during Parseghian's years.

The Trojans came into the contest riding a 23-game unbeaten streak, and their star tailback Anthony Davis ran all over Notre Dame the previous year for 6 touchdowns when USC claimed a 45-23 Trojan victory at home. Adding to the mystique of this Notre Dame home game, despite terrific seasons and near National Championships, Parseghian's teams had not outright beaten USC since 1966.

The Irish defense was ready and would not be denied. They responded to the challenge, limiting Davis to just 55 yards on 19 carries. The star tailback of the day was Notre Dame's Penick, who found the holes and ran for 118 yards, which was 50 yards more than the entire Trojan team. No part of the game was easy but the Irish offense and defense played at its best level. Nothing was easy but the Irish won the contest W 23-14 and Parseghian's squad won its remaining games.

The other 1973 Notre Dame victories on the way to the National Championship included: Purdue away W (20-7), Michigan State at home W (14-10), Navy at home W (44-7), Pittsburgh away W (31-10), Airforce at home W (48-15), and Miami away W (44-0).

1973 Sugar Bowl

Notre Dame accepted the Sugar Bowl bid, which set the stage for a real national championship game. Alabama was awarded the UPI title before the bowl season, but it was Notre Dame that had won the championship head to head against Alabama on the field, (24-23) in a nail-biting thriller that saw six lead changes.

Alabama's Paul W. (Bear) Bryant and Notre Dame's Ara Parseghian meet on the field of Tulane Stadium prior to the Sugar Bowl on Dec. 31, 1973. On Dec. 31, 1973, two of college football's most fabled programs met for the first time on the gridiron with nothing less at stake than the national championship. As the kickoff approached the Alabama Crimson was ranked No. 1 in the country, the Notre Dame Fighting Irish were No. 3 and both were undefeated. Anticipation was at a fever pitch and, as the game unfolded, absolutely warranted.

The result: Notre Dame beats Alabama, 24-23, for the 1973 national title. What happened? Both had perfect records, and the Tide came in No. 1 and the Irish No. 3 (No. 2 Oklahoma was on probation); this was the first meeting in history between the teams, and it took place on New Year's Eve. Alabama scored a TD to take a 23-21 lead early in the fourth quarter but missed the extra point. Notre Dame's Bob Thomas kicked a 19-yard field goal with 10:34 left to give the Irish a 24-23 lead. Late in the game, Alabama downed a punt at Notre Dame's 1. On third-and-8 from the 3 and with little more than two minutes left, Irish backup TE Robin Weber basically was left uncovered because of a blown coverage and hauled in a 37-yard reception from Miller-Digby Award recipient: # 2 Tom Clements, Notre Dame quarterback, to seal the win and the No. 1 ranking.

Notre Dame jumped to a 6-0 in front of 85,161 excited fans at Tulane Stadium in New Orleans. However, Alabama quickly answered with a Randy Billingsley 6-yard touchdown run. After Notre Dame's Al Hunter scored on a crowd dazzling 93-yard kick-off return, Alabama scored 10 straight points. In the fourth quarter, three turnovers occurred in 90 seconds, with Alabama getting the best of the action.

The Crimson Tide capitalized on a halfback pass from Mike Stock to quarterback Richard Todd for a 25-yard touchdown to take a slim 23-21 lead, but they missed the crucial extra point. Notre Dame responded and fought its way down the field with Tom Clements driving the Irish 79 yards in 11 plays. This set up a potential field goal on a clutch 15-yard pass to tight end Dave Casper. Irish kicker Bob Thomas kicked the field goal to give Notre Dame a slim victory W (24-23) and the AP national title.

1974 Notre Dame Football Season Coach Ara Parseghian

Great Player: Tom Clements, QB, 1972-1974

Tom Clements was an athlete and played many sports at Canevin High School in Pittsburgh. He was even recruited to be a point guard for the mighty Tar Heels. When Tom Clements arrived at Notre Dame, he was not permitted to play as a Freshman. Those who came the year after him until today, got to play four years.

After Coach Parseghian and Offensive Coordinator Tom Pagna could not really deal with ND QB prospects for 1972, along came Tom Clements. He had it all.

Clements could run, throw and scramble. He was also able to become a great team leader. More than any other QB candidate, he was the quarterback most suited to deploy the full array of the Parseghian/Pagna Offense.

As a QB, he would rush for over 1,000 yards in his three years as a starter and he would score 12 rushing touchdowns to complement his 22 passing TDs. Wow!

Clements came on the scene with a big burst in 1972. He immediately established Notre Dame as a powerhouse with which to be reckoned. He led early victories over Northwestern in Evanston, 37-0, 35-14 over Purdue in South Bend, and then 16-0 over the Spartans in East Lansing. This was even before walloping Pitt, 42-16 in South Bend.

It looked preordained for a while but then the train derailed in a stunning 30-26 upset loss to the Missouri Tigers, coached by Al Onofrio in South Bend. The previous week Mizzou had been whacked 62-0 by Nebraska in Lincoln. Somehow something sure went wrong for ND and right for Mizzou for this game.

There were some big defensive issues nobody expected. Freshman Steve Niehaus had been anchoring the defense until mid-season. Then, he injured his knee while warming up for a workout. The bulwark of the "D" was lost for the season.

In its last two games, the Irish D yielded a total of 85 points to USC and Nebraska, first watching Anthony Davis score 6 TDS) in the Coliseum and then watching Johnny Rodgers excel in the Orange Bowl. So, there was no championship to be had in 1972. But, 1973 was the next year.

In 1973, Tom Clements knew the job. He has settled in. Niehaus was all healed and back bigger and better than ever. Two talented freshmen, Ross Browner and Luther Bradley joined the defense and added more strength and power. The Irish went unbeaten, and were just about untouchable. They even broke the six-year jinx with USC. The 14-10 win over Michigan State was the only victory by less than a touchdown.

Notre Dame kept winning and it was with ease. The title game was set. New Year's Eve, Deep South, New Orleans, in the old Tulane Stadium. Paul "Bear" Bryant, the Prince of the South and the King of the SEC. Bryant seemed to have had a Notre Dame burr under his saddle from way back when Paul Hornung was recruited to ND instead of the Crimson Tide.

The battle raged. It even exceeded the hype. Late in the game, just when the dew was beginning to cover Dixie, and Bryant's Red Elephants were ready to move in for the kill, Tom Clements dropped back into his own end zone, with great aplomb, and dropped the ball into the waiting arms of Tight End Robin Weber some 36 yards downfield. First and 10 Irish. The Irish ran out the clock. Notre Dame 24-Bama 23. As an aside, the game received a 25.3 Nielsen

Rating, making it one of the highest-rated college football games of all time.

1974 turned out to be Ara's last year. The Irish suffered what some call a strange loss to Purdue early in the year. When they went to the Coliseum, they quickly shot to a 24-6 lead over a talented USC squad. Then, in a surreal comeback, USC came back with 49 points in a row defeating the Fighting Irish L (24-55).

Ara announced he was going to retire, and was looking for a good win. Again, it was Alabama and the "Bear" still had not had his fill of revenge. He brought his Crimson Tide team to be the Irish opponent. This game was the Orange bowl. Notre Dame 13-Alabama 11.
Tom Clements is the only quarterback EVER to defeat Bear Bryant twice in bowl games.

In 1974 Clements won All-America honors and finished fourth in the Heisman voting behind running backs Archie Griffin of Ohio State, Anthony Davis of USC and Joe Washington of Oklahoma. He was quite a great player.

The 1974 Notre Dame Fighting Irish football team was the 11th season coached by Ara Parseghian It would be Coach Parseghian's final season as Notre Dame Head Coach. As all Parseghian seasons, this 1974 season was also a great one. I recall in my mid-twenties in 1974, missing Ara as soon as his departure was announced.

There is a lot of good fortune in winning a championship. It is not all skill but that surely is the best ingredient. To say it just a bit differently, there is a lot of skill and good fortune to win two great championships, especially in the Parseghian era as all football teams were toughening up and the competition was nothing to sneeze at.

Let's look quickly at the 1974 season and then go back a bit and wrap up the Parseghian era, as much as it pains me. Writing about Ara Parseghian has been a real treat for me. It was fun the first time living it, and fun again each time I relive this chapter. I hope reading this chapter has given you the same good feeling.

All my life – at least the part that remembers Notre Dame games, I hated it when ND was playing either Purdue or Southern Cal (USC). No matter how good the Fighting Irish were, there were always blips on the radar whenever ND was having an excellent season and were playing Purdue or USC. The Boilermakers and the Trojans were always better teams when they faced the Irish.

If it were not for these two teams, Notre Dame would have had many more national championship seasons and the mystery and the hard-fought battles extend even to today.

This particular year that we are examining, 1974 was typical. The prior year, 1973 was atypical. The Fifth Dimension used to sing about the moon being in the seventh house and Jupiter being aligned with Mars. That always needed to happen along with God's favor for the Irish to have an undefeated season no matter how good the coach or the team might be.

Either God or Lucifer placed USC and Purdue on this earth as more cuss words were yelled at TV screens in my day from Irish fans when these two teams played the Fighting Irish of Notre Dame. In 1974, there was no alignment and there was no seventh house and as so many times before Purdue L (20-34) and USC L (24-55) both beat Notre Dame and together stole what could have been an undefeated season. Ara Parseghian must have felt the same frustration as all ND Fans.

In 1974, the Irish were #4 in the coaches' poll and #6 in the AP. Their regular season record was 9-2 and they won the Orange Bowl again against Alabama (13-11). The season began earlier than normal on a Monday night, September 9 in a game against the Georgia Tech Yellow Jackets at Grant Field in Georgia. The Irish won W (31-7). It was not all downhill from there.

The End of the Ara Era

Ara Parseghian is shown here running out on the field with a number of players including Tom Clements, # 2.

Ara quit coaching all teams after the 1974 season for "health reasons." He began a broadcasting career calling college football games for ABC and CBS.

He also dedicated himself to medical causes later in life after his daughter was diagnosed with multiple sclerosis and three of his grandchildren died of a rare genetic disease.

This great coach was inducted into the College Football Hall of Fame as a coach in 1980. His career coaching record is 170–58–6. 1974 was his last season as Notre Dame Coach. Like Rockne and Leahy, this great coach made his mark and was missed from his first day of retirement. Thank you for a great job, Coach!

Thankfully, Mr. Parseghian is still around and still attending Notre Dame games. It is reported that he and Coach Brian Kelly have a great relationship. Long live Ara Parseghian, one of the great ones in life.

Chapter 17 Coach Dan Devine 1975-1980

Coach # 23
One National Championship -- 1977

Rockne, Leahy, Parseghian, Devine—Four Greats—National Championships

1975	Dan Devine	8–3
1976	Dan Devine	9–3
1977	Dan Devine	11–1*
1978	Dan Devine	9–3
1979	Dan Devine	7–4
1980	Dan Devine	9–2–1

Introduction to the Dan Devine Era

When Ara Parseghian called it quits after the 1974 season, Notre Dame was forced into what seemed to many to be a common situation for the Irish—having to replace another legend. Like other not-too-shabby coaches before and after him, Dan Devine, a great coach—the only Notre Dame coach who in just six seasons brought home a national championship—stepped into this unenviable situation.

Father Hesburgh and Father Joyce had tasked Dan Devine with taking over the football program. He had been head coach of the Green Bay Packers for three years at the time, but his heart was always in college football.

Before Green Bay, he was head coach at both Arizona State and Missouri. At ASU, he compiled a nice 27-3-1 record, including an undefeated season in 1957. He then moved on to Mizzou where his success continued, including one undefeated season (1960) and four top 10 finishes in the AP Poll (1960. Devine was a great college coach. He was so good that in 1963, he was almost offered the Notre Dame job after the 1963 season and right before Ara Parseghian accepted the position.

Maybe, just maybe that would have been OK, but few would ever replace Ara Parseghian with anybody else, ever—under any conditions.

Though Parseghian had not died like Rockne did ever so tragically, the Notre Dame faithful and the scribes at the Student Newspaper seemed to have identified at the time, a major disturbance in the "FORCE." I don't know how else to say it. The predestination of an immortal taking Notre Dame to an undefeated season again seems to be in the front of this thinking, but, additionally, something morose seemed to have overtaken the campus at this time. How could anybody think Dan Devine was anything but great?

1975 Notre Dame Football Season Coach Dan Devine

The 1975 Notre Dame Fighting Irish football team was coached by Dan Devine in his first year. Devine had taken over for the retired Ara Parseghian, and he had mostly a Parseghian selected team to work with in 1975. The team finished 8-3.

Devine led the Irish into its first "Holy War." The Holy War is an American rivalry between the Boston College Eagles and University of Notre Dame Fighting Irish. In 1975 it became a new nonconference rivalry in college football. Unfortunately, for the Irish, in years to come, BC would add itself to the list which includes USC and Purdue as major ND championship spoilers, I regret to say. For 1975, the Irish did well with an 8-3 finish.

1976 Notre Dame Football Season Coach Dan Devine

Dan Devine was the University of Notre Dame Head Football Coach in 1976. From Irish standards, his first year had not gone well, though when compared to regular mortal men, it was not too bad at all. His squad lost three games in 1975 and did not go to a bowl game. Bowl games are a dime a dozen today but in 1975, there were only 11 bowl games. The Irish finished 9-3 in 1976. Still no cigar, but not too bad.

The administration decided to accept a Gator Bowl bid this time around and the players were ready to play ball. ND signed up to play Joe Paterno's storied Penn State team in the Gator Bowl, hoping to build momentum for what was expected to be another fine ND team in 1977.

Devine's team took full advantage of the opportunity, with the Browner-led defense playing a great football game. Notre Dame won the Gator Bowl v the Nittany Lions, W 20-9.

1977 Notre Dame Football Season Coach Dan Devine

The 1977 Notre Dame Fighting Irish football team was coached by Dan Devine in his third year as head coach This Notre Dame football team was ranked third in the country to start the season. Its veteran defense was again expected to do well with returning Outland Trophy winner Ross Browner at defensive end.

Great Player: Ross Browner, DE 1973-1977

Ross Browner was the mainstay of Notre Dame's Defense in the 1970's. He was a Consensus All-America pick in 1976 and '77 and was inducted into National Football Foundation Hall of Fame in 1999.

He was a four-year Irish starter who played on 1973 and 1977 national championship team. In 1976, he was the Outland Trophy recipient and 1977 the Lombardi Trophy winner.

Browner was unanimous first-team All-America end in both 1976 and '77. He finished fifth in '77 Heisman Trophy voting. Browner for years has held Notre Dame records for tackles by front four linemen (since 1956) in a career with 340. He also leads on tackles for minus yardage (since 1967) in a single season with 28 for 203 yards. He is tops with tackles for minus yardage in a career with 77 for 515 yards.

Browner also likes to recover fumbles and at ND, he recovered 12. Seventy-seven of his 340 career tackles resulted in total losses of over 515 yards. He broke up 10 passes, recovered eight fumbles, blocked two kicks, scored two safeties and one touchdown. He also played in the 1978 Japan Bowl and Hula Bowl.

After Notre Dame, Browner kept on going and was the eighth overall selection in the 1979 NFL draft as the first-round pick of Cincinnati Bengals. He played through '87 season. He is ranked No. 84 in college football.com's top 100 players of all-time. He was voted into Gator Bowl Hall of Fame in '99. He also won the Robert Maxwell trophy. Overall, Browner had a great football career as he was definitely one of Notre Dame's great players.

Great Player: Joe Montana QB, 1974-1978

Joe Montana did not pop into Dan Devine's mind as his next quarterback when he took over the ND team from Ara Parseghian. Joe Montana had yet to become Joe Montana.

When he finally became Joe Montana, it was clear that he was one of the best QB's that had ever lived at the college and pro levels. Montana proved it every time he took the field.

Joe Montana won a national championship at Notre Dame and four Super Bowls with the San Francisco 49ers. Just this year, Tom Brady broke his Super Bowl record. Congratulations Mr. Brady. Montana played quarterback with an imperturbable spirit even under pressure. It made him synonymous with big-game excellence.

"If you had one game you had to win, Joe Montana is your quarterback," 49ers teammate Randy Cross said.

"I was one of about seven freshman quarterbacks, and I played my way down to seventh string," Montana recalled of his 1974 ND arrival. "I didn't doubt my ability, but I wondered whether I was ready for a place like Notre Dame. Everybody else was good, and really big -- especially the defensive guys."

The great Ara Parseghian had recruited Montana out of Western Pennsylvania, where they have been known to grow great quarterbacks. When Ara retired and Dan Devine showed up for work, Montana's future was in doubt, Why would Devine pick Montana? Even Joe did not know the answer to that one. Musing, Montana thought:

"Devine probably wondered why I was recruited."

Montana fortunately made two buddies on campus—the Irish fencing coach Mike DeCicco and his son. Mike also served as an academic advisor to Notre Dame athletes. Additionally, he was the dad of Joe's teammate/roommate Nick DeCicco. Nick had convinced Montana to stick around when Devine came to campus. He convinced him that his day would come. And it did.

As a sophomore in 1975, Joe Montana was able to direct the Irish to comeback victories over North Carolina and Air Force.

In these two games, the sophomore QB had shown what he had and it was good. But, he encountered another setback. He injured his shoulder and it cost him the 1976 season and he thus had no place in Dan Devine's mind or heart.

He became #3 on the depth chart going into 1977. Nobody was looking to give Joe a chance, Devine felt his fortunes were best met with another player. Yet, Montana nonetheless got his chance in the third game when the Irish were losing 24-14 against Purdue. Devine inserted Montana into the game and Joe delivered 154 passing yards and 17 points in the final 11 minutes for a 31-24 victory.

"The players were practically jumping up and down when Joe came into the game. They started slapping him on the back before he had taken a snap," recalled Roger Valdiserri, Notre Dame's longtime media relations director. "I was sitting next to my Purdue counterpart, and he asked me what was going on. I said, `That's Joe Montana, and you guys are in trouble.'"

The Irish would not lose again that season, nailing down the national championship with a 38-10 thumping of top-ranked Texas in the Cotton Bowl. The one-time scared, skinny, homesick freshman was now a poised, accomplished star, partly because Mike DeCicco's belief in him overcame Montana's self-doubt.

"Notre Dame is a hard place to leave, fortunately," he said. "It's not really big, but it's sort of overwhelming because it's Notre Dame, and you're always mindful of what that means. You want to be the best, and you want to prove it by playing against the best."

An early-season loss to Missouri derailed Notre Dame's hopes of repeating as national champion in 1978, but two more vintage comebacks enhanced the Montana legend. The rest of the Montana story is scattered in with the rest of the 1977 season and are told below in this section of this book on ND's great players. Joe Montana had finally found his day in the sun.

Great Player: Ken MacAfee, TE 1974-1977

Whereas Penn State is clearly Linebacker U, more and more experts suggest that Notre Dame is now "Tight End U." For such a legacy, Ken MacAfee is exactly the kind of player that comes to mind.

He was a consensus All-American for both the 1976 and 1977 seasons. In the 1977 season as a senior, MacAfee caught 54 passes for 797 yards and six touchdowns. Not too shabby!

How does three-time first-team All-American in 1975-77 sound along with a unanimous pick in 1977 as senior. Ken MacAfee is a 1997 National Football Foundation Hall of Fame inductee who finished third in the 1977 Heisman Trophy voting.

Additionally, he is the first lineman to win the Walter Camp Player of the Year Award in 1977. As noted but worth repeating as it is remarkable, during 1977 national championship season MacAfee caught 54 passes for 797 yards and six touchdowns.

In total, he caught 128 career passes for 1,759 yards and 15 TDs, ranking third on Notre Dame career receiving chart. He was pleased to go to Hawaii for the 1978 Hula Bowl and to the Japan Bowl. How about being a first-round pick by San Francisco in 1978 NFL draft.

After ND, MacAfee played with the San Francisco 49ers in 1978-79 after being drafted seventh overall in the first round of the 1978 NFL Draft. He was a starter in his rookie season, catching 22 passes with one going for a touchdown. He was also a starter in his second season, 1979 and caught 24 passes for 4 touchdowns.

In 1980 MacAfee was asked to play guard for the 49ers, and not feeling suited to play that position, he left football and began dental school, and became Dr. Macafee. After the season his rights as a player in the NFL were traded to the Minnesota Vikings, but he never played a regular season game with them. He was placed on injured reserve in September, 1981. I do not think it was a toothache.

If my teeth were not so perfect, I would look him up and ask him to make sure they were perfect. Ken MacAfee is a man's man. It's nice to see there are still some of us around.

Great Player: Luther Bradley DB 1973-1977

Luther Bradley was a great football player, period. He was a consensus All-American pick in 1977 He played on some great teams including the 1973 and 1977 Irish national championship teams. in 1975, he intercepted a pass vs. Purdue and returned it 99 yards for a touchdown for the second-longest interception return in Notre Dame history.

He had 153 career tackles (five for 30 yards in losses), broke up 27 passes, recovered two fumbles, and in his spare time, he blocked two kicks. Bradley holds the all-time Notre Dame individual record for most interceptions in a career with 17 for 218 yards; most yards gained by interceptions (one game) with 103 vs. Purdue.

He also has the highest average for yardage by interception return (one game) with 51.5 and in a season with 33.8. He was pleased to participate in the 1978 Japan Bowl. He was drafted in the first round in 1978 by Detroit and he played through 1981.

In 1977 on Dan Devine's great championship team, Willie Fry was on the other end and Luther Bradley was the Irish key defensive back. The position coach in the secondary was the late Jim Johnson, a great defensive coach. Johnson was at the beginning of a career that would see him become the renowned defensive coordinator for the Philadelphia Eagles' best teams in the early 2000s.

This was a great season but it did have a major burp in the second game against Ole Miss. Devine brought the Irish to 10-1 regular season and a win in the Cotton Bowl Classic against Texas W (38-10). The 1977 squad became the tenth Irish team to win the national title and were led by All-Americans Ken MacAfee, Ross Browner, Luther Bradley, and Bob Golic. Junior Joe Montana, a future Pro Football Hall of Fame member, was the starting quarterback on this team.

Third year coach Dan Devine expected great things from his talent-rich Notre Dame team after a well-played 9-3 season and 20-9 Gator Bowl win over Penn State the previous year. The team needed experience and they got it and in 1977 they were ready for big things.

Starting the year off in a firestorm, Notre Dame, with a preseason ranking of #3, had no choice but to play its best. The first opponent was the Pitt Panthers, who were the defending national champions. The Panthers had won in South Bend while moving towards their national championship in 1976.

Things were brighter for the Irish in 1977 for the Irish because Heisman winner Tony Dorsett was gone. Dorsett was starring as an NFL rookie in Dallas. Notre Dame won the opener W (19-9), but immediately gave it back with a very surprising loss at home to Ole Miss L (13-20). The masses were asking: Was it the end of championship hopes in the Devine Era?

Notre Dame fans do not like things to go wrong and they were grumbling all over the country after the Ole Miss loss. After two-three-loss campaigns, another three-loss season would be clearly unacceptable. Even today, that is not acceptable at Notre Dame, where the pleasant scent of a National Title has been lost for some time now. It certainly was not OK in 1977.

The offense was playing poorly as junior quarterback Rusty Lisch, who started the first three games for Devine was struggling, and then he got hurt. Second-stringer Gary Forsythe got the chance against Purdue and Notre Dame fell behind 24-14. Devine was not pleased and looked to the bench and found another junior waiting to play. The new QB was their third-stringer—a kid named Joe Montana.

Montana had played well in some relief work as a freshman in 1975, then he missed the 1976 season with a shoulder injury. Montana proved his mettle at Notre Dame and in pro-football. Before immediately was up, he had led the Irish back to a win away over the Boilermakers W (31-24). He then led consecutive wins over Michigan State at home W (16-6) and Army away, W (24-0). Those wins set the stage for a mid-October date with fifth-ranked USC, a team with the gift of having the Irish's number. Doing well against USC would bring relevance back to the ND program.

The 1977 Notre Dame-USC game has a special place in Fighting Irish lore. The Blue and Gold team was not going to wear blue and gold. When Notre Dame returned to their lockers after the pre-game warmups, to get their "Devine" pep talk, there was something different there. It was in their lockers already. The Irish saw something—Kelly green jerseys. On this day, Kelly green would replace the traditional dark navy customarily worn. It electrified the team and when they came running out of the tunnel again, the crowd went berserk.

As simple as the change to green jerseys may have been, it gave the Fighting Irish a huge emotional lift and there was no question about the outcome of the game from the moment the Irish took the field. They pummeled USC (49-19).

Led by Montana and tight end Ken MacAfee, a third-place Heisman candidate, Notre Dame would finish its season with five straight wins to finish. Their 10-1 record was amazing considering the slow start. There was still one more challenge. On November 12, at Clemson a tough Tigers team took a lead and had Notre Dame down by double-digits.

Montana put his helmet back on and began to lead the Irish back to victory. Joe Montana was able to add another early chapter to his comeback legend. He got it done when it counted and led the Irish back to a win W (21-17) against Clemson.

A Buried Montana Sneaks Ball in for Game Winner at Clemson

Notre Dame concluded the season ranked #5 in the country and got an invitation to play #1 Texas in the Cotton Bowl.

On the way to the Cotton Bowl after USC, ND stopped Navy at home W (43-10), and then the next week crushed Georgia Tech W (69-14). After Clemson, it was Air Force at home W (49-0), and Miami at Miami W (48-10).

The Cotton Bowl was played on Sunday January 2 since New Year's Day was Saturday on the "long" football weekend. Few thought that a Notre Dame New Year's Day run to a national title was likely, but it was theoretically possible. ND had a fine season with the one burp being Ole Miss.

At the time, four teams were ahead of Notre Dame in the rankings—in addition to Texas, there was Oklahoma, Michigan and Alabama—all were in separate bowl games, so the Irish could hope to pull off a miraculous turnaround. It would be as easy to bring about as a completed "Hail Mary" pass for a touchdown. But then again. Notre Dame was named after Mary, the Mother of Jesus, so all things were possible.

In 1977, there were no BCS champions and the bowl games were the end of the season. The AP and the UPI determined the champions and there were times that they did not even wait until the bowl games to make their decrees. So, without a BCS, in 1977, it was possible for the national championship to be determined on New Year's Day or even January 2 if it were a Sunday game.

On this January 2, a Sunday, playing against Texas, it was well known that the Cowboys from Texas had won the NFC championship the day before so the Texans were hoping for a two-for weekend. It sure would be nice for them if UT added a nice national championship to the Texas picture.

The Longhorns had an exceptional runner who had just won the Heisman Trophy, notably Earl Campbell. He was a powerful runner with some of the biggest muscular thighs ever seen on a back. Campbell had a great big NFL career ahead of him.

The good news for Notre Dame in the game was that its defense was able to prevent Earl Campbell from getting it going. Texas helped things by turning the ball over time and again. The Longhorns got the fans going by scoring first for a 3-0 lead, Notre Dame had stopped their advance for a touchdown.

Joe Montana, along with running backs Jerome Heavens, Vagas Ferguson and Ken MacAfee kept scoring after that. The final score was W 38-10, well worthy of a national championship, but it was not assured as other teams were also in the hunt.

Other than Alabama, who handily had beaten a 9-2 Ohio State team in the Sugar Bowl, all other teams seemed to eventually lose their place in the championship line. Michigan was upset by four-loss Washington and quarterback Warren Moon in the Rose Bowl. The heavily favored Sooners were an almost sure bid for the national championship title if they were able to defeat Arkansas.

Oklahoma found Arkansas weakened when Razorbacks coach Lou Holtz suspended three players for disciplinary reasons prior to the game. Yet, somehow, the Razorbacks were not going to lie down.

Despite not having his key players, who had scored more than 75% of the season's points playing in the game, Hogs coach Lou Holtz made his first mark on South Bend history even before he arrived to coach the 1986 season. Holtz's Arkansas smoked OU 31-6 and it was then down to Notre Dame or Alabama for the national championship. The pundits would have to decide.

The pundits were chatting that it would have been an ideal time for a plus-one format after the bowls, because the Irish and Tide both appeared to be deserving of championship status. Alabama had played a consistently tougher schedule and their September loss to Nebraska was infinitely more defensible than Notre Dame's defeat at Ole Miss.

But the Tide had mostly close games that were nothing like the ND blowouts. Alabama had no great runaways like the wins—shall I say the catastrophes—Notre Dame had hung on USC and Texas, beating two highly regarded opponents by a combined 58 points.

The Voters do like "trophy wins" over a consistently steady long haul. In the end, the fact that Notre Dame had in fact buried the consensus #1 team in a bowl game only heightened the Notre Dame case. And, so the Fighting Irish won the national championship, and just like Parseghian before him and Holtz after him, Devine had done it in his third year. Congratulations Coach Devine.

Notre Dame Quarterback Joe Montana attempts a pass during the January 2, 1978 Cotton Bowl against Texas

January 2, 1978 Cotton Bowl v Texas from Scholastic, ND's Student Magazine

The Irish used their most time-consuming drive of the first half (3:19) 'to eat up the rest of the clock giving Texas a last chance at their own 32-yard line 'with 20 seconds left. As inept as McEachern was for 29 1/2 minutes of the first half, he came alive, when Texas had their backs to the wall with a little help from sloppy play in the Irish secondary. With two seconds left, the Texas quarterback threw in desperation to Ronnie Miksch. Although his pass was way off target, Jim Browner interfered, giving the Longhorns one last try from ND's 13- yard line with no time remaining on the clock. The Irish had been too generous as the Longhorns managed to score, on a pass to Mike Lockett. The touch down left a sour taste in the' mouths of, Irish fans as Akers' club got back in a ball game they would have been out of, with the halftime score reading 24-10.

The' momentum shifted more toward Texas when the Irish took the ensuing-kickoff and drove 60 yards only to have a field goal attempt go wide, but the Longhorn players must not have been listening well during halftime as McEachern was intercepted by Steve Heimkreiter, a turnover that sealed the Texans' fate. The game was as good as over when Vagas Ferguson crossed the goal line with 6:54 remaining in the third quarter giving Notre Dame an insurmountable 31-10 lead.

Dan Devine's squad wrapped-up the scoring when Ferguson made a slashing 26-yard run for his third touchdown of the afternoon leaving the final score 38 --10. The Irish spared Texas another touchdown when Rusty Lisch directed a last second drive to the two-yard line but did not call time out. Devine figured his team had proved; enough on the field this day to be called the number-one team in the nation. "

"This puts us where Texas was, number one. We earned it on the field. We played number one, and we beat them," the Irish coach later commented. "At this point, I do not think, there is anybody that could beat our football team." Hours later, a host of media backed up these words as - Notre Dame took top honors in both the AP and UPI polls and was honored with, the MacArthur Bowl, symbolic of the National Championship.

While everyone expected the game to be dominated by the running of Earl Campbell, it was a Notre Dame back that played the best game of his short collegiate career. Sophomore Vagas Ferguson rushed for 100 yards and two touchdowns and hauled in three passes for another TD. His performance this day was good enough to earn him Most Valuable Offensive Player of the game. Jerome Heavens also picked up 100 yards on the day putting him well over the 1000-yard mark for the season.

On the other side of the line, Bob Golic played a game that was typical of his weekly performances this season. His 17 tackles earned him the Defensive Player of the Game award ahead of runner-up, Ross Browner. The Notre Dame defense allowed Campbell 118 yards on, 29 carries (only 30 in the second half). The highly-touted senior played a tough game. "Campbell' is the best offensive 'back' in the country," praised Luther Bradley. "But he is no match for Ross Browner, Willie Fry, Bob Golic, and the· rest of our defensive squad." Browner and Fry, the Irish bookends, totaled 15 tackles (five for losses) and two fumble recoveries between them.

Dan Devine brought his team up before Christmas to prepare for this all-important game, and it proved perfect timing as mental attitude played a large role in the outcome. After the game, Devine was asked a question about himself and how he prepared for this game, and he responded, "Thank you for asking, but Dan Devine is not important." The Texas Longhorns must join Notre' Dame's demanding fans and insist that indeed, Dan Devine is important.

1978 Notre Dame Football Season Coach Dan Devine

The 1978 Notre Dame Fighting Irish football team was coached by Dan Devine. His squad went 8-3 in the regular season and Notre Dame Also won the Cotton Bowl against Houston (35-34), ending the season at 9-3.

After the 1977 Championship season, Notre Dame was on a continual high, which lasted into the fall of 1978. The ND basketball team had also made it to the Final Four. The high would end abruptly as the football season began. Notre Dame suffered two quick home losses to open the season, L (0-3) September 9 against Missouri, and L (14-28) September 23 against Michigan.

Great Player: Bob Golic LB, 1975-1978

Bob Golic was a unanimous All-American as senior captain in 1978. He was also a member of the 1977 national championship team who made 146 tackles, broke up five passes, blocked one kick, made three interceptions and returned one punt that season.

Golic added another 152 tackles in 1978.

He was also one of nation's top wrestlers with a three-year record of 54-4-1 - finishing third in NCAA meet in 1976 and fourth in 1977.

In his ND football career, Bob made 479 tackles; broke up eight passes; made six interceptions for 22 return yards; recovered two fumbles; blocked one kick and returned one punt 16 yards. Whew!

He was a 1979 participant in Hula Bowl and Japan Bowl and he was declared the defensive player of game in Hula Bowl.

In his pro career, he was a second-round selection by New England Patriots in 1979 NFL draft. He had a nice career from 1979-92 with New England, Cleveland and Los Angeles Raiders. He then became an NFL analyst for NBC Sports and also sports radio work in Los Angeles. His brother Mike is cohost on the Mike and Mike Rado Show.

More on Joe Montana QB

Joe Montana was at quarterback for his senior year and the Irish were ranked #5 to begin the season. Losing two at home was a less than stellar start to the season.

In the Missouri game, Montana had trouble with the ball and committed three red-zone turnovers. The Irish were stopped on fourth down in another scoring opportunity. On another, the Irish were very close and on another fourth-down attempt, they shanked an easy field goal.

One mistake after another with nothing positive in between gave Missouri a L (0-3) shutout of the Irish. ND quickly fell to #14 in the polls.

Michigan came in and took advantage of ND not having its act together. The Wolverines walked out of Notre Dame Stadium with a win L (14-28). Then came Purdue and Michigan State back to back. These Big Ten stalwarts would each win eight games and finish second and third in the league. The Irish came back at home against Purdue to win W (10-6) and in another four-point game, they squeaked out a win against the Spartans at Spartan Stadium W (29-25).

Pitt came to South Bend on October 14. The Panthers were at an "in-between" spot in their program history. Tony Dorsett was no longer there to assure their attack and Dan Marino had yet to arrive on campus. The 1978 Panthers still had a lot of spark and were ranked when they came to Notre Dame Stadium to play the Irish. Pitt took a 17-7 lead into the fourth quarter.

Comeback Kid Joe Montana Strikes Again!

It was time for the "comeback kid," a nickname owned by Joe Montana for being able to bring the Irish victory from the open jaws of defeat. This would be the start of a number of 1978 comebacks for Montana. He fired seven straight fourth quarter completions, including two touchdowns that gave Notre Dame a win W (26-17). The Irish had been unranked since the Michigan loss. The victory over # 9 Pitt brought ND back to the national rankings at # 20.

Feeling pretty good about themselves, the Irish defeated Air Force away W (38-15) and the victory over Miami W (20-0) nudged Notre Dame up to the #15 rank.

Navy was enjoying a big year in 1978 and was 7-0, ranked 11th in the country, when they met Notre Dame in a neutral-site game in Cleveland. The Irish showed how far they had progressed, rolling to a win W (27-7). The Irish then had another decisive victory W (31-7) over a struggling Tennessee team at home. Following this, the Irish went south to Atlanta and disposed of bowl-bound Georgia Tech by W (38-21).

The string of wins, well played, brought Notre Dame back into the Top 10. Running backs Vagas Ferguson and Jerome Heavens both were each having good years. Ferguson accumulated over 1,100 yards and Heavens chipping in over 700. Offensive center Dave Huffman made All-American as did Bob Golic on defense.

Montana did not make All-American. Chuck Fusina, the great QB for Penn State got those honors and Fusina also was # 2 in Heisman voting. Fusina had led Penn State to an undefeated regular season in 1978. Nonetheless, Montana remained the foremost author of comebacks.

In the season finale at USC, the Irish fell behind 24-6. Montana put himself into comeback gear and led a fourth-quarter rally that put ND ahead 25-24. The win appeared to be in the books when USC quarterback Paul McDonald was sacked and fumbled on the final possession. But a Pac-10 official ruled that McDonald had his arm going forward and the pass was ruled as incomplete. Soon, USC was in field goal range and a perfect kick brought them the game L (25-27). This was the first of two straight games that USC would win with help from officiating that was—at best—shaky.

As for Notre Dame, they were still #10 in the country and were preparing for the Cotton Bowl against Houston to be played in Dallas. Dan Devine was a great coach for sure.

Cotton Bowl in Houston

Forever known as the "Chicken Soup Game" because of frigid temperatures, heavy winds and a frozen Irish quarterback, Notre Dame trailed 34-12 in the fourth quarter at Austin, Texas.

With quarterback Joe Montana battling the flu and back in the locker room trying to fight off hypothermia, hopes looked bleak for the # 10 Irish to come back against the No. 9 Cougars.

It was so cold and wet at game time that Montana suffered from a hypothermia attack and could not function. Notre Dame's star quarterback was kept in the locker room for safety purposes, eating hot chicken soup while covered with blankets. He was not expected to play at all.

The rescue efforts to make Montana OK were more than successful as he recovered before the end of the game. But, by this time, the Irish were well behind 34-12. Montana emerged from the locker room and he excited the ND crowd by being back in the game with just 7:37 to play. The comeback kid was on the field. The adrenalin overcame the cold.

Tony Belden started the comeback for Notre Dame by blocking a punt that Steve Cichy returned for a touchdown. Montana converted the two-point play. The score was then 34-20. Notre Dame got the ball back and Montana led a 61-yard touchdown drive and gained another two-point conversion and suddenly it was 34-28 and there was still 4:15 to play. The comeback kid was at it again.

Notre Dame got the ball back, but Montana fumbled on the Houston 20 with 1:50 left. It looked like fate had caught up with the Irish and even chicken soup could not pull this game from the nether world.

The Cougars, however, with great ND defense soon were faced with 4th-and-1, and decided to go for it on their own 29-yard line. Facing a heavy wind, this was a defensible decision—they weren't going to get more than 10-15 net yards on a punt in these conditions. The Irish defense did not give an inch.

A still-warm Joe Montana led the team to the eight-yard line with six seconds to play. His first pass to Kris Haines in the left corner of the end zone was incomplete. Because he released so quickly, there was at least another second on the clock.

Devine and Montana went back to the same play, and this time Montana hit Haines. The final score was W 35-34. The comeback kid had brought Notre Dame back again for a victory. If it were today, somebody would have figured out how to take Montana's injury season and give the senior a fifth year. But, then again, Joe Montana's big opportunities were about to present themselves in the

NFL. Montana was warm at the end but you get a feeling for how cold it was by looking at Dean Devine shivering out a few comments to the Comeback Kid in the epic below. If it were today, somebody would have photoshopped Devine to make it look like he was clean-shaven. These guys were in it for keeps.

Notre Dame's quarterback Joe Montana shown during the 1979 Cotton Bowl. Montana led Irish to a final second win. The team was coached by Dan Devine.

This great player, Chicken Soup Joe, the Comeback Kid, who had been on the bench his first two seasons at Notre Dame under Joe Kuharich, would go on to win four Super Bowl rings with the San Francisco 49ers. Pundits at the time who wrote about the Irish after Montana noted that Notre Dame didn't have quite that many great moments in its future after Montana moved on.

However, all of the future ND moments would add to the lore. Together, a storied school and a legendary quarterback made the 1978 Notre Dame football season one to remember. Lou Holtz, the great one would be called on in a few years to add zip once again to Notre Dame. Dan Devine was already putting on a good show for the Irish. The show, only an immortal could put on!

1979 Notre Dame Football Season Coach Dan Devine

The 1979 Notre Dame Fighting Irish football team was coached by Dan Devine in his fifth season. Notre Dame finished with a regular season record of 6-4 and with its Bowl victory in Japan against Miami (40-15), overall the Irish finished the season at 7-4.

Great Player: Vagas Ferguson, RB, 1976-1979

Ferguson was from the small town of Richmond, Indiana- but he was ready to make a huge splash, and he did. He became the all-time leading rusher in Notre Dame school history by the time he left with 3472 yards and 32 sweet touchdowns. Vagas Ferguson holds the Notre Dame record for attempts in a season with 301 rushes and he holds the single season rushing record with 1437 yards (130 avg.). He is quite a guy and he is very resilient.

He was an All-American pick in 1979, finishing his career as Notre Dame's all-time leading ground-gainer with 3,472 rushing yards and 32 touchdowns. I love repeating that. Ferguson was the first ND rusher to gain more than 1,000 yards in consecutive seasons with 1,437 in 1979 following 1,192 in '78. He was a member of the 1977 national championship team.

The following year, Vagas was named outstanding offensive player of 1the 978 Cotton Bowl with 100 rushing yards and three TDs. His record called attention to all the pundits as he finished fifth in 1979 Heisman Trophy voting.

Ferguson is not Johnny Come Lately, he holds the all-time record for rushing yards in a game with 255 vs. Georgia Tech in 1978, and in a season with 1,437 (an average of 130.6 per game). He holds the record for rushing attempts in a season with 301 as well as per-game record at 27.4.

Vagas was pleased to participate in the 1980 East-West Shrine game and the Japan Bowl. It was a big honor.

He was selected in first round of 1980 NFL draft by New England Patriots as 25th overall pick and he had the opportunity to play four years in NFL with New England, Houston and Cleveland. He finished up as Athletic Director at Richmond (Ind.) High School, his alma mater. Nice!

1980 Notre Dame Football Season Coach Dan Devine

The 1980 Notre Dame Fighting Irish football team was coached by Dan Devine in his sixth and last season. As was customary, all home games were played at Notre Dame Stadium in South Bend, Indiana. The 1980 season would be Dan Devine's last as Notre Dame's head coach. Notre Dame finished a very respectable 9-2-1.

Great Player: John Scully, C, 1977-1980
John Scully was a tough football player. He made consensus All-American in 1980 .as a result of his great work as the Notre Dame starting center in 1979 and 1980 and as tri-captain of 1980 team.

In 1977, John played backup tackle for the Dan Devine national championship team. In 1978, he played as backup left tackle. Devine moved him to center in 1979 and he started all 11 games. He received an invitation to play in East-West Shrine game showcasing his football talents.

When he was finished with college football in 1981, Scully was a fourth-round NFL draft pick in 1981 by Atlanta and he played with Falcons until 1990. He has another life besides football. He was co-producer of a CD and music video titled 'Here Come the Irish,' a collection of Irish-style songs about Notre Dame. I think Mr. Scully enjoyed playing football the most but he was good wherever his talents led him.

In August, Dan Devine had announced that the upcoming season would be his last. Notre Dame had a good six seasons with Dan Devine including a national championship. This year, the offense scored 248, while the defense gave up 128 points. Dan Devine goes down in ND History as one of the Fighting Irish's finest coaches. He is the least known of the "immortals," who have brought the Fighting Irish great national championship seasons.

Classified as an EPIC game, The Notre Dame 1980 writing team wrote this about the Michigan game, a classic:

1980 MICHIGAN

In one of the greatest late-game see-saw affairs on this list, No. 8 Notre Dame and No. 14 Michigan swapped the lead three times in the second half before the smallest and most unlikely of heroes emerged with the game-winning play under the most difficult circumstances.

Pinned at his own 20-yard line with only 40 seconds remaining -- all while working against a steady 15 mph wind and trailing 27-26 -- Irish head coach Dan Devine benched his starting quarterback and called on confident big-armed freshman, Blair Kiel, to lead the final drive.

A couple of clutch passes -- and the help of a fortuitous 32-yard pass interference call -- helped Kiel move his team to Michigan's 34-yard line with only 0:04 remaining on the clock to set up Irish kicker Harry Oliver's impossible 51-yard field goal attempt for the win.

"I just remember thinking this wind is very strong and half-thinking, `I don't have a chance at making this thing,'" the late Oliver would recount in a 2004 interview with Irish Sports Report.

Call it luck of the Irish, or a just a well-timed weather break, legend has it the winds calmed just long enough for the 5-11, 185-pound Oliver to boot the kick and clear the crossbar by inches as the clock expired, delivering arguably the most memorable field goal in Notre Dame history for a 29-27 Irish win.

1980 Cover Michigan V Notre Dame Devine's last Season

1981 Sugar Bowl

Notre Dame had locked in to the Sugar Bowl and had a shot at moving up in the polls by derailing Georgia's Bulldogs and their sensational freshman running back, Herschel Walker. In the Sugar Bowl game. Notre Dame's defense was almost perfect as it controlled the line of scrimmage and the Irish got an early field goal from Oliver to take a 3-0 lead. Unfortunately, that was the end of the good news for Notre Dame.

The Fighting Irish had a miscommunication on who would field a kickoff return and this gave Georgia the ball on the 1-yard line. Additionally, ND committed four other turnovers. One miscue after another and a win cannot be had. ND also missed field goals. And in spite of Georgia completing just one pass all game long, the Irish lost L (10-17). The final ranking for Notre Dame was #10 in the coaches' poll and # 9 in the AP. Nobody could call that a slouch season but surely it could have been better.

Wrap-Up Article on Dan Devine

There is a great wrap-up article on the Devine era for those wanting to read more about this great coach. This Washington Post article by John Feinstein describes the ups and downs of Dan' Devine as a college coach and as the coach of Notre Dame.

https://www.washingtonpost.com/archive/sports/1980/11/12/dan-devine-38/aaa07da9-0865-41ca-85e1-4cfa5f0a906e/?utm_term=.6a669afb8019

God bless Dan Devine RIP, who passed away at the age of 77 on May 9, 2002. He was a great college coach in my book.

Dan Devine, a fine man and a fine coach, R.I.P.

Chapter 18 Coach Gerry Faust: 1981-1985

Coach # 24

Tough Road for Faust

1981	Gerry Faust	5–6
1982	Gerry Faust	6–4–1
1983	Gerry Faust	7–5
1984	Gerry Faust	7–5
1985	Gerry Faust	5–6

Former Notre Dame Football Coach Gerry Faust stands on the sidelines in South Bend, Ind. during the 1983 season. (AP Photo/Joe Raymond)

Article from the Washington Post on Faust's appointment

The best introduction to the Gerry Faust years at Notre Dame would be to display the hype as it was in 1980 for Gerry Faust, when he was sought after to be the coach of the University of Notre Dame football team. He was hired to succeed retiring coach Dan Devine. Here it is:

Notre Dame Picks Faust, Ohio High School Coach

November 25, 1980

Reprinted from the Washington Post with thanks.

> *Gerry Faust, who guided Cincinnati Moeller High School to national prominence during the past 18 years, was named Notre Dame football coach today, succeeding Dan Devine.*
>
> *Notre Dame President Rev. Theodore Hesburgh made the announcement of the appointment of Faust, whose teams have compiled a 174-17-2 record since 1963. They also have won 70 of their last 71 games.*
>
> *Edmund P. Joyce, executive vice president, said Faust was chosen because of his record on the high school level.*
>
> *"We feel quite strongly that Gerry Faust is the perfect individual to carry on the great tradition associated with athletics at the University of Notre Dame," Joyce said. "I don't know of anyone acquainted with Gerry who doesn't have the greatest respect and admiration for him and his accomplishments."*
>
> *Faust's teams have won five of the last six Ohio Class 3A championships, including the latest one on Sunday when his Crusader team finished a 13-0 season by defeating Massillon, 30-7.*
>
> *"I'm extremely pleased and tremendously honored to have been chosen to come to Notre Dame," said Faust, 45, whose teams have sent 250 players into the college ranks.*

"I said several years ago, the only job other than the one at Moeller in which I would be interested in would be at Notre Dame and I meant that sincerely."

Faust, whose team had a 33-game winning streak, explained why he decided to leave Moeller to take the Notre Dame job.

"I am a strong believer in tradition and discipline in educating your people," said the Dayton University graduate. "I don't believe there is a university in the country that combines those two items along with academic and athletic excellence better than Notre Dame does."

Devine announced his resignation before the start of the season, citing personal reasons, including the health of his wife.

The Irish, currently ranked No. 2 in the nation, are 9-0-1 on the season, giving Devine a 53-14-1 mark entering the regular-season finale at Southern California Dec. 6.

Notre Dame also has a shot at the national championship with a date against top-ranked Georgia Jan. 1 at the Sugar Bowl.

"We felt that whoever took over at Notre Dame," Devine explained, "they would be inheriting a veteran squad. This is a great bunch of young men and we know that the transition will be that much easier."

Faust will become the 24th head coach in the history of the tradition-rich Midwest independent dating back to 1894.

At Moeller, Faust has been turning out college-looking teams for years at Cincinnati Moeller High.

Faust's high school team never looked more collegiate than on Sunday. Some of Faust's players suspected then that their coach was Notre Dame-bound.

"We dedicated this game to Coach Faust because it might have been his last game at Moeller," fullback Mark Brooks said immediately after Sunday's game.

Gerry Faust was a great high school coach. It is easy to see with the credentials noted in this introductory article how Notre Dame would see in Faust both a great coach and a great man. Perhaps he was the perfect coach to take Notre Dame to another championship, but it probably was not this year, and it probably was not without more college experience.

1981 Notre Dame Football Season Coach Gerry Faust

The 1981 Notre Dame Fighting Irish football team was coached by Gerry Faust in his first year as head football coach. The 1981 offense scored 232 points, while the defense allowed 160 points. Despite Dan Devine's feeling that he had left his successor a solid team, it was Notre Dame's first losing season (5-6) in 18 years. There were no bowl offers and no rankings.

1982 Notre Dame Football Season Coach Gerry Faust

The 1982 Notre Dame Fighting Irish football team was coached by Gerry Faust in his second year as head football coach. Faust was no longer in awe of Division I coaching and teams and he did better plotting how to become victorious against them. Notre Dame's record was 6-4-1. The team was unranked throughout the season, and it was not invited to play in a bowl game.

Great Player: Bob Crable, LB, 1979-1981

Bob Crable was an animal during his time at Notre Dame. Crable was a unanimous All-American in 1980 and 1981 and an absolute workhorse. Crable had 521 career tackles with 187 of those coming in 1979 (a record). Also in 1979, Bob Crable had a NCAA record 26 tackles against Clemson.

If there was one defensive player in that era that defined what a Notre Dame player should be, it was Bob Crable. He was all over the field and he put ball carriers and their buts on that same field at a record pace.

Bob Crable was a near unanimous All-American pick in both 1980 and 1981. He was not an animal but he sure could have fooled the opposition. He recorded a massive 521 career tackles -- still a Notre Dame record. He still holds the ND records for most tackles in a season (187 in 1979); in a game (26 vs. Clemson in 1979), and his 26 tackles also ties the NCAA record.

<<< Bob Crable

Some highlights of game he helped win include when he recovered a Houston fumble in the 1979 Cotton Bowl which led to Irish TD and comeback victory. In 1979, Bob literally won the Michigan game with a last-second field goal block. For all of this he was well honored including being invited and being a 1982 participant in the Hula Bowl.

Crable was a first-round draft pick of the NFL New York Jets in 1982. After that, he played three years with Jets until injury cut his career short. He became a head football coach and teacher at Cincinnati Moeller High School. Hope he is still happy in football and outside of its realm.

1982 Pittsburgh Game ... Nice

Faust's crowning achievement of the season was against Pittsburgh. How did unranked Notre Dame defeat Pittsburgh with Dan Marino at the Pitt QB slot?

Pitt had not seen anything like Allen Pinkett since Tony Dorsett but Pinkett was playing for Notre Dame. A

The Irish defense forced a number of Pitt punts. On one series, Dame put together one of its most impressive drives of the 1982 campaign to seal the Panthers' fate. Joe Howard raced around end for 18 yards on first down from the Irish 35.

After Pinkett picked up four more yards, Moriarty exploded into the secondary on a quick opener for 29 yards to the Pitt 14. Pinkett, who registered his second consecutive 100-yard game, capped off the six-play, 65-yard drive with a seven-yard scoring romp. Johnston's conversion finished the scoring with 4:06 left. This was the best game of the 1982 season for Notre Dame.

1983 Notre Dame Football Season Coach Gerry Faust

The 1983 Notre Dame Fighting Irish football team was the third season for head coach Gerry Faust. ND finished at 7-5. Notre Dame's big 1983 moment was that it had made it to the Liberty Bowl where they faced Boston College and the Eagle's prized quarterback Doug Flutie.

In the Liberty Bowl, Boston College scored first on a 13-yard touchdown pass but missed the extra point. Notre Dame came back as Allen Pinkett and Chris Smith each rushed for 100-plus yards. Pinkett scored two touchdowns as Notre Dame beat Boston College, 19–18, to win its first bowl game since the 1979 Cotton Bowl. The ND record in 1983 was (7-5) which included the Liberty Bowl win. Though the season was positive, ND fans and alumni were not looking for just OK seasons.

ND v BC in Liberty Bowl. Head to Head Play

1984 Notre Dame Football Season Coach Gerry Faust

The 1984 Notre Dame Fighting Irish football team was coached by Gerry Faust in his fourth season. The Fighting Irish were 7-5 and finished # 17.

1985 Notre Dame Football Season Coach Gerry Faust

The 1985 Notre Dame Fighting Irish football team was coached by Gerry Faust in his fifth and final season with Notre Dame. This was the second losing Season (5-6) with Coach Faust. Irish fans were getting restless with the lack of long-term solid play.

Great Player: Allen Pinckett, RB, 1983 – 1985

Allen Pinkett was simply great. He was a two-time All-American at Notre Dame. In 1985, he was eighth in the Heisman balloting. He was Notre Dame's career rushing leader with 4,131 yards until Autry Denson broke his record in 1998, with 4,318 yards. Pinkett was the first Notre Dame player ever to rush for 1,000 yards in three consecutive seasons. He had 1,179 in 1983, 1,268 in 1984 and 1,176 in 1985.

Allen Pinkett

He remains the Irish career scoring leader with 53 touchdowns, including 49 rushing. He is tied with Vagas Ferguson (1976–1979) for the most rushing TDs in a single season. Pinkett had 17 TDs in 1984 and Ferguson had 17 in 1979.

Pinkett scored 4 TDs against Penn State at Happy Valley on November 12, 1983 and scored 3 against the Nittany Lions at Notre Dame Stadium on November 17, 1984.

Pinkett was drafted by the Houston Oilers with whom he played six seasons from 1986-1991. In his career with the Oilers, he gained

2,624 yards rushing with 21 TDs, and he caught 119 passes and 5 TDs. He was the team's leading rusher in his final year, 1991, with 720 yards.

For years, Pinkett was the color commentator for Notre Dame's football games broadcast by IMG College

---

1985: Faust's Last Season

Farewell to Gerry Faust. May God, bless you as you are a good man. Here is a link to a closing article to summarize the Faust years as written by the New York Times:

http://www.nytimes.com/1985/11/27/sports/embattled-faust-resigns-as-coach-of-notre-dame.html

Chapter 19 Coach Lou Holtz: 1986-1996

Coach # 25
National Championship 1988

Rockne, Leahy, Parseghian, Devine, Holtz—Five Greats—with National Championships

1986	Lou Holtz	5–6
1987	Lou Holtz	8–4
1988	Lou Holtz	12–0
1989	Lou Holtz	12–1
1990	Lou Holtz	9–3
1991	Lou Holtz	10–3
1992	Lou Holtz	10–1–1
1993	Lou Holtz	11–1
1994	Lou Holtz	6–5–1
1995	Lou Holtz	9–3
1996	Lou Holtz	8–3

As you can see by his record, Lou Holtz is one of the best coaches ever at Notre Dame. He is one of the elite. He is one of the immortals. He fits in with the Notre Dame immortals as he is one.

1986 Notre Dame Football Season Coach Lou Holtz

The 1986 Notre Dame Fighting Irish football team was coached by Lou Holtz. It was clearly a rebuilding year for Coach Holtz. Notre Dame produced a 5-6 record under first-year coach Holtz. Despite the poor record, the moxie that Notre Dame showed all season long, even in defeat, lifted the spirits of the fans as we all knew that Notre Dame was in for something good.

1987 Notre Dame Football Season Coach Lou Holtz

The 1987 Notre Dame Fighting Irish football team was coached by Lou Holtz in his second year as Notre Dame Head Coach. Tony Rice became the starting quarterback for Notre Dame following an injury to Terry Andrysiak. Rice would become one of the Notre Dame stars that few fans would ever forget.

This year Tim Brown would end ND's 23 year Heisman drought (John Huarte) as he would pick up the sixth **Heisman Trophy** for Notre Dame. The Irish would finish the season 8-4 and they earned a berth to the Cotton Bowl Classic for the first time since the 1978 season. But, unfortunately, the Irish lost L (10-35) the game against Texas A & M.

Nobody denied that it was the best season since Dan Devine had retired.

Great Player: Tim Brown, Flanker, 1984-1987

One of Lou Holtz major bright spots in his first two years as ND Head Coach was a great player named Tim Brown. Though the first two years were not as spectacular as year 3, it was not because Tim Brown was not out there every day giving it all for Notre Dame. He was a spectacular player for Lou Holtz.

Brown appeared on the scene in 1986 as a junior with a brilliant season-ending performance in a come-from-behind upset of USC, then used back-to-back punt returns for touchdowns in an early-season 1987 game against Michigan State to cement his Heisman bid.

Though he was listed as a flanker, Brown did it all. He used his ability as a pass receiver, rusher out of a full-house backfield and punt and kickoff returner to rank third nationally in all-purpose yardage as a junior (176.5 per game) and then he was at the top again (sixth) as a senior (167.9). He finished his junior campaign with 254 all-purpose yards in the 38-37 win at USC (including a 56-yard punt return that set up the winning field goal), then returned punts for 66 and 71 yards for a pair of touchdowns in an early romp over eventual Big Ten and Rose Bowl champion Michigan State.

Tim Brown finished his career as Notre Dame's all-time leader in pass reception yards (2493) while also returning six kicks for touchdowns (three punts, three kickoffs). Despite constant double and triple coverage as a senior, Brown earned a reputation as the most dangerous player in college football. Brown was a first-round pick of the Los Angeles Raiders (sixth player chosen overall) in the '88 NFL draft. A great college player and a great pro, Tim Brown was selected to play in the NFL Pro Bowl nine times.

1988 Notre Dame Football Season Coach Lou Holtz

The 1988 Notre Dame Fighting Irish football team was coached by Lou Holtz in his third year. This magical and mythical Holtz-led ND squad ended the season with 12 wins and no losses and no ties, winning the national championship. In other words, the Fighting Irish were unbeaten and they were good enough to convince all the Notre Dame haters in the world that they were worthy of being voted the # 1 team in the country.

The Fighting Irish had nothing handed to it, nor had it ever. The Irish won the title by defeating the previously unbeaten and No. 3 ranked West Virginia Mountaineers in the Sunkist Fiesta Bowl in Tempe, Arizona by a score of a 34-21. This powerful 1988 squad, one of 11 national title squads for the Irish, and a squad coached by the eternally great Lou Holtz, is considered to be one of the best undefeated teams in the history of college football.

The Irish always had tough schedules and that is why some of us think that they missed out on a few past titles. This time, there was no choice. Notre Dame beat teams which had finished the season ranked #2, #4, #5, and #7 in the AP Poll. How about that?

They also won 10 of 12 games by double digits. This phenomenal 1988 squad may best be remembered for its 31-30 upset of No. 1 ranked Miami, when Miami was at its best in Miami. It was Coach Jimmy Johnson's last year of his dynasty. Johnson had built a powerhouse that won and won and won and won. Notre Dame ended Johnson's and Miami's 36-game regular season winning streak. According to Irish fans, it was Notre Dame's landmark 31-30 win over top-rated Miami in 1988 in a game that keynoted that Irish national championship season.

The notion of *"Catholics vs. Convicts"* came from an ND student who put it on a t-shirt. The students liked it and he made money printing more and more and more. They sold like hotcakes during the buildup for the Top 5 showdown.

The teams really did not like each other and it seemed there was no love lost between the coaches. There was a pre-game fight between the two teams outside of the entrance tunnel lead credence to the slogan on the shirts. Both teams—players and coaches—wanted the victory badly. The fans seemed to want it even more.

The game has gone down as one of the most memorable in all of college football. Other than their loss to Notre Dame in South Bend, Miami would have been undefeated as they literally ripped through all of their other opponents. Miami and Jimmy Johnson, a coach people loved to hate, and many still do, did not have what it took in 1988. Notre Dame beat the Hurricanes and that is that.

This game has gone down in history as Good v. Evil. It was the Midwestern choirboys vs. South Beach renegades. It was the Catholics v. Convicts. It was ND V UM: Football at its best and worst.

Miami was #1 and Notre Dame #4 (5 wins, 0 losses) when they met in South Bend on Oct.15. Miami was the defending national champion. They came in with a 36-game regular season winning streak. The Irish, led by Tony Rice, held a 31–21 lead in the third quarter, but the Hurricanes rallied to within 31–30 on a touchdown with 45 seconds left in the game. The Canes went for the two-point conversion and missed. ND won the game W (31-30)

Great Player: Tony Rice QB 1987-1989

Tony Rice was one of the cornerstones on Notre Dame's 1988 national championship team which went 12-0 and defeated West Virginia in the Fiesta Bowl. He holds the school records for rushing yardage by a quarterback in a season (884 in 1989) and a career (1,921), ranking 15th among all Irish players in the latter category. Rice also stands sixth in school history with 4,882 yards of total offense.

From **Scholastic**

When ND won the Championship for Lou Holtz in 1988

<<< Tony Rice

Every college quarterback has a style. But not all of them get the job done with it. The true quarterback mold and Notre Dame's Tony Rice just don't fit. Quarterbacks are supposed to be smooth operators. Coaches want them cool, a little cocky, and to play the part. Rice can look more like a runaway colt. The only thing classic about the Irish junior seems to be the results. He can go 100 miles-an-hour all day, get dirty, and get excited. He can make a major college stadium seem like his personal sandlot. Somewhere inside Tony Rice burns a Jim McMahon attitude. He came to Notre Dame from small-school country in South Carolina with winner stamped on his forehead and question marks everywhere else. **Sept. 4, 1988 South Bend Tribune**

Notre Dame football fans expect a lot of improvement this season from quarterback Tony Rice. What they forget is how far he already has come. Rice took over at halftime of the Pittsburgh game last season when starter Terry Andrysiak limped into the locker room with a broken collarbone. "I came out of the· huddle for the first time in the second half and lined up under guard instead of center," said Rice. "I guess I was kind of nervous at first." Coach Lou Holtz doesn't ask his quarterbacks to win games. He demands they not lose them. **Sept. 9, 1988 Indianapolis Star**

His passes aren't Hall of Fame spirals, like Joe Montana's or Joe Theismann's. He won't win a Heisman Trophy, like Paul Hornung or John Huarte. The name "Tony Rice" will never roll off Notre Dame lips with the magic of "Johnny Lujack." But look at his W's. With this uncommon, uncelebrated Irish quarterback at the throttle,

America's No. 1 college team puffed its record to 9-0, taking a 54-11 Saturday stroll against a wonderful Texas university with a woeful 0-8 football team that also happens to play under the name of Rice (no kin). **Nov. 6, 1988 St. Petersburg Times.**

Great Player Raghib "Rocket" Ismael, Flanker, 1988-1990

The Rocket went to my high school and was coached by Mickey Gorham, a 1959 Notre Dame scholarship tackle, and my one-time football coach at Wilkes-Barre Meyers High School.

There is a great high school story about Meyers playing at Dallas in 1987, one of the best teams in the Wyoming Valley Conference. Coach Ted Jackson of Dallas knew the speed of the Ismael brothers, Raghib (Rocket) and Qadry (Missile)—Quadry went to Syracuse and Raghib went to ND), Jackson knew they would rip his team apart with their blinding speed. Both were great high school football players and phenomenally fast track stars. To negate the speed of the Ismael's, Jackson had a trick that in 1987 was perfectly legal.

Some say Coach Ted Jackson refused to permit the grass to be cut at Dallas, PA Stadium before the Meyers game. Consequently, the Ismael's were in essence, "caged in," by the high grass and were easy pickings for Dallas Defenders.

The folklore says the grass was knee high. "Maintenance made a mistake," joked Dallas head coach Ted Jackson. "They cut the grass. Fire that guy." Jackson was a win at all costs kind of coach at the high-school level and very lever. Jackson beat another great coach, an ND graduate Mickey Gorham, who was the Rocket's coach.

Notre Dame's web site: http://www.und.com/sports/ highlights Ismael's career and it was a great one. He was two-time first-team All-American as sophomore in '89 and junior in '90 and a unanimous pick in '90 when he finished second in Heisman Trophy voting behind BYU's Ty Detmer.

The "Rocket" became a starter on the 1988 National Championship squad with 12 catches for 331 yards and two touchdowns, while returning 12 kickoffs for 433 yards and two TDs. He had 64 rushing carries for 478 yards and two TDs in '89 and caught 27 passes for 535 yards. Always great in the return department, Ismael returned 20 kickoffs for 502 yards and two TDs with seven punt returns for 113 yards and one TD in '89.

Raghib was the Walter Camp Player of the Year in '90 with 67 rushing carries for 537 yards and three TDs in, 32 pass receptions for 699 yards and two TDs, 14 kickoff-returns for 336 yards and one TD while returning 13 punts for 151 yards.

His career totals included 273 all-purpose attempts for 4,187 yards and 15 TDs-- a 15.3 yards-per-attempt average. Ismael holds records for pass reception yards per catch in a career with 22.0 (71 for 1565); kickoff returns for touchdowns in a game with two (vs. Michigan in 1989 and again vs. Rice in 1988) and in a career with five; and kick return yards per attempt in a career with 22.6 (17 for 1607). Raghib "Rocket" Ismael is listed as the 75th greatest football player of all-time by collegefootball.com.

Let's check out the 1988 all-win ND record on the next page:

The home games were against the following: Michigan W (19-17). Purdue W (52-7), Stanford W (42-14), Miami W (31-30), Air Force W (31-13), Rice W (54-11), Penn State W (21-3).

Regular season away games were at Michigan State W (20-3), at Pitt W (30-20), at Navy W (22-7), and the big one at #2 USC W (27-10)

The Fiesta Bowl was going to either eliminate Note Dame as the "shoe-in" National Champion or affirm the Irish as the best team in the country. It was an important game. It was played in Sun Devil Stadium in Tempe Arizona against a very powerful # 3 West Virginia Team. Notre Dame won the game 34-21.

A great account of the bowl game in Tempe is at the following link

http://archives.nd.edu/Football/Football-1988s.pdf.

Go IRISH!

1989 Notre Dame Football Season Coach Lou Holtz

The 1989 Notre Dame Fighting Irish football team was the fourth ND squad coached by Lou Holtz. The Irish played its home games at Notre Dame Stadium in South Bend, Indiana. This was the perfect follow-up season to a National Championship year, except for one thing—# 7 Miami L (10-27), a team that finished the season 11-1. Jimmy Johnson, the long-time Miami Coach stepped down unnoticed in 1988 to coach Dallas as the new 1989 Hurricanes coach Dennis Erickson did not miss a single beat.

On January 1, Notre Dame went back to the Orange Bowl venue where they had lost to Miami and they beat # 4 ranked Colorado W (21-6) to end the season. If it were not for Miami, a team that also finished 12-1, Holtz's Fighting Irish would have been crowned #1.

1990 Notre Dame Football Season Coach Lou Holtz

The 1990 Notre Dame Fighting Irish football team was coached by Lou Holtz in his fifth season with the Irish. The Irish finished 9-3.

Notre Dame at #6 (9-2), were invited to play (10-1-1) Colorado, the #1 ranked team in the Country at the time in the Orange Bowl. It was a game with little offense.

Both defenses were strong but Colorado had just a little bit more in them than the Irish as they beat Notre Dame L (9-10), bringing Notre Dame's season record down to 9-3 and the Irish ranking to #6. Another year with title hopes unmet but a fine year by anybody's standards.

Great Player Todd Lyght, CB, 1987 -1990

Todd Lyght was a three-year starter at cornerback and 4-year monogram winner from 1987-1990. He led the team in tackles in the Fiesta Bowl against West Virginia to help the Irish win the game and the national championship. He was a consensus All-American in 1989 and 1990 and he was a finalist for the Jim Thorpe Award. Lyght captured 1 career interceptions with one of those returned for a touchdown. In an era that was still predominantly consumed by the running game, Todd Lyght was as a guy who could stop it all. The offense loved him.

Lyght was a two-time consensus All-American in 1989 and 1990 who was unanimous as a pick in his junior year 1989. Because he played so well, he had more playing time in 1987 than any other freshman, making 29 tackles, causing one fumble, breaking up two passes and making one interception.

He started for three years at cornerback from 1988-90. He unapologetically led the team in tackles in '89 Fiesta Bowl win over West Virginia for the national championship.

Notre Dame coaches loved him and he was named one of the captains for 1990 season and he became a finalist for the 1989 Jim Thorpe Award.

Lyght had 161 career tackles; caused one fumble; broke up 20.5 passes; had 11 interceptions for 55 return yards and one TD.

He was quite a player.

Additionally, he ranked eighth in final NCAA standings in '89 for interceptions. He played in the 1991 Hula Bowl and the Japan Bowl. And, after all that, he was a first-round pick of the Los Angeles Rams in 1991 NFL draft and he later played for the Detroit Lions. You have to be really good to get such a record.

Great Player: Michael Stonebreaker LB, 1986-1990

Michael Stonebreaker was a charter member of the Three Amigos on Notre Dame's 1988 National Championship team. Stonebreaker was a blue-collar, in your face, hard nose... well pick any other idiom for a tough guy playing linebacker and that's him.

Stonebreaker was a two-time consensus All-American for the 1988 and 1990 seasons. For his career, Michael had 220 tackles, 5 sacks and 5 interceptions.

In summary, Stonebreaker was a two-time consensus Irish all-star and a unanimous first-team All-America selection in 1990. He finished third in the balloting for Butkus Award as top linebacker nationally in 1990.

In 1990, he started all 12 games for the Irish, ranking second on squad in tackles with 104 that season. The was the top Irish tackler in '90 with 95; had 220 career tackles with eight passes broken up. He enjoyed his five interceptions for 103 yards and one touchdown, and he loved causing those four fumbles. He recovered two fumbles and had five sacks for minus-29 yards. Michael played in the 1991 Japan Bowl and Hula Bowl games.

After ND football, he was drafted in 1991 by the Chicago Bears, then signed with Atlanta in 1993 and New Orleans in 1994. After he moved on from the NFL, he played for the World League in Switzerland in '95. He then became a member of the NCSA advisory board.

Great Player: Chris Zorich, NT, 1988-1990

It is really hard for me to believe that I am getting old. It has been almost 30 years since I heard the drumbeat of Chris Zorich's name as the pain was being inflicted on ND opponents.

Chris was the winner of the 1990 Lombardi Award for defensive acumen. He was the two-time consensus all-star selection in 1989 and 1990 and a unanimous first-team All-American as senior in 1990. He loves football and he like any of us loved being recognized for his abilities.

Chris started at nose tackle in 1988 on Lou Holtz's national championship team. He made 70 tackles plus 3.5 sacks for minus-17 yards. He was named the United Press International (UPI) Lineman of the Year for 1989 and the College Lineman of the Year by the Touchdown Club of Washington, D.C. He stacked well as a finalist for the 1989 Lombardi Award. Zorich was chosen by CBS Sports/Chevrolet as the Defensive Player of the Year for 1990 and was a major finalist for '90 Outland Trophy.

<<< Chis Zorich's career totals are staggering. They include 219 tackles (21 for minus-56 yards).

He played in the NFL including the last half of the 1997 season with Washington Redskins. He had been drafted in the second round by the Chicago Bears in 1991.

He is president of the Chris Zorich Foundation in Chicago. He graduated from law school at the University of Notre Dame in 2002. Chris finds obstacles in his way as challenged to overcome. He does.

1991 Notre Dame Football Season Coach Lou Holtz

The 1991 Notre Dame Fighting Irish football team was coached by Lou Holtz in his sixth year as head coach. In 1991 with Lou Holtz at the helm, there was no concern about interest in the Notre Dame program.

Notre Dame had another banner year but with a record of 10-3, the Irish came up short again in its attempt for a second Holtz championship. At season end, the Fighting Irish finished #12 in the coaches' poll and #13 in the AP.

Great Player: Jerome Bettis, RB, 1990-1992

Jerome Bettis is one of the Best ND Football players ever. Lou Holtz had no doubts. Wherever he played, he was one of the greatest football players ever. Ask Pittsburgh!

A budding journalist at Notre Dame noticed that Jerome Bettis had a tendency to carry would-be tacklers down the field as if they were passengers along for the ride. From this he became "the Bus!"

The "Bus" is one of the most humble and heralded fullbacks in Notre Dame history. He played three seasons in an Irish uniform compiling 2,356 career yards (1,927 rushing, 429 receiving) and 27 TDs during his collegiate career. During the 1991 season, Bettis established program records for most TDs (20) and points (121) in a season. He additionally led the Irish in rushing yards (977) during his sophomore year.

Bettis holds Notre Dame's bowl game records in rushing yards (150) and rushing TDs (three) after leading the Irish to a 39-28 win over Florida in the 1992 Sugar Bowl. He left for the pros after his Junior Year.

Sugar Bowl

The 58th Annual Sugar Bowl Classic has authored its own write-up of its January 1, 1992 game. I stole all my facts about "the Bus" from their wonderful write-up. This game is classic Betttis.

The game featured a good ND team running in 18th place at a 9-3-0 pace against a #3 Florida team that was 10-1. Things would change by the end of the game. ND was # 13 (10-3-0), and Florida, just beaten by Notre Dame were ranked at #7 (10-2-0).

Jerome Bettis enjoys telling the story of how he listened and believed in his coach. Why would he not? The coach was Lou Holtz and he never lied. Some say that a football coach's orders had never been carried out so perfectly. Bettis did not mind telling the real story after the game.

Lou Holtz would have liked nothing more than to turn the clock back on his legs, add some ballast to his body and go play all positions because by half-time, he could not figure out why ND was not winning the game. Bettis offered his version of the coach's halftime speech:

"Coach (Lou) Holtz told us we could move the ball on the ground—and that we WOULD move the ball on the ground in the second half."

That was that. The observation and the command.

At halftime, ND was behind 16-7, and had not done the job rushing. The accountants had the Irish down for a grand total of just 34 yards. Holtz speech must have awakened the echoes of the immortals as the coach tells his story:

"At the half, I came in and I just didn't think we were in sync," said Holtz. "Our defense had been on the field too long so I made the decision to go to more power and control football. We wanted to go back to Notre Dame football."

Jerome Bettis heard every word and every inflection, and he understood the body language. More than that... Bettis took Holtz's orders to heart. In the dying minutes of the game—in an imagination-stretching span of 2:44—Jerome Bettis, one of the great ones, whose echoes will be heard by others over time, broke loose for three touchdown runs of 3, 49 and 39 yards.

He rushed for an even 100 yards, and with the help of some ND friends, he brought Notre Dame back from the jaws of defeat, to a magnificent but deceiving 39-28 victory. It was nothing less than an uphill grind all night for the Irish.

Notre Dame finished with 279 yards for the night, of which 141 came in the fourth quarter; 100 from Bettis in just several minutes. The Gators were not lying down for ND. They were doing great and yet struggling. For the game, the Gators had gained an eye-popping 511 total yards. Their major flaw was that they could not muster up the ability to punch in touchdowns when the team got so close to the end zone that they could smell the grass on the other side of the line.

Coach Holtz took a few respectable bows for his resilient team after the game. I bet he was thinking about Jerome Bettis. Some say it was Notre Dame and Holtz who had the last laughs. Bettis was pleased that he had come through for the team. Holtz offered these comments:

"We aren't a bad football team," said Lou Holtz. "People say that we didn't deserve to be here, but I've got to tell you, I'm proud of this team. We beat the No. 3 team in the nation, and didn't have a lot of help -- they didn't fumble; they didn't turn the ball over."

The facts in this section honoring the contribution of Jerome Bettis to Notre Dame football were from the book "Sugar Bowl Classic: A History" by Marty Mulé, who covered the game and the organization for decades for the New Orleans Times-Picayune.

Bettis did very well as a pro at Pittsburgh, and as a Pennsylvanian, I enjoyed watching him there. He retired in 2006 after the Steelers won Super Bowl XL in his native Detroit, Michigan. Mr. Bettis (the Bus) was inducted into the Pro Football Hall of Fame in 2015.

Few players on any team ever performed as well as Jerome Bettis while at Notre Dame. For Bettis, it was just another day's work. "Can't everybody do this?" God bless the "BUS."

1992 Notre Dame Football Season Coach Lou Holtz

The 1992 Notre Dame Fighting Irish football team was coached by Lou Holtz in his seventh year as head coach. Notre Dame had a nice-looking squad ready to go and they were ranked # 3 in the preseason polls. There was always hope for another championship. Rick Mirer was quarterback and he also served as captain of the fighting Irish.

When #22 Penn State came to South Bend and played a really close match W (17-16). Here is a recap of the PSU game:

The Snow Bowl

In this 1992 season, ND had just won the Holy War and now Penn State was coming to Notre Dame. The Irish were ranked # 8 and Paterno's PSU was at # 22. The series was going on hiatus after this game and nobody knew when the next game might be. Penn State had won eight of the last eleven games and held a slight edge in the series 8-7-1. The word on campus was that the Irish had this game circled all season long, wanting a big victory on Senior Day. As you can see from the picture it was snowing and to some this is still known as "The Snow Bowl."

The score was knotted at half-time, 6-6. The weather had improved by the second-half kickoff and the Irish D came up with a big stop. Notre Dame took a 9-6 lead before Penn State drove to the goal line. The Irish knew they needed a monumental goal-line stand to keep the game on the Irish side.

They rallied behind captain Demetrius DeBose, and executed what some have called a picturesque goal line stand. This forced the Nittany Lions to kick a field goal. As the teams prepared to play the fourth quarter, the score was still tied at 9-9.

Penn State scored another touchdown and Notre Dame had some time on the clock but not much. They had to get a TD to tie or go ahead. There was 4:16 left in the game. As the Irish advanced the clock was ticking. Now behind 16-9 with fourth down at the three-yard line, Notre Dame called judiciously called time out with twenty-five seconds remaining.

Snow Bowl – 1992 Encounter between Penn State and Notre Dame

Coach Holtz called a play normally reserved for two point conversions and that had never been used in a game before. Rick Mirer checked to his last option and told Jerome Bettis to go out. The "Bus" caught the touchdown pass in the middle of the end zone. Notre Dame then trailed 16-15. Under Holtz's leadership, the Irish were already once booed at home after a tie so it was clear that they needed to put the game on the line and go for two.

In what looked like a broken play, Mirer rolled to his right and Brooks mirrored him in the end zone. Brooks caught his third collegiate pass for the two points. The gutsy two-point conversion was successful. Notre Dame led 17-16 and withstood three Penn State passes after the kickoff before time expired. At the end of this game, the seniors had gotten their victory and the series was then tied 8-8-1.

"It was kind of weird because [Holtz] basically came up with a play on the fly," said Brooks, who only had two previous career pass receptions. "And we never even thought twice about going out and executing it."

The teams met again in 2006 at Notre Dame and 2007 in Beaver Stadium. Both teams won their home games and the series remains tied 9-9-1.

Notre Dame at # 5, then played rival USC, then ranked #23 at the Coliseum in a game in which anything could happen. The Irish won W (31-23). Notre Dame finished at 9-1-1 and were ranked #5 before playing in the Cotton Bowl against #3 Texas A&M. Notre Dame dominated the Cotton Bowl and won W (28-3) for a 10-1-1 season and a #4 ranking in the coaches' and the AP polls.

Great Player: Rick Mirer, QB 1989-19828

Right in the middle of Lou Holtz's eleven years at Notre Dame came Rick Mirer.

He was a great QB at ND and his 41-career touchdown passes ranks him third on Notre Dame's all-time list behind Brady Quinn (58) and Ron Powlus (52). Nobody passed as much then and Mirer's 41 are arguably the result of a balanced offense. Lou Holtz was his coach, and so one thing we know. Mirer never once felt sorry for himself. Self-pity was not in Holtz' playbook.

I have written a number of times about the PSU ND Snow bowl. When you are from PA, seeing snow all winter long, you think it is nothing. But, when you are playing football, it is really something.

Rick Mirer was a phenomenon and he was the QB for ND in the Snow Bowl v PSU. The Nittany Lions who play in bad weather all the time were not impressed that Coach Holtz could conjure up some snow to make the game more difficult for them. They were probably not on familiar terms with Ara Parseghian or they could have asked Ara to stop it!

Penn State made its trip to ND on November 16, 1992 in the classic, which immediately became known in Notre Dame lore as "The Snow Bowl." Look at the pictures. Mirer led the Irish steadily downfield, but with 25 seconds remaining, it was fourth-and-goal from the Penn State three. The touchdown came relatively easy, as Mirer hit a wide-open Jerome Bettis, pulling the Irish to within one point.

Rather than go for a tie, Notre Dame Head Coach Lou Holtz decided upon a two-point conversion. Mirer lofted the ball over a rapidly closing Penn State lineman. The ball sailed high toward the shortest player on the field. With fans tightly packed around the perimeter of the field, some in the press box were unable to even see whether Brooks caught the pass.

Mirer didn't have to wait for the crowd to go nuts to learn whether his pass had found its mark.

"I knew he was going to catch it," recalls the former All-American quarterback, who still ranks third on Notre Dame's career total offense list. "Reggie's effort was what that whole drive was all about.

"It wasn't the prettiest game on offense, although our defense played great. Sometimes, you just need to have your back to the wall. We had one shot, and that was it.

Rick Mirer is a standout person and an outstanding football player. He went on to spend over a decade in the NFL. He was a great Notre Dame prospect, a great Notre Dame football player, and he was a great player in the NFL. He was always a pleasure to watch do his magic against ND opponents. I am very pleased that a good guy like Rick Mirer got to be coached by a good guy like Lou Holtz. Go Irish!

1993 Notre Dame Football Season Coach Lou Holtz

The 1993 Notre Dame Fighting Irish football team was coached by Lou Holtz in his eighth year. Paul Failla and Kevin McDougal shared the QB duties. Backup Failla got time when McDougal hurt his shoulder. The season went so well that it surely looked like Lou Holtz was about to get his second national title at Notre Dame. Just two points and a Holy War later and things looked different.

On November 13, Notre Dame played Florida State in a late-season matchup of "unbeatens." The winner of this game, at Notre Dame Stadium in South Bend, Indiana, was certain to play #3 Nebraska (which would then move up to #2) in the Orange Bowl for the National Championship. What could stop that eventuality?

Let's look at the write-up from EPIC ND games to see a nice story about this game and then I may offer my few additional words:

When ND and Florida State met that day, the game had been hyped by many as the "Game of the Century". This much-acclaimed clash between #1 and #2 did not fail to live up to expectations. With Notre Dame, ahead by a touchdown and Florida State driving, hoping for a tie, or two to win. Irish defensive back Shawn Wooden batted down a Charlie Ward pass in the end zone with three seconds left to play. Notre Dame won the battle W (31-24).

Nothing but a holy war

Boston College was ranked # 12 when the next week, the Eagles came roaring to Notre Dame Stadium for the continuation of the Holy Wars. It was one of the best games of the year. The Notre Dame offense piled up 427 yards of offense, scored 5 touchdowns, including 22 points in the last 11 minutes. Yet, the game would forever be remembered on Boston College's last drive as their kicker David Gordon hit a 41-yard field goal as time expired to win it L (39-41), ending Notre Dame's bid for a national title.

Notre Dame fans were understandably upset that Florida State was playing for the national title with one loss, since that one loss was a whooping given to the squad by none other than the Fighting Irish.

West Virginia fans were also upset that FSU was playing for the national title with one loss, as the Mountaineers finishing the season undefeated. This kind of problem makes the BCS seem like a great solution.

Notre Dame dominated Florida State the whole game. A late FSU rally brought the score to 31-24. Bowden was happy to get out of South Bend with his respect and clearly did not expect a coronation to the national title ahead of Notre Dame.

On Nov. 24, 2000, Scott Merkin wrote a special to the Chicago Tribune that captures Notre Dame fans' sentiments on the game and on the voting snow-job. Here is an excerpt:

"One 42-yard field goal by a little-known left-footed kicker from Boston College prevented Kevin McDougal from leading Notre Dame to the 1993 national championship. One kick and some questionable pre-BCS voting that put Florida State ahead of Notre Dame in the final polls. "If we beat Florida State, like we did, and Boston College beat us, it just means Florida State should have been behind both of us in the voting," McDougal explained. "I still think we should have won the..."

Great Player: Jeff Burris, FS, 1990-1993

Jeff Burris was a consensus All-American in 1993 in a season that saw the Irish go 11-1 and truth be told... hosed out of a national championship. Burris was a one of a kind type of talent that was used to perfection by Lou Holtz.

He was a 1993 tri-captain of the Irish squad that went 11-1 and finished "second" in final polls. Burris led the 1992 team in interceptions and minutes played. He consistently ranked nationally in 1991 as punt returner with a final 12.6-yard average. Hard as it is to believe, Jeff Burris played more minutes in 1993 than any other Irish defensive player.

Jeff was voted National Monogram Club MVP by team in 1993 . . . with his greats statistics in career totals: 89 tackles; 14 passes broken up; 10 interceptions for 67 yards; 29 carries for 136 yards and 10 TDs as goal-line tailback; one pass reception for three yards and TD; 11 kickoff returns for 132 yards; 19 punt returns for 287 yards and one TD.

Jeff was selected Irish MVP in the Irish' 1993 win over top-rated Florida State. He played in Senior Bowl. After all the college action. Burris was a first-round selection in 1994 by the Buffalo Bills. He is currently a member of the Cincinnati Bengals.

Great Player: Aaron Taylor, OT 1990-1993

Aaron Taylor was a mountain of a man on the field for sure. At 6'4", 280 pounds, he was one of the biggest lineman in the country when he played in the early 1990's for the Irish.

Taylor was a unanimous first-team All-America selection in 1993 as senior offensive tackle after earning consensus honors as a junior in '92 as offensive guard. He was the winner of the 1993 Lombardi Award and was one of three finalists for Outland Trophy. He was also a Lombardi finalist as junior in '92.

He received the Notre Dame Lineman of the Year Award from the Moose Krause Chapter of the National Football Foundation and Hall of Fame in '93. He was voted by his teammates as recipient of the Nick Pietrosante Award, which is given to the player who best exemplifies courage, dedication and pride of the late All-America fullback.

Taylor was captain of the ND Football Team in his senior season, starting 30 games straight to the end of his career. He was also a member of the 1994 Hula Bowl team.

Always destined for pro-football, Taylor was drafted by the Green Bay Packers in the first round of 1994 NFL selections. He played on the team that won the Super Bowl in 1997. He also played for the San Diego Chargers in 1998 and 1999 before he chose to retire from professional football. He was voted one of the top 25 players form 1970-present. He was one heck of a football player.

1994 Notre Dame Football Season Coach Lou Holtz

The 1994 Notre Dame Fighting Irish football team was coached by Lou Holtz in his ninth year. Ron Powlus was the ND Quarterback. This year brought the worst record for Coach Holtz since his first season. The Irish were unranked at 6-5-1 and struggled all year.

Great Player: Bobby Taylor CB 1992-1994

Bobby Taylor was an uncommon cornerback. They are often smaller. He was 6'1" and over 200 pounds suggesting that he might be a better fit for a free safety position. He had played that role in his freshman year. However, the wiry speedster Texan moved to cornerback and showed off his phenomenally appreciated coverage skills.

Taylor was named the 1994 Defensive Back of the Year by the Columbus (Ohio) Touchdown Club. He was a consensus All-America pick during the 1994 season, earning accolades from the American Football Coaches Association, United Press International, Walter Camp Foundation, College and Pro Football Newsweekly, The Sporting News and Football News

Taylor was a player and stayed healthy and played games. He started 28 games over his three-year career, eventually moving into the free safety position as a freshman. He had five career interceptions, returning one for a touchdown against Navy.

He was a second-round draft choice of the Philadelphia Eagles in 1995 and 50th pick overall.

1995 Notre Dame Football Season Coach Lou Holtz

The Notre Dame Fighting Irish football team with its ten-year coach Lou Holtz played its 1995 home games at Notre Dame Stadium in South Bend, Indiana. The team compiled a 9-3 record and finished # 13 in the coaches' poll and # 11 in the AP.

Northwestern coach Gary Barnett and Notre Dame coach Lou Holtz shake hands after Northwestern's upset win on Sept. 2, 1995 in South Bend. (Phil Greer /Chicago Tribune)

Notre Dame was immediately surprised to begin the season when Northwestern came into South Bend and beat the Irish L (15-17).

At the end of the season, the #9 Fighting Irish were invited to the Orange Bowl to play Florida State. The Seminoles won the close game L (26-31).

1996 Notre Dame Football Season Coach Lou Holtz

The 1996 Fighting Irish football team was coached by Lou Holtz in his eleventh and final year as Notre Dame Head football coach. The Irish had a fine record at 8-3 and ND was # 21 in the Coaches' Poll and # 19 in the AP.

Lou Holtz Resigns as ND Football Coach

On Monday, November 18, 1996, Lou Holtz met with his team and gave them the news first of his decision to leave Notre Dame and pursue coaching opportunities elsewhere. In much the same way that he could not explain his feelings about the Golden Gophers two years after leaving Minnesota, Holtz had a tough time explaining why he was leaving Notre Dame.

Holtz said: "You have no idea how proud I have been to hear, 'He's the coach at Notre Dame,' " he said. "That's something you just can't buy."

This link to a November 20, 1996 piece written by Mike Jensen of the Philadelphia Inquirer does a nice job of putting Holtz tenure and his departure in perspective as we sign off from the Lou Holtz coaching era in this book. Enjoy:

http://articles.philly.com/1996-11-20/sports/25649667_1_lou-holtz-emmett-mosley-job-in-college-football

Notre Dame Students love Lou Holtz!

In their Football wrap-up, the Student Magazine, Scholastic had some very nice words for Coach Holtz. They clearly loved him and knew they would miss him. He is one of the great ones. This was not missed on anybody from Notre Dame.

God bless Lou Holtz, forever. Dear Lord, please keep him and his supporting family healthy!

Chapter 20 Coach Bob Davie: 1997–2001

Bob Davie Coach # 26
George O'Leary Coach # 27

Served as Holtz Defensive Whiz

1997	Bob Davie	7–6
1998	Bob Davie	9–3
1999	Bob Davie	5–7
2000	Bob Davie	9–3
2001	Bob Davie	5–6
2001	George O'Leary	0–0

In 1994, Lou Holtz asked Bob Davie to come to Notre Dame to serve as Defensive Coordinator. Davie did nothing less than a great job. Under Davie, the defense improved so much that in 1996, the team set a school record for number of sacks and allowed the lowest total yardage of any Notre Dame team since 1980. Holtz liked Davie and when in September 1995, Holtz had surgery and missed one game, he asked Davie to be the interim head coach. Under Davie, Notre Dame beat <u>Vanderbilt</u>, 41–0. Technically, if he had never become head coach, Bob Davie would have been the only undefeated and untied coach who ever won a game as head coach for Notre Dame. Now, let's take a look at Bob Davie's time as head coach of the University of Notre Dame:

1997 Notre Dame Football Season Coach Bob Davie

The 1997 Notre Dame Fighting Irish football team was coached by Bob Davie in his first season. His record was not too impressive at 7-6. Since Davie had been part of Holtz's team as defensive coordinator, despite there being a new coach, the Irish had high expectations. The team was ranked eleventh in the pre-season polls.

Great Player: Ron Powlus, QB 1994-1997

Ron Powlus is the current Director of Player Development for Notre Dame University. He was a four-year starter at quarterback for the Irish from 1994-97. He was the most recruited high school player in the country in 1993-1994.

He was a two-time captain who set 20 school records at Notre Dame.
He started all 44 regular-season games (plus two bowl games) in which he played and completed 558 of 969 passes for 7,602 yards and 52 TDs.

He signed as a free agent in 1998 with the Tennessee Oilers and then was on the Detroit Lions' preseason roster in 1999 and the Philadelphia Eagles' roster in 2000.

A native of Berwick, Pennsylvania, Powlus earned his bachelor's degree in marketing from Notre Dame in 1997. He and his wife, Sara, are parents of two sons, Ronnie and Tommy.

1998 Notre Dame Football Season Coach Bob Davie

The 1998 Notre Dame Fighting Irish football team was coached by Bob Davie in his second season. This year's record was 9-2 in the regular season and Notre Dame lost to Georgia Tech in the Gator Bowl. The Irish finished 9-3, and #22 in the Nation. Notre Dame started the season with some inertia and confidence from the last five regular season games of 1997 going down in the win column. Things looked promising.

Ron Powlus had graduated and Jarious Jackson was the clear starter. Jackson led the Irish, ranked # 22 against the # 5 ranked Wolverines with a win W (36-20) at home to start the season. Michigan was the defending co-national champion. What a game for Bob Davie. The Wolverines were led by future NFL great Tom Brady, but even he could not make up for poor play. Notre Dame pulled off a smart 36-20 upset. Were the Irish on their way?

1998 Gator Bowl

In the Gator Bowl, Notre Dame got behind early to the Georgia Tech Yellow Jackets with two long touchdowns. Though making a close game out of it by reducing the gap to a touchdown in the fourth quarter, the Irish were unable to move the ball on their last two drives and they lost their fourth straight bowl game L (28-35). Overall, the season ranking was # 22.

Great Player Autrey Denson RB, 1995-1998

Denson came from Nova High School in Davie, Florida
High School: Nova High School to major at ND in Business Administration. He received his degree in 1999.

From 1995-98, he was a record holding running back for the Fighting Irish. He starred in four bowl games. He earned 1999 Gator Bowl Most Valuable Player

As a four-year monogram winner, he was a three-year starter and two-time Most Valuable Player at Notre Dame from 1995-98. He is still the all-time leading rusher (4,318 yards) in school history. He recorded 43 career rushing TDs and 5,327 all-purpose yards, both of which rank second in Notre Dame annals. He gained more than 1,000 yards rushing over each of his final three years with the Irish. He was an Associated Press All-America selection as a senior in 1998.

1999 Notre Dame Football Season Coach Bob Davie

The 1999 Notre Dame Fighting Irish football team was coached by Bob Davie in his third season as head coach. This year's record was 5-7 in the regular season and Notre Dame was not invited to a Bowl game and the Irish were unranked in both polls.

2000 Notre Dame Football Season Coach Bob Davie

The 2000 Notre Dame Fighting Irish football team was coached by Bob Davie in his fourth season as head coach. This year's record was a very respectable 9-2 in the regular season and Notre Dame was invited to the BCS Fiesta Bowl to play Oregon State. Notre Dame had a much better year than in 1999. With the Fiesta Bowl loss, the team finished the season at 9-3, ranked # 16 in the coaches' poll and 15 in the AP.

2001 Notre Dame Football Season Coach Bob Davie

The 2001 Notre Dame Fighting Irish football team was coached by Bob Davie in his fifth season as head coach. Davie had just signed a five-year extension to his contract and after the 9-3 season in 2000, despite the bowl blowout, Notre Dame had great expectations of the team but they were not realized.

After being 9-3, and slipping to 5-6, there was some obvious inconsistency with the team. At the end of the 2001 season, there were no bowl offers and ND was unranked.

Davie Fired by Irish

Post Script on Bob Davie

Everybody knew when Lou Holtz recommended Bob Davie for the job of head coach at ND when Holtz stepped down, that Bob Davie was a good man. In his early forties at the time, Davie had not necessarily had the time to get gritty and tough enough to consistently win at Notre Dame. Ara Parseghian had offered 100% accurate advice when Davie took the job: *"Worry about one thing, and that's winning."* Davie did not win consistently at Notre Dame and he lost the job because of that one pesky requirement—*winning*.

George O'Leary

On December 9, 2001, Notre Dame hired George O'Leary away from Georgia Tech. to replace Bob Davie. However, New Hampshire Union Leader reporter Jim Fennell, while he was researching for a piece about a "local boy done good!" story on

O'Leary, uncovered misrepresentations in O'Leary's resume. These were severe enough that they had influenced the administration's decision to hire him.

The resulting media scandal embarrassed Notre Dame officials, and tainted O'Leary. The coach resigned five days later, before coaching a single practice, recruiting a single player, or hiring a single assistant coach. Yet, he is credited as a Notre Dame head coach in this book and others. George O'Leary's tenure is the shortest of any head coach in FBS history. He would go on to become the head football coach at UCF.

No ND players played for George O'Leary

Chapter 21 Coach Tyrone Willingham: 2002 – 2004

Willingham Coach # 28
Baer Coach #29

Willingham had great credentials

2002	Tyrone Willingham	10–3
2003	Tyrone Willingham	5–7
2004	Tyrone Willingham	6–5
2004	Kent Baer	0–1

2002 Notre Dame Football Season Coach Tyrone Willingham

The 2002 Notre Dame Fighting Irish football team was coached by Tyrone Willingham in his first year as head coach. The Fighting Irish were ranked #17 in the coaches' poll and #17 in the AP with a

10-3 record. Not too—too bad! Willingham's Irish were invited to the 2003 Gator Bowl in Alltel Stadium.

After Bob Davie's 5-6 2001 season, Notre Dame was looking for good news and Tyrone Willingham was delivering that good news for the Irish almost every week all season long. Notre Dame had green t-shirts printed with "Return to Glory." The Kelly family of Wilkes-Barre, PA proudly wore those T-shirts. They were classics.

ND *Return to Glory* T-shirt decal in Willingham's time

The 2002 season became known as a "Return to Glory" for the Irish. You can see the phrase in the T-shirt image above.

Great Player: Shane Walton: DC, 1997-2002

Shane Walton was a great defensive cornerback back for Notre Dame but he was never supposed to have had his feet on the gridiron. Walton was not in South Bend to play football at Notre Dame. Shane was there on scholarship to play soccer for the Fighting Irish, and in 1998 he led the Irish soccer team in scoring and was named Big East Freshman of the Year.

Enter Bob Davie. Davie saw Walton's quick feet and he proved that he could recognize defensive talent even on a different type of field. Tyrone Willingham benefited from Davie's keen instincts on talent.

Almost any soccer player that has ever been "drafted" by their school to play football, became the kicker. In Walton's case, he was a cornerback and received All-American status in 2002 as a key part of a devastating defense that had to bail out the offense throughout most of the season.

2002 was his big year. He was recognized as a unanimous first-team All-American as a senior. Walton finished the year with 68 tackles (46 solo), seven interceptions (two returned for touchdowns) and seven pass breakups. Nice find!

The 2002 Season Football Games

It is hard to believe in recollection and now even with the facts in front of me that Notre Dame did not score an offensive touchdown in its first game against Maryland W (22-0) at Giants stadium in the Kickoff Classic. Additionally, the Irish equaled that mark the following week against Purdue W (24-17) at home. After two weeks, still no offensive scores.

2003 Gator Bowl

The Irish had won 10 games in 2002, but had messed up late in the season instead of earlier. Consequently, Notre Dame was not invited to a BCS bowl game. Instead, the team accepted a bid to play North Carolina State in the Gator Bowl. Though it was better than Joe Smith's Happy Bowl at a high school stadium in Wilkes-Barre, PA, it was not something for which ND was hoping.

Quarterback Pat Dillingham #9 of the Notre Dame Fighting Irish prepares to hand-off the ball against the North Carolina State University Wolfpack in the Toyota Gator Bowl at Alltel Stadium on January 1, 2003 in Jacksonville.

The Irish played the bowl game tentatively, not as tough as expected, as if they were outmatched both on offense and defense. The Wolfpack won the game solidly L (6-28), giving the Irish its sixth consecutive bowl loss. Despite the three losses at the end of the season, the Irish salvaged a top-20 ranking at # 17 in both the Associated Press (AP) and Coaches' Polls.

Willingham, had it made but hanging on to a national championship is not a task for mere mortals. Just a few more perfect games and Willingham's picture would have been among the immortals. Everybody in the world was rooting for Notre Dame to keep winning.

After the season, some Irish players received honors for their fine play. Arnaz Battle was named by one foundation as their sportsman of the year, while Shane Walton was named as a Consensus All-American. Additionally, Tyrone Willingham, who had a successful yet disappointing season, was honored with two Coach of the Year awards—Sporting News as "Sportsman of the Year," and the Irish coach was the only coach listed by Sporting News as one of their "Most Powerful People in Sports."

Congratulations Coach Willingham.

What a difference a year makes!

2003 Notre Dame Football Season Coach Tyrone Willingham

The 2003 Notre Dame Fighting Irish football team was coached by Tyrone Willingham in his second year as ND Head Football Coach. Despite great expectations, Notre Dame had a less than sterling season. For ND faithful; it was startling but not sterling. The Irish finished the season unranked at 5–7 and failed to become bowl eligible. Few actually know what had happened between a successful season and a less than mediocre effort.

Notre Dame Fans simply do not like losses and unless there is a real reason that is understandable, and it is not an eternal notion, there will be grumblings.

2004 Notre Dame Football Season   Coach Tyrone Willingham
2004 Notre Dame Football Bowl Game   Coach Kent Baer

The 2004 Notre Dame Fighting Irish football team was coached by Tyrone Willingham in his third season. Notre Dame finished the regular season 6-5 under Willingham. The only good part of the record was that it was above the .500 mark. At 6-5, with all of the new bowl games added to post-season college play, teams in 2004 needed to win just six games to be invited to a post-season game.

Hoping to claim another win for the "Gipper," Willingham's Notre Dame accepted an invitation with its six-win qualification, to the Insight Bowl. Tyrone Willingham would not get to coach this bowl game. He was released at the end of the 2004 season before playing the bowl game. Assistant Coach / Defensive Coordinator Kent Baer, a good guy—never expecting to have to do the University a favor—was asked to coach the Irish in its bowl game appearance. He agreed because he is a good guy.

The Irish, with a dismal 6-5 record were invited and in turn accepted a bowl bid to play in the Insight Bowl, However, the administration had succumbed to great pressure from Fans and Alumni to stop the bleeding.

Willingham Fired

In a move highly criticized by those who believe football should be played with flags in back pockets and each team should be granted the opportunity for as many as ten apologies for seemingly aggressive plays, Notre Dame decided that it needed a new head coach. Tyrone Willingham had proven to be a great man but not as great a football coach.

The Insight Bowl

Two days after the USC trouncing, ND fired a great guy, Tyrone Willingham, whose major fault was that he did not bring wins into the football program as quickly as he had promised. Defensive coordinator, Kent Baer, led the Irish after the firing to prepare the team for the Insight Bowl. Many at Notre Dame hoped that Baer would "win one for Ty." Even another great guy like Kent Baer could not make this particular 2004 Notre Dame Team work well enough to win its last bowl game

Chapter 22 Coach Charlie Weis 2005–2009

Coach # 30

Weiss early on was treated like a god

2005 Charlie Weis 9–3
2006 Charlie Weis 10–3
2007 Charlie Weis 3–9
2008 Charlie Weis 7–6
2009 Charlie Weis 6–6

New coach had great credentials

Notre Dame is always excited when the University takes a not-so-productive coach and replaces him. The new guy is always going to save the program and every now and then, he actually does.

After Tyrone Willingham produced two poorly played seasons in a row, his time had passed at Notre Dame, and when Notre Dame started looking, they forgot that their best coaches were former head coaches. Nonetheless, when they hired Charlie Weiss, he was the brains of the New England Patriots' offense and despite the difference in jobs between being a strategist and a coach, Weiss got the nod at Notre Dame because the Patriots were doing so well, and perhaps because Bill Belichick does not hire anything other than the best.

Weis served as offensive coordinator for the Patriots under head coach Bill Belichick from 2000 through 2004, and he did some commendable work. He installed what is known as the Erhardt-Perkins offensive system, and assisted the Patriots in three Super Bowl victories— (XXXVI, XXXVIII, XXXIX).

Therefore, anybody who hired Charlie Weiss, knew they would not be hiring a *Johnny-come-lately*. Yet, other than a one year stint as head coach at a high school before his pro career, Charlie Weis never had full control of all the marbles for a football team.

From his record at Notre Dame, it apparently would have served him better if he had more field coaching experience at a college level. Here is an introductory article I selected from the Washington Post. You and I would more than likely have been pleased to hire Charlie Weiss in 2005 after reading this:

http://www.washingtonpost.com/wp-dyn/articles/A58013-2004Dec11.html?referrer=email

Patriots' Weis to Coach Notre Dame

By Mark Schlabach
Washington Post Staff Writer
Sunday, December 12, 2004

> "New England Patriots offensive coordinator Charlie Weis agreed to become football coach at Notre Dame and will receive a six-year contract that will pay him nearly $2 million annually, a source close to the search said last night. Weis becomes the first Notre Dame alumnus to coach the Fighting Irish since Hugh Devore in 1963.
>
> Notre Dame, which fired coach Tyrone Willingham on Nov. 30 after three seasons, is expected to announce Weis's hiring at a Monday news conference in South Bend, Ind. The Patriots play the Cincinnati Bengals today in Foxboro, Mass.

Willingham's controversial dismissal left only two black head coaches -- Karl Dorrell at UCLA and Sylvester Croom at Mississippi State -- among the 117 at the Division I-A level.

Weis, 48, who is white, has worked the past 15 years as an NFL assistant, spending the past five seasons as the Patriots' offensive coordinator. He is credited with the development of quarterback Tom Brady, a sixth-round draft choice who has led the team to two Super Bowl victories. Weis, who hasn't coached in college since 1989, has won three Super Bowl rings -- one with the New York Giants and two with the Patriots.

A Notre Dame committee of trustees and boosters, which voted to fire Willingham over the objections of the Rev. Edward "Monk" Malloy, the school's outgoing president, and Athletics Director Kevin White, met again yesterday. The committee chose to begin negotiations with Weis after selecting him over former Fighting Irish quarterback Tom Clements, now offensive coordinator of the Buffalo Bills, and Washington Redskins defensive coordinator Greg Blache, a former defensive back at Notre Dame.

Clements was informed yesterday morning that he wouldn't be hired by Notre Dame; associates of Blache said he withdrew his name from the search.

Blache -- who declined to comment through a Redskins spokesman -- was initially considered a long-shot candidate. However, he interviewed extremely well during a meeting with school officials early this past week. Redskins Vice President Vinny Cerrato, Notre Dame's recruiting coordinator from 1986 to 1990, played a role in the interview, according to one source who requested anonymity.

Two days after firing Willingham, White and incoming Notre Dame president John Jenkins flew to Salt Lake City to interview Utah Coach Urban Meyer, who had already begun contract negotiations with Florida. On Dec. 3, Meyer signed a seven-year contract to replace Gators Coach Ron Zook, who was fired in October. The Irish also contacted Detroit Lions Coach Steve Mariucci, Denver Broncos Coach Mike Shanahan and Iowa's Kirk Ferentz about replacing Willingham, but they all indicated they weren't interested.

Weis, who nearly died two years ago, from complications of gastro-intestinal surgery, is expected to finish the season with the Patriots, the defending Super Bowl champions, who are 11-1 going into today's game. If the Patriots advance to their third Super Bowl in four years, their season wouldn't end until Feb. 7 -- one day after both Super Bowl XXXIX in Jacksonville and college football's national signing day.

Weis was expected to leave the Patriots after this season even if he didn't accept the Notre Dame job. He is in the final year of his contract with the team and was upset that the Patriots didn't extend his deal before this season. Weis is paid about $500,000 per year—about half of what other top NFL coordinators are being paid. He also has grown increasingly frustrated about his inability to land an NFL head-coaching job despite the Patriots' success. NFL sources said he would have been hired as coach of the Buffalo Bills after last season, but the Bills were unwilling to wait until after the Super Bowl to interview him.

Staff writers Nunyo Demasio and Mark Maske contributed to this report.

2005 Notre Dame Football Season Coach Charlie Weis

The 2005 Notre Dame Fighting Irish football team was coached by Charlie Weis in his first year as head coach. Weis's Irish, after a dismal (6-6) 2004 season, took Tyrone Willingham's team at 6-6 in 2004, and with Charlie Weiss, former offensive coordinator with the Patriots, an ND grad, were happy to make him the first successful Notre Dame alumnus to coach the team since 1963.

2005 Great Player Jeff Samardzija WR, 2005-2006

Samardzija is also known as "The Shark." Jeff Samardzija was supposed to become a great baseball player. Maybe he has. But in 2005, he had the first of two-great all-time time great back to back seasons as a wide receiver in Notre Dame history.

He had a breakout season in his junior year with 77 receptions for 1249 yards and 15 touchdowns. And in 2006, he added 78 catches for 1,017 yards and 12 touchdowns.

Samardzija was more than just a stat collector, he was a threat and a savior. He made a huge number of clutch catches throughout the 2005 and 2006 seasons. Quinn would throw it up and

Jeff would bring it down. He was a big-time receiver in big time games, and he really started a run at Notre Dame where the school had a legitimate Bilitnikoff Award candidate every year.

2005 Games leading to the Fiesta Bowl

With 9 wins, 2 losses, and a ranking of #6 in the BCS polls, the Weis Irish were invited to the Fiesta Bowl, held in Sun Devil Stadium in Tempe Arizona. Their opponent was the ever-powerful #4 ranked Ohio State Buckeyes. This was just the second BCS appearance for the Irish and the first since a 2000 loss to the Oregon State Beavers in the Fiesta Bowl.

Jim Tressel, always a tough coach was at the helm for the Buckeyes. The score was 21-7 for the Buckeyes at the half. Ohio had a 24-13 lead going into the fourth quarter. Huston added another field goal, and Walker ran for a third touchdown, before Antonio Pittman ran for a 60-yard touchdown for the final score of the game. The Buckeyes won L (20-34), giving the Irish their NCAA record-tying 8th straight bowl game loss. Sorry Charley!

2006 Notre Dame Football Season Coach Charlie Weis

The 2006 Notre Dame Fighting Irish football team was coached by Charlie Weis in his second year as head coach. After a nice 9-3 start in his first season, Weis brought in a #19 finish with ten wins and three losses. The ND regular season record of 10-2 was enough for the Notre Dame Fighting Irish to be invited to the prestigious Sugar Bowl.

Five offensive starters, three defensive starters, and placekicker D.J. Fitzpatrick had already gone to the NFL after the 2005 season. Many key Irish returned such as quarterback Brady Quinn, wide receiver Jeff Samardzija, running back Darius Walker, and safety Tom Zbikowski. The Irish were given a lot of pre-season hype about being possible national championship contenders. Weis, in 2006, still had god-like status at Notre Dame.

Charlie Weis had a great recruiting year in 2006 with 28 recruits. It was a top ten ranked recruiting class, included three five star recruits on offense and 14 four star recruits with eight on offense and six on defense. Things were looking good for the future.

Georgia Tech & Penn State

The Irish were ranked # 2 when they pulled into Bobby Dodd Stadium in Atlanta to play Georgia Tech. The Yellow Jackets drew first blood when quarterback Reggie Ball connected on a four-yard touchdown pass with receiver Calvin Johnson at the end of the first quarter. Georgia Tech's defense was up to the challenge as it did the job holding back an experienced Notre Dame offense. Travis Bell's field goal put Tech's lead up to 10-0. This was the ND wake-up call as Georgia Tech would not score again. Quinn launched a magnificent 14-play, 80-yard drive right before the half, culminating in a five-yard rushing touchdown by the QB.

After a Weis halftime adjustment, the running and passing games began to work. But, as both defenses tightened, the teams were trading punts until, with a 4th-and-1 on the Tech 47-yard line with 1:10 left to play, Weis gambled and Quinn picked up the yard on a quarterback sneak.

The Irish got the first down and then ran out the clock for the victory W (14-10) victory. Quinn had completed 23 of 38 passes for 246 yards.

Penn State was next and they came to Notre Dame for the first time since the 1992 Snow Bowl game between the two teams. Until the second quarter, it was a tight defensive battle. Things opened up in the second quarter as Quinn connected on two TD passes and with a second field goal, the Irish were up 20-0 at halftime.

Notre Dame scored 21 more and Penn State got 14 in the second half. The Irish won (41-17). This victory would be Charlie Weis' lone 2006 win over a team that finished ranked in the AP Poll.

Michigan, Michigan State & Purdue

Michigan outplayed the Irish and won the game with a big score L (21-47). V Michigan State, this game remains tied for the 7th biggest comeback in ND history. The Irish won W (40-37). Ten came

Purdie which visited #12 Notre Dame undefeated on Sept. 30, and played their normal tough game against the Irish. Though undefeated, they were the underdogs. The Irish won the game W (35-21). It still looked like Weis was a demagogue.

Stanford, UCLA, Navy, North Carolina

On October 7, winless Stanford came and lost W (31-10). UCLA was not looking good, ranked # 9 when they came into Notre Dame Stadium for the game. The Bruins suffered from another great ND finish. which not only helped the ND lore but in 2006, it kept alive the Bowl Championship Series hopes of the 10th-ranked Fighting Irish W (20-17).

Charlie Weis was elated: "Good teams win games like that...Good teams at the end of the game somehow, good teams make a play at the end of the game to win."

Air Force, Army, & USC

ND wearing their splashy green jerseys against Army

Army came into South Bend to play #6 ranked Notre Dame in the Irish's final home game for the team's senior class. The Irish wore their special green jerseys. ND won handily W (41-9)

The season finale for Notre Dame with a trip to the LA Coliseum is often a close call, no matter who wins. T

Marching Band on the field at the Los Angeles Memorial Coliseum got the crowd going at the start of the 2006 #3 USC vs. #6 ranked Notre Dame football game

When a late game onside kick failed. USC scored again and the Irish lost L (24-44). Notre Dame finished the regular season 10-2.

Great Player: Brady Quinn, QB, 2003-2006

QB Brady Quinn holds many records as a top quarterback for Notre Dame in the Charlie Weis Era.

After an outstanding career at Dublin Coffman High School in Dublin, Ohio, listed # 20 on ESPN's list of the nation's top 100 prospects, Quinn was offered a scholarship from Notre Dame. The story is that he came to Notre Dame after a tip from fellow recruit Chinedum Ndukwe's father

Quinn accepted the offer to attend Notre Dame, and then the fun started. He set 36 ND records during his four seasons with the team. There were ten career records, twelve single-season records, four single-game records and ten miscellaneous records broken by Quinn throughout those four years, including the record for career pass attempts with 1,602; completions with 929; yards-per-game with 239.6; touchdown passes with 95, and the Irish's lowest interception percentage with 2.43.

Quinn won 29 games as a starter at Notre Dame, which tied him with other ND stalwarts such as Ron Powlus and Tom Clements for the most in ND history.

When Charlie Weis came to Notre Dame, Quinn was let loose and he was terrific. He averaged 110 more passing yards per game than he had as a sophomore as starting quarterback, while increasing his number of touchdown passes from 17 in 2004 to 32 in 2005.

He was named to the 2005 AP All-America Team as a third-team quarterback and the 2006 SI.com All-American Team as a second-team quarterback. He also received the Sammy Baugh Trophy as the nation's top passer of the 2005 season. At the end of the season, Notre Dame faced Ohio State in the Fiesta Bowl. Quinn had 29 completions in 45 pass attempts for 286 yards in a 34–20 loss to Ohio State.

Quinn finished the 2006 season with 3,426 yards on 289 completions out of 467 attempts for a completion percentage of 61.9% and 7.34 yards per attempt. He threw 37 touchdowns to only 7 interceptions, and was sacked 31 times. He finished the regular season with a passing efficiency rating of 146.65—18th in the country.

Notre Dame was invited to the 2007 Sugar Bowl, played on January 3, 2007, against LSU. Quinn was held to 148 passing yards. Quinn threw two touchdown passes, both of which were in the first half. LSU was tough and held Notre Dame scoreless through the second half of the game, defeating the Fighting Irish 41–14.

After the season, Brady Quinn received a number of awards. They included the Johnny Unitas Golden Arm Award for the best college quarterback in the nation and the Maxwell Award for the best college football player. Quinn was also named the Cingular All-America Player of the Year and was named to the 2006 AP All-America Team as a second-team quarterback.

Quinn graduated from Notre Dame with dual degrees in political science and finance. He was drafted early by Cleveland and played a number of years for the Browns. In 2017, he is working on a comeback. Let's wish him the best.

2007 Notre Dame Football Season Coach Charlie Weis

The 2007 Notre Dame Fighting Irish football team was coached by Charlie Weis in his third year as head coach. Notre Dame opened the season with five losses without a win. It was the team's worst opening prior to 2007 (0–3). The Irish would go on to compile the worst record in team history (3-9)

Their nine-loss season was also a school record. Few expected such a season as for two years with Brady Quinn as a starter, Weis' team played well most of the time if we choose to ignore the bowl losses. How could this happen?

Alumni were not pleased for sure but Weiss had just renewed a ten-year contract. It would cost Notre Dame a ton if there was an abrupt termination of the contract. But, this season was nothing less than terrible and most were blaming Weis for the trouble.

2008 Notre Dame Football Season Coach Charlie Weis

The 2008 Notre Dame Fighting Irish football team's head football coach was Charlie Weis. This was Weis's fourth season as Notre Dame's head coach. He entered the season with a 22–15 record, coming off a 3–9 season after having posted back-to-back BCS level seasons in his first two years. In 2008, the Irish had to show some life after the 3-9 finish. No Irish coach had ever been fired mid-season.

The team started 4–1, but hit some tough times and completed the regular season 6-6.

The Irish ended the 2008 season on a positive note. They had lost nine bowl games in a row. This year, they beat Hawaii W (49–21) in the Hawaii Bowl.

Boston College was ready!

For the November 8 Saturday night game, my entire family drove six hours to Wellesley, MA, just outside of Boston for the 2008 version of the BC / ND Holy War game. The girls went to Boston shopping while the guys went to the game in the rain. Now, who's smart? To assure having seats together, I had earlier bought six season tickets for the family. ND tickets are hard to get.

The season tickets seemed more affordable than scalper rates on game night, and we were assured of seats together. My son Mike and nephews Scott and Merek Piotroski and my brother-in law, Mitch Bornstein and my nephew Matt Bornstein, drove with me in the rain from the Bornstein home where we all were staying. We bravely sought a parking spot.

We were mentally prepared for the chilly, wet, and damp night game that we would experience. We parked after a long search for a spot in the pitch-black dark. We had passed the stadium in our search for a spot but were on the main drag. We walked quite a few blocks from our lucky parking spot to our reserved seats at Alumni stadium.

We did this all to watch a sluggish and seemingly exhausted Notre Dame team and a distressed coach give it up to the Boston College Eagles L (0-17). Unranked BC pitched a shutout against unranked (5-3) Notre Dame. As much as I love Notre Dame and Notre Dame Football, I found little enjoyment watching this poorly played game under my small, but functioning umbrella and my extremely cheap game-time poncho.

ND Coach Charlie Weis Hapless at BC

The Eagle's fans near us were very nice. That was the best part of the experience. The Eagles were not supposed to make a game out of it but like many of the Holy Wars between the Jesuits and the CSC, what is supposed to happen does not happen.

The Stadium was so small, I got a good look at Coach Weis during the game and it actually made me sad. He looked hapless and helpless and his look spilled over onto the ND team. I felt that the team had little choice but to play in a miserable, luckless, sloppy fashion. Something had to change soon in South Bend. It was too late for this particular holy War.

Notre Dame came back from this unexpected loss to beat the Midshipmen the following week at M & T Stadium in Baltimore in a close one W (27-21). Syracuse was next on the schedule.

In just a few years of playing the Irish, Syracuse had become a nemesis team. For years as President of the IBM Club in Scranton, I ran bus trips from Scranton to Syracuse's Carrier Dome to see the Orangemen play teams like Penn State, Pitt, Army, and other legacy teams, I knew Syracuse's team were always scrappers. I watched them clip off Notre Dame's wings in 2004 at the Dome in Willingham's last year. Yet, in 2008, I did not expect Charley Weis' team to be beaten by a weak Syracuse team at home. Yet, ND could not win this one and were beaten in a close game. L (23-24).

Notre Dame was hurting so bad for victories that I knew in my heart that when the Irish traveled to the Coliseum against USC this year that it was not going to be pretty. Yet, I always hoped things would be good. For this game, USC was ranked # 5 and Notre Dame was unranked. The Trojans never gave Notre Dame a chance in the game and they solidly beat The Fighting Irish L (3-38). The Irish finished the regular season at 6-6 and thus qualified for a minor bowl game—the Hawaii Bowl.

The Hawaii Bowl

I would have loved to have accompanied the Irish to Hawaii to see the game but for the 121st time in ND history, nobody called to make arrangements. I hoped for a victory. Sometimes good hopes materialize into good outcomes. This was one of those years. The Irish won at Hawaii 49-21 and broke a bunch of records along the way. I was happy for the Fighting Irish, and as always, I hoped for more of the same in 2009. Over time, Irish fans have developed a wary eye about these ups and downs.

Notre Dame soundly beat Hawaii 49–21 in its first bowl victory since the Irish defeated Texas A&M in the 1994 Cotton Bowl Classic to end the 1993 season.

In 2008, Irish quarterback Jimmy Clausen broke loose and with that breakout, he broke school bowl game records by passing for 401 yards and five touchdowns. Clausen was on the money. His 84.6% completion rate was the second-best completion percentage for any player ever in any bowl game in NCAA history.

Wide receiver Golden Tate was golden as usual. He also set Irish bowl records by catching three touchdowns and passes for 177 yards. Both players were honored as co-MVPs of the game.

For a team that had struggled all year, there was a lot in this game for the players. The Irish broke 9 bowl records. it was not just Clausen and Tate, who had record days, the Fighting Irish were fighting all day and they set bowl records in total offense (481 yards), scoring (49 points), and longest kick return (96 yards by Allen). Clausen had a 69-yard connection to Tate, which also became a new record. All parts of the team were well oiled and functioning. It had become a different team than the one I saw first-hand in Boston.

Perhaps Notre Dame should play home games in Hawaii, and yes, if invited, I would come. The ND defense also did its job, accumulating a whopping 8 sacks and an interception. Notre Dame and ND fans had this game to chew upon in the off-season as it tied the 1978 Cotton Bowl Classic for Notre Dame's largest margin of victory in a bowl game at 28 points.

2009 Notre Dame Football Season Coach Charlie Weis

The 2009 Notre Dame Fighting Irish football team was coached by Charlie Weis who had entered his fifth season as head coach. This season for Weis had an asterisk in the beginning. The ND Administration knew things were not copacetic but they also knew they could become OK with a great season.

So, they hoped that the coach, Charlie Weis would help the team recover from the last two bad years. Weis had unexpectedly become an underachiever. It was hoped by many ND faithful that he would finally blossom as a college coach. With two bad years behind him, Charlie Weis surely knew there was an "or else," attached to everybody's well wishes for his improvement.

When two entities engage in an arrangement in which both have a stake, such as marriage, both must bring something of reasonably equal value to the table. Notre Dame had paid the agreed upon salary for four years and were paying it again for the fifth year while its marriage partner in this case had been failing in his part of the covenant. Notre Dame Officials, to begin the 2009 season, did not need help from the alumni or from fans to remind Coach Weis what his part of the deal was. It was clear. Win!

Great Player: Jimmy Clausen, QB, 2007-2009

Jimmy Clausen had a spectacular high school and prep school career and was well recruited by Notre Dame and many others. He graduated from high school one semester early and enrolled at Notre Dame on January 16. He was a mystery to the press. In 2007, during ND's only preseason practice open to the media, Jimmy threw only a number of short passes. Pundits expressed some concern at this point about the strength of his arm after having had off-season elbow surgery.

When the Irish lost to Georgia Tech in fall, 2007 in the opener, Clausen was named the starting quarterback. But, he would win just one of his first six starts. He was replaced by Evan Sharpley while ND was losing to BC on Oct. 13, 2007. After sitting out Notre Dame's losses to USC and Navy, Clausen was again named the starter for their game against Air Force.

Clausen finished his freshman year completing 56.3% of his passes for 1,254 yards, with 7 touchdowns (plus two rushing TDs). He was intercepted 6 times and he was sacked a team-record 34 times.

As a sophomore, he improved to a 60.9% of his passes completed for 3172 yards, 25 touchdowns and 17 interceptions. He was the 44th ranked quarterback in NCAA Division I FBS. He led the Fighting Irish to a 7-6 record, culminating in a 49-21 victory against Hawaii in the Hawaii Bowl.

In his junior season, he was looking good. Clausen was named midseason All-American by The Sporting News. He finished the season big with 3,722 yards passing, a 68.8% completion rate, 161.42 passer rating, 28 touchdowns, and four interceptions.[28] In December, 2009, Clausen declared that he would forgo his senior season at Notre Dame and entered the NFL draft following news of the firing of head coach Charlie Weis.

He was drafted by the Carolina Panthers and played 13 games in 2010. He played six games with the Chicago Bears over two years and in 2014 he was traded to the Baltimore Ravens. He played two games with the Ravens in 2015 and has not played since then. Clausen returned to Notre Dame during the 2011 off-season to finish his degree in sociology.[

Great Player: Golden Tate WR, 2007-2009

Golden Tate was one of the best receivers in Notre Dame Football. In fact, he was one of the most electrifying wide receivers for the Irish in recent memory. He blossomed into the top playmaker on the team in 2008. He provided Notre Dame's offense with a bona fide threat to score every time the ball was in his hands.

He caught 64 passes for 1,211 yards (18.9 average) and 11 touchdowns, tops on the Irish in his last two seasons. He ranked 10th all-time at Notre Dame in touchdown receptions. Tate gained at least 100 receiving yards in six games during his career. He tied for fifth most in school history with Jim Seymour and Tim Brown.

Golden Tate recorded 22 receptions of at least 20 yards in his first two seasons and 17 of his catches gained at least 30 yards. With his quick feet, he even did some rushing, gaining 41 rushing yards on six carries with one TD.

As a flexible player, Tate also returned kickoffs. He averaged 20.7 yards on 41 kickoff returns, which ranks eighth in kickoff returns and ninth in kickoff return yardage in ND program history. He got his yards in whatever way he could and in the end, had tallied 2,215 all-purpose yards. Tate was an all-around athlete and a mainstay left fielder on the Irish Baseball Team and so he missed missed most of spring practices due to his starting roles.

He was identified as ready to be great and he was great. He was selected to Phil Steele's 2009 preseason first-team All-America squad; named to Sporting News' preseason All-America third team, and he was tabbed by Steele as the sixth-best wide receiver and

19th-best punt returner in college football for 2009. Lindy's labeled him the 15th-best wide receiver in 2009 preseason. One thing for sure—Golden Tate was a fine football player. He was one of Notre Dame's great ones.

Great Player: Kyle Rudolph TE 2008-2010

Remember that Notre Dame is "Tight End U." So, one would expect some of the finest top tight ends in nation matriculate to Notre Dame to become one of the best at the position on a team that loves the position of tight end. Kyle Rudolph is one of the best tight ends to ever play for Notre dame. Despite only being a junior when he came to prominence, his combination of great size 6'6", 265, and strength with deceptive speed and tremendous ball skills when attempting to snatch football out of air made him as good as he was.

The was the only sophomore in 2009 to get the John Mackey Award. He was a semifinalist. Of eight Mackey Award semifinalists, only Rudolph returned in 2010.

He caught 62 passes for 704 yards with five touchdowns in his career ... has started 22 of 23 career games played ... established freshman receiving records at Notre Dame and became first tight end in Irish history to start every game in first season ... had surgery on shoulder in offseason and was somewhat limited in spring practice.

There were big expectations for Rudolph for a promising 2010 junior season. But they were derailed midseason when he was afflicted by a hamstring injury. The injury ended his season after 6 games. On September 11, he had set a Notre Dame record for most receiving yards in a game by a tight end against Michigan with 164 yards on 8 receptions, with more than half of the yardage coming after he hauled in the second-longest pass play in school history with a 95-yard touchdown.

Rudolph finished his final season before going pro with 28 receptions for 328 yards and three touchdowns, ending his 3-season career at Notre Dame ranked among the all-time leading tight ends in school history.

His 90 career receptions were the fourth-most by a tight end in school history and his 1,032 career receiving yards are also fourth-most. His pair of 8-catch games fell 1 reception short of the school record for a tight end of 9 receptions in a game and was only the fourth Irish tight end to break the 1,000-yard career yardage plateau. On January 4, 2011,

Rudolph decided to forgo his senior season and declared for the 2011 NFL Draft.

Rudolph didn't participate in the 2011 NFL combine because of his torn hamstring, but posted a 4.78 40-yard dash time only three weeks after being medically cleared to participate at Notre Dame's Pro Day in South Bend, Indiana. He was selected by the Minnesota Vikings with the 43rd overall pick in the second round of the 2011 NFL Draft.

He was the first tight end selected in the draft and is the second-highest drafted tight end in Vikings history behind Hal Bedsole (chosen in the first round, 19th overall) in the 1964 NFL Draft. He started 8 games as a rookie and in 2012 he had his breakout year. So far, since 2011, he has played in 80 pro games and has 265 catches for 2621 yards. Kyle Rudolph is the real deal.

Even Starkist couldn't stop this "Sorry Charlie!"

Weis took the medicine he knew was coming as he was summarily fired as head coach the Monday after the Stanford loss at the end of the season. Notre Dame was embarrassed that 6-6 was the best it could do with so much talent and so much invested.

Though the Irish team was bowl eligible with 6 wins, nobody felt like playing a consolation bowl game. Rather than play in a loser's version of a winner's bowl, Notre Dame used its energy to move its program forward.

Athletic director Jack Swarbrick hired Cincinnati head coach Brian Kelly after a 10-day coaching search. It just happens that I have the very same first and last name as Coach Kelly. Like most other real Irish fans, I am very pleased that the "the real Brian Kelly" is the head coach at Notre Dame. One day when we get to talk, and after a few gifts of books that I have written, we will know each other; but not now and that is OK!

Weis's last season with the Irish was unremarkable. My personal glimpse of the coach on the field in the Boston College game the year before had told me that it was all over for ND if Weis were retained indefinitely as the coach. If I were a great football analyst, I could deduce what was wrong with Charley Weis as a coach. I have some thoughts that I would prefer not to share. I wish Coach Weis the best and sure hope he has a fruitful life.

After the season, Notre Dame Athletic Director Jack Swarbrick, when asked about what his biggest disappointment had been that season, took a long pause, then said, "The Navy outcome." He was not ready to evaluate the football season until season's end, but he knew that "Up until the Navy game we were in the BCS conversation." The Navy game, however, was the first of the tragic season-ending four-game losing skid.

Swartbrick fired Weis as head coach the Monday after the Stanford loss. At the same time, he announced that wide receiver coach Rob Lanello would take charge of football operations, including recruiting, *until Brian Kelly was names head coach.*

As I like to do in this book, in order to close out coaching eras, I searched for an appropriate piece to end the Charley Weis era, and this chapter. Most Notre Dame fans could have written an appropriate piece about Charlie as he had represented a lot of hope and then some results and hope; more hope, and then mental anguish. Chicago news outlets normally have a way of getting to the core of the matter so I selected this piece.

Check it out when you have time:

http://chicago.suntimes.com/news/7/71/805420/charlie-weis-fired-at-notre-dame-in-shortest-coaching-death-watch-ever

Chapter 23 Coach Brian Kelly 2010–2016

Coach # 31

Kelly is ND's Head Football Coach (2016)

2010	Brian Kelly	8–5
2011	Brian Kelly	8–5
2012	Brian Kelly	12–1
2013	Brian Kelly	9–4
2014	Brian Kelly	8–5
2015	Brian Kelly	10–3
2016	Brian Kelly	4-8

Assumption writes re: alumnus Brian Kelly

We now all have the opportunity to read about the last coach of the modern era, as I present the Brian Kelly Era of Notre Dame Football. The lead article comes from his alma mater. Many of us already have deified Kelly as one of the great immortals, not unlike those greats, who have brought national championships to Notre Dame. I predict that his day will come. I for one am happy to wait. I am very pleased that Coach Kelly is on the job for all the Notre Dame faithful. Brian Kelly is a fine coach. Notre Dame has done well and will do even better under his leadership.

I spent several hours at the beginning of this chapter trying to find a Chicago or LA or NY article on Coach Brian Kelly but when I found this online article from Kelly's college alma-mater, I was very pleased and I stopped researching. It is a nicely written piece about Coach Kelly's appointment to Notre Dame's head coaching position. It was written by the college from which he graduated, Assumption College:

https://www.assumption.edu/news/brian-kelly-%E2%80%9983-named-head-coach-notre-dame-football-team

Brian Kelly '83 Named Head Coach of Notre Dame Football team

Assumption alumnus and former defensive coordinator Brian K. Kelly '83, who recently took the University of Cincinnati Bearcats to two consecutive Bowl Championship Series appearances and a perfect 12-0 regular season in 2009, has been named the 29th head football coach at the University of Notre Dame.

Notre Dame's president, Rev. John I. Jenkins, C.S.C., praised Kelly in an announcement on the school's website. "I am absolutely delighted to welcome Brian and his family to the Notre Dame family. He brings to us a long and successful career as a head coach, and I am confident that he will have even greater success here. I'm also very pleased that he has put considerable emphasis on excellence in the classroom and that his student-athletes graduate at a rate well above the norm."

As an Assumption football player Kelly played at middle linebacker for the Greyhounds and graduated from Assumption College with a B.A. in Political Science. His football career at Assumption included 19 tackles in the final game of the 1981 season and he captained the two of the most successful club football teams in Hounds' history for Hall of Fame Coach Paul Cantiani '73. Kelly earned all conference honors in the New England Collegiate Football Conference as both a junior and senior and left with a school-record 314 tackles (currently seventh). His record 214 assists stood until 2005 when broken by Chris Grogan '06.

Kelly served as defensive coordinator at Assumption for four seasons under Hall of Famer Bernie Gaughan, raising the team's level of play before leaving to coach for Grand Valley. At same time, he coached women's softball and ushered the Assumption team to 20-plus and entrance into the postseason regional rankings. Kelly's winning ways were recognized when he was named to the Assumption Alumni-Athletics Hall of Fame in 2006.

A native of Chelsea, MA, Kelly graduated from St. John's Prep (Danvers, MA), where he starred in three sports: football, hockey and baseball. Brian and his wife, Paqui, have three children - Patrick Liam, Grace Marie and Kenzel Michael.

Notre Dame's webpage has the official announcement.
http://www.und.com/sports/m-footbl/spec-rel/121009aaq.html

Great Player: Michale Floyd , WR 2008-2011

As a true freshman at Notre Dame, Floyd played in 11 of Notre Dame's 13 games in 2008, only missing the final two games of the regular season (Syracuse and USC) due to an injury sustained early against Navy. He recorded seven touchdown receptions on the year, breaking the record for an Irish freshman (previously held by teammate Duval Kamara's four TDs in 2007), while catching 48 balls to break another Notre Dame freshman record in receptions (Kamara had 32 in 2007). His 719 receiving yards set the mark for Notre Dame first-year players (Tony Hunter had 690 in 1979).

Michael Floyd was one of the top college football wide receivers in the nation during his full career with Notre Dame. He has totaled 271 receptions for 3,689 yards and 28 touchdowns while starting 41 of 42 games played in an Irish uniform. He is listed on the NCAA FBS active career charts in receiving touchdowns (37), receiving yards per game (87.8), receiving yards (3689) and receptions per game.

His 37 TD receptions is a school record. He recorded 13 100-yard receiving games in his career, tied for second in Notre Dame history. He is the ninth Notre Dame wideout to ever register 2,000 career receiving yards. He is the third wideout in Irish history to have two separate seasons ranking in the top 10 for receiving touchdowns in a single season. Additionally, he is the only ND wideout to ever register four games with at least 10 receptions.

Floyd caught two or more touchdowns passes seven times in his career. He is the third Irish wide-receiver to have three or more touchdown receptions in multiple games. Floyd is also the first player in school history to register multiple touchdown catches of at least 80 yards. He had a reception in 29 of the 30 games in which he played for ND. The only game he failed to make a reception came against Navy in 2008 when he was injured early in the first quarter while blocking downfield.

Michael Floyd set freshman records at Notre Dame for receptions, receiving yards and receiving TDs. He then became fourth Irish freshman in last 20 years to score a TD on his first career catch, joining Raghib "Rocket" Ismail and Derek Brown in 1988 and Derrick Mayes in 1992.

Michael Floyd was snagged by the Arizona Cardinals 13th overall in the 2012 NFL Draft. He began 2012 as a backup wide receiver. His first career reception was an eight-yard touchdown off a deflected pass in a 27-6 win against the Philadelphia Eagles. He played in all 16 games with three starts recording 45 receptions for 562 yards and two touchdowns.

In t 2013 season, Floyd started all 16 games recording 65 receptions for 1,041 yards and five touchdowns. Floyd was released by Cardinals on December 14, 2016 following a DUI arrest.

Michael was claimed off waivers by the New England Patriots on December 15. Floyd recorded his first catch as a Patriot in the team's Week 16 blowout win over the New York Jets, a six-yard throw from Patriots backup QB Jimmy Garopolo. On January 1, 2017, Floyd caught his first touchdown as a Patriot against the Miami Dolphins. He also assisted fellow wide receiver Julian Edelman on his 77-yard touchdown catch and run by delivering a block to Dolphins cornerback Tony Lippett. He was inactive for the first two playoff games as his team advanced to an NFL Record 9th Super Bowl appearance.

The Patriots won Super Bowl LI when they defeated the Atlanta Falcons 34-28 despite Floyd not playing. The Patriots trailed 28-3 in the third quarter, but rallied all the way back to win the game which featured the first overtime game in Super Bowl history and the largest comeback in the Super Bowl.

2010 Notre Dame Football Season Coach Brian Kelly

The 2010 Notre Dame Fighting Irish football team was coached by Brian Kelly in his first year as head coach. This was Kelly's first season as Notre Dame's head coach, after leading the Cincinnati Bearcats to a 12–0 regular season and a BCS bowl berth.

In 2010, Notre Dame's regular season schedule was ranked the most difficult schedule in the nation with a Team Opposition Record Percentage of .6529. This poll was published by the NCAA and it only included wins against Division I teams.

Notre Dame finished the first Kelly season with a very healthy 8–5 record. Better than that, the Irish defeated Miami (FL) 33–17 showing that their resurgence was not a fluke.

Brian Kelly replaced Charley Weis on Dec 10, 2009 in time to work hard to bring in recruits to help the team. Two of the Irish's bright spots, Jimmy Clausen and Golden Tate chose not to play their final years and declared for the 2010 NFL draft. Graduation was another factor that caused a number of players to move-on. Weis had a good team... but.

Being hired in the off-season, if there is such a thing anymore for a collegiate head coach, Kelly's first mission was recruiting. In his first attempt at recruiting a class for Notre Dame, he was quite successful with 23 signed commitments from high school players across the United States. Five early enrollees included Quarterback Tommy Rees, Wide Receiver Tai-ler Jones, Cornerback Lo Wood,

Cornerback Spencer Boyd and Safety Chris Badger. Things were lining up for a successful Irish run.

Kelly liked Junior Dayne Crist as his QB for 2010. Crist executed well in completing 59.2 percent of his passes, for 2,033 yards, 15 touchdowns and 7 interceptions. The QB then suffered a major injury against Tulsa, the ninth game, and this ended his season. Tommy Rees, a resilient, dedicated, hard-working, but young quarterback came in for Crist, finishing the Tulsa game. Rees was very effective but could not deliver a victory as the Irish lost L (27-28)

This Utah game is listed as one of the top Notre Dame games of all time. The pundits identified the essence of this game as: "The punt block that saved a season." Things were bleak for the 4-5 Irish coming off consecutive losses to Navy and Tulsa. Both # 15 Utah and unranked Notre Dame each started out by gaining just 14 yards on their first 3 offensive series. Utah then got a field goal, which would be their only score in the game.

ND cornerback Robert Blanton (12) celebrates his TD run back on a blocked punt against Utah during the first quarter at ND Stadium.

The Irish were down 3-0 late in the 1st quarter when Robert Blanton blocked a punt and returned it for a touchdown. This was the spark that helped the Irish grab momentum. Tommy Rees threw a touchdown in the 2nd quarter and then hit Duval Kamara for another score to open the 3rd quarter after Utah fumbled the second half kickoff. On the next series, Rees found Kamara again and the route was on W (27-3).

New Year's Eve 2010 Sun Bowl

Tommy Rees and Michael Floyd were the game heroes as Notre Dame beat Miami W (33-17) in the Sun Bowl. Notre Dame claimed the victory after Reese passed for 201 yards and two touchdowns to Michael Floyd.

After a 20-year hiatus in the good-guy / bad-guy series, the Catholics were again playing the Convicts, but the monikers had all gone away. It was just smash-mouth football on an anything but quiet New Year's Eve afternoon in Texas.

The Irish hit pay-dirt three of their first four possessions. Rees was on the mark passing 3 and then 34 yards to Floyd when Cierre Wood broke free on a 34-yard scoring run.

David Ruffer had a good kicking day, pounding three in from 40, 50 and 19 yards. The Irish defense was also on full alert, picking off Miami starting quarterback Jacoby Harris 3 times and chalking up 4 total interceptions in the first half to help the team grab a quick 27-0 lead.

2011 Notre Dame Football Season Coach Brian Kelly

The 2011 Notre Dame Fighting Irish football team was led by second year head coach Brian Kelly. Every year Notre Dame's football program competes as an independent. They are not affiliated with any conference. But in 2015, ND agreed to play five ACC games each year as other ND sports teams had become integral parts of the ACC.

This particular year, 2011, Notre Dame had a better regular season than in 2010. However, they finished with the same overall record as the team's venture into the Champs Sports Bowl led to a defeat by a rejuvenated Florida State Team L (14-18)

2012 Notre Dame Football Season Coach Brian Kelly

The 2012 Notre Dame Fighting Irish football team, led by third year head coach Brian Kelly, played home games at Notre Dame Stadium. They competed as an independent. Despite starting the season unranked, the Fighting Irish finished the regular season at 12-0, and #1 in all major polls. Manti Te'o kept the Irish defense in control of most games as the Notre Dame finished the season with the number one defense in the country.

ND gave up just 10.3 points per game. They played in the BCS National Championship Game with a chance to win their first national title since 1988, but were defeated by the Alabama Crimson Tide. Brian Kelly had gone undefeated and untied 12-0 in his third season prior to the bowl game. This was a tremendous accomplishment. Most of his predecessors, who won national championships in their third years as Head Coach were not expected to play or win a bowl game.

Great Player: Manti Te'o: LB, 2009-2012

In his time on the field, Manti Te'o was the undisputed leader of the Fighting Irish and he was a huge defensive nightmare for opposing offenses. With a lot of spirit Te'o's defense led Notre Dame back into the spotlight with its highest national ranking since 2006. He is the school's 17th NFF National Scholar-Athlete.

Te'o graduated with a degree in graphic design, the Laie, Hawaii, native gained many honors for his fine play at the school of Our Lady. He was named the 2011 Notre Dame Football Student-Athlete of the Year. He was also selected as a Second Team Academic All-American and First Team All-District honoree as a junior.

Te'o achieved Second Team All-America honors two times and he also won the Lott IMPACT Player of the Week three times in his last season. He received national acclaim for his standout performance versus Michigan State, having lost both his grandmother and girlfriend within a 24-hour period the week prior.

Te'o was a finalist for the prestigious Butkus Award and the Lott Trophy as a junior. He was captain of the Irish two years in a row. His defensive cat-like prowess led the team to consecutive bowl berths, including a win in the 2010 Sun Bowl.

His 133 tackles in 2010 were the most by a Notre Dame player in 27 years, and he recorded the third-most tackles (66) ever by an Irish freshman. In his senior year, he led the Irish in tackles again. He also was an interception leader.

He had been a volunteer for the South Bend Center for the Homeless and for the Tackle the Arts initiative. In this role, Te'o was a three-year participant in Christmas parties for ill children. He also read to patients in the hematology/oncology unit at the local hospital.

He was selected in the second round (38th overall) of the 2013 NFL Draft by the San Diego Chargers. He is the highest selected Notre Dame linebacker since Demetrius DuBose in 1993. It was on May 10, 2013, Te'o signed a four-year contract with the Chargers. The deal included a $2,141,768 signing bonus and was worth just over $5 million with over $3.1 million in guaranteed money.

Specifically, Te'o earned his first NFL sack by sacking Colin Kaepernick--coincidentally, the first player Te'o tackled in his collegiate career--on a 4th down play. He finished the 2014 season with 61 tackles, 1 sack, 1 interception, and 3 pass deflections.

In 2015, Te'o had 63 tackles, one interception, and one forced fumble. He missed four games in mid-season due to an ankle injury. On September 5, 2016, Te'o was named one of the San Diego Chargers team captains for the 2016 season [55] On

September 28, 2016, he was placed on injured reserve with a torn Achilles. We're looking for more from Manti as he heals.

Great Player Tyler Eifert, TE 2009-2012

Tyler Eifert played for the Notre Dame football team from 2009 to 2012. As a freshman in 2009, he got in just one game after suffering a back injury. As a sophomore in 2010, he was a backup to Kyle Rudolph but he had to assume the duty when Rudolph suffered a season-ending injury.

Eifert finished 2010 with 27 receptions for 352 yards and two touchdowns in 11 games. In his junior season, he took over the starting position. As a starter, Eifert had 63 receptions for 803 yards and five touchdowns.

As a fine member of Notre Dame's "Tight End U," Eifert broke the school's tight end single-season receptions and receiving yards' record, previously held by Ken MacAfee.

He was named a 2011 Mackey Award finalist but did not win the award. As a senior, he had 50 receptions for 685 yards with 4 touchdowns. He also won the 2012 Mackey Award after being named a finalist the year before and was also named second- team All-American by the Associated Press.

After a 42–14 loss to the Alabama Crimson Tide in the 2013 BCS National Championship Game, Eifert decided to forgo his final season of eligibility and declared his intentions to enter the 2013 NFL Draft. He did and he is having a fine time of it – if only he can stay well.

So Far, in his four years Eifert has had a great pro career On September 8, 2013, Eifert made his NFL debut, recording 5 receptions for 47 yards against the Chicago Bears.[10] On September 7, 2014. during his first game of the 2014 season against the Baltimore Ravens, Eifert suffered a dislocated elbow after landing awkwardly on his arm while trying to twist out of a leg tackle by safety Darian Stewart. He was placed on injured reserve on September 10, 2014, and ended up being out for the season.

In 2015, he played in 13 games and caught 52 passes for 615 yards. In 2016, he played just eight games with 29 receptions and 394 yards. He was on injured reserve half the season with a back injury. Let's wish him well for next year.

The multi-talented Everett Golson was Brian Kelly's designated starting quarterback for 2012 and he did a great job most of the time during the season. Pundits who have examined Junior Tommy Rees's performance in 2012 suggest that there would have been no magic, no 12-1 stellar season, if backup Rees were not available to come off the bench to save the Irish against Purdue, Michigan and Stanford. These were major relief roles and Rees was on target in each of them.

Rees survived and pulled the Irish to victory in really tough situations this season. Golson led the Irish for most of their touchdowns and his athleticism helped him squirm out of situations in which the Irish would have otherwise been stymied.

In terms of recruiting, this Kelly class was a bit lighter than others. Coach Kelly received 17 commitments in his second full recruiting class. Those included commitments from three early-enrollees: defensive tackle Sheldon Day, quarterback Gunner Kiel, and cornerback Tee Shepard.

Michigan at Home

For the second game in a row, Notre Dame's Tommy Rees came off the bench to spark the Notre Dame offense in a 13-6 win over the Wolverines. Rees was drawn into action when Everett Golson was ineffective against the tough Michigan defense. Kelly substituted Rees midway through the second quarter.

Denard Robinson, who had been a one man wrecking crew against the Irish in years past, was also ineffective, but Michigan kept him in the game. Robinson felt his play was so below par that he apologized to the Michigan fans after the game and said it would not happen again. Robinson threw four interceptions against the Irish.

Rees finished 8 for 11 passing for 115 yards. More importantly, he did not commit a turnover.

ND Coach Brian Kelly speaks with QB Tommy Rees during the game against Michigan in 2012.

Notre Dame ran out the clock after a Michigan field goal with 3:27 left in the game had cut Notre Dame's lead to 13-6. Rees then connected with Tyler Eifert on a 38-yard pass down the sideline on a critical third down. Then an 8-yard run on a 3rd & 8 play with one minute left by Theo Riddick put the game away.

"It's a great feeling any time you can beat Michigan," Rees said. "It's a great environment ... a lot of fun."

BCS Championship Bowl

For such a great season, #1 ranked Notre Dame got to play #2 ranked Alabama in the BCS championship Bowl at Sun Life Stadium in Miami Gardens, FL. The six-week wait to play this game took seemed to take the edge off the Irish and they were defeated by the Crimson Tide L (14-42).

Before a record, Sun Life Stadium crowd of 80,120 that definitely included more green than crimson, The Crimson Tide's star running back, Eddie Lacy, ran right through the Irish on a 20-yard touchdown run before the game was 3 minutes old.

This capped off a punishing 82-yard drive that was the longest of the season given up by the Fighting Irish. That was the complexion of the game until it ended with an Alabama victory.

2013 Notre Dame Football Season Coach Brian Kelly

The 2013 Notre Dame Fighting Irish football team was led by fourth year head coach Brian Kelly.

Everett Golson, to the chagrin of his fellow teammates, was out on academic suspension for the year. Senior Tommy Rees stepped in as the starting 2013 quarterback. The Fighting Irish finished the 2013 regular season 9-4. They were # 21 in the coaches' poll and # 25 in the AP. ND was invited to the Pinstripe Bowl at Yankee Stadium and they defeated Rutgers W (29-16)

Pinstripe Bowl v Rutgers December 28, 2013

Tommy Rees is always a positive guy. There are many who would suggest this final game for Rees as a graduating senior from Notre Dame University is typical of his great play and the perfect descriptor for his four years of leading Notre Dame to victory after victory. It was not all easy. But, Tommy Rees made it seem that way when he ran the game.

Rees threw for 319 yards and no interceptions in his final college game, leading No. 25 Notre Dame to a 29-16 victory against

Rutgers. The game was far from pretty but ultimately successful. Rees's performance was solid, going 27 for 47.

Known as the Closer because he saved or won many games for the Irish with late drives, against Rutgers, Rees was mistake-free and productive. He missed a few throws that could have broken open the game, but, he came through. "I'm a Tommy Rees fan for life," Coach Brian Kelly said. Kelly also said that it was "a good season that could have been a great season." Kelly said.

Great Player: Tommy Rees, QB, 2010-2013

Tommy Rees was the next-guy-in for Notre Dame for three of his four years with the team, and more often than not, or so it seems, he was called in to save the day. From 2009 to his senior season, the Notre Dame Football highlights for most games have featured his name as his utility value to the team was so high.

Rees was not necessarily the greatest but he sure was one of the greats and deserves his spot in this book. More than most, he proved his greatness many times in his career. He is responsible more than anybody else for Notre Dame's undefeated regular season in 2012 and their shot at the BCS championship. Tommy still holds the single-game consecutive completion record at ND—14—, which he achieved on Nov. 12, 2011 vs. Maryland, He is still # 2 in single-game pass completions—33--, which he set on Oct. 30, 2010 vs. Tulsa as a freshman.

As a senior, Tommy started all thirteen games. He threw for 3,257 yards and 27 touchdowns. He was just the third QB in school history to eclipse the 3,000-yard passing mark in a season and only two other ND quarterbacks ever registered more touchdown passes in a year. He threw at least two touchdown passes in 10 games and completed 54.1-percent of his passes (224-of-414) for 3,257 yards and 27 touchdowns ... registered a passing efficiency of 135.4. He had a 23-8 (.742) career record as the Irish starting quarterback. His career victories are seventh-best in school history. I can keep going and will for a bit more

He was just the second Irish quarterback ever to throw two 80-yard touchdown passes in the same season (joining Dayne Crist in 2010) and the only one to ever do it on the road each time. He was ranked 11th in the nation for most yards per completion (14.54), 19th in passing touchdowns (27), 24th in passing yards (3,257), 30th in passing yards/game (250.5), 35th in point responsibility (162) and 45th in point responsibility/game (12.5).

He had five 300- yard passing games this season, matching Brady Quinn (2005) for the second-most in school history in a single season. He closed out his great school record with 319 yards passing in the 29-16 victory over Rutgers (Dec. 28) in the New Era Pinstripe Bowl. He completed 27-of-47 passes and did not toss an interception. In fact, his 47 passes without an interception is the most without a pick in single-game school history.

Tommy Rees engineered a string of eight straight scoring drives (six touchdowns and two field goals) between the Air Force (Oct. 26) and Navy (Nov. 2) games, excepting a series of kneel-downs at the conclusion of Notre Dame's visit to Colorado Springs. Rees threw three touchdown passes in the 37-34 victory over Arizona State on Oct. 5. This marked his seventh career game with at least three touchdown passes. He had another one at Air Force on Oct. 26, where he completed 17-of-22 passes for 284 yards and five touchdowns against the Falcons. His 260.71 passing efficiency rating against Air Force is the eighth-best in the nation this year against an FBS team ... etc. etc. etc. indeed!

2014 Notre Dame Football Season Coach Brian Kelly

The 2014 Notre Dame Fighting Irish football team was led by fifth-year head coach Brian Kelly. The Irish were two different teams this season. Team One played the first six games with all players well and ready to play. Team Two lost half of its defense mostly through major injuries and yet, they went out each week and did their best. However, in a depleted condition, Team 2 often did not do well enough to bring home the victory.

ND started the season with a 6–0 record, ranked as high as #5 in both the AP Poll and the Coaches' Poll. They suffered a major setback with many player injuries in the second half of the season. They lost five of their last six games. They finished the regular season at 7–5.

I don't want to make excuses for ND but everybody saw that Kelly lost half the defense or more by the second half of the season. It was so bad that if it were not for the freshman class, ND would have had to forfeit games.

I watched this season as every season very closely and it was very painful. Of course, it was even more painful for Coach Kelly to watch one player after another being taken out of action with major injuries. Thankfully all players eventually recovered after the season had ended.

The Music City Bowl Notre Dame v LSU

Just because Notre Dame has something to say, lets' let ND say it about this well-played bowl game. Enjoy reading the official word:

2015 LSU (MUSIC CITY BOWL) v NOTRE DAME

Under the category of "nobody saw this coming," and in only the second bowl game that makes the list, unranked Notre Dame came into this matchup reeling, disappointed, and left for dead after losing its last four regular-season games.

But calling on the pride of a program, a two-quarterback system, and the leg of a struggling kicker, unranked Notre Dame overcame long odds and a 28-21 third-quarter deficit to defeat No. 22 LSU 31-28 to win the 2015 Music City Bowl on the last play of the game.

With 5:41 remaining and the score tied at 28, the Irish took their final possession at their own 15. In relative ease and precision -- only two third-down conversions necessary -- the quarterback tandem of freshman starter Malik Zaire *and experienced senior* Everett Golson *moved 71 yards to set up a 32-yard field goal attempt for senior placekicker Kyle Brindza.*

Brindza, who had missed six of his previous nine field goal attempts, calmly capped his career with a last-second game winner and the memory of a lifetime.

"To leave a program so historic like this in this kind of fashion is great," Brindza said immediately afterward. "It's a blessing for me, but also to be able to help win a game for all my teammates is a bigger blessing."

This comeback doesn't stand with some of the classics of yesteryear, but it remains "music" to Irish ears, an important win during the Brian Kelly era, and a start to a fresh list of fantastic photo finishes.

2015 Notre Dame Football Season Coach Brian Kelly

The 2015 Notre Dame Fighting Irish football team was led by sixth-year head coach Brian Kelly.

What a great team ND put together under Brian Kelly for the 2015 season. It can be argued that the 2015 team is the most explosive offense that Brian Kelly has coached at Notre Dame. But for four points in two games, the 2015 season would have been dramatically different.

During the regular season, the Irish were one of twenty-one schools in the country to average 200 or more passing yards and rushing yards per game. The Irish had fourteen plays of over 50 yards during the season. This ranked 13th in the country and was a Notre Dame school record. The Fighting Irish were fun to watch.

During this season, ND also had two touchdowns of over 90 yards. C.J. Prosise contributed a 91 yarder and Josh Adams gave the Irish a 98-yard touchdown. In 126 years of previous Notre Dame Football games, the Fighting Irish had only two such runs before 2015.

The 2015 running game was dominant in its success against opposing defenses. At 5.76 yards per carry, the Irish ranked fifth in the country. Finishing the regular season averaging 34 points per game, including a 62-point effort against UMass, the most points in an ND game since 1996; the point output was phenomenal.

Ohio State has always been a great team. Urban Myer's team was as great in 2015 as those of the past but they had lost a late season game to Michigan State, which kept them from winning the Big Ten Championship. Notre Dame had also lost a big game against Clemson earlier in the season and then again late season against Stanford. Add up the Irish loss total in the regular season and you get four points…just four points. How much is two plus two?

The ND 2015 season ended on a heartbreaking note, as the Irish were defeated by Ohio State University in the Fiesta Bowl by a score of L (28-44). The resident Indiana Irish have a few things to prove to their neighbors in Ohio as ND has not beaten the Buckeyes since 1936. Brian Kelly had another great recruiting class. He received 24 commitments in his fifth full recruiting class including one five-star, Aliz'e Jones. The class included student-athletes from 13 different states.

Great Player: Sheldon Day, DL 2012-2015

Sheldon Day played as a true freshman at Notre Dame in 2012, appearing in all 13 games. He collected 23 tackles and two sacks. As a sophomore, he did even better in 11 games and made eight starts. Day recorded 33 tackles and a half sack. In the 11-game schedule of his junior year, Day had 40 tackles and one sack.

Following the end of the season, Sheldon Day announced that he would return for his senior season, foregoing the 2015 NFL Draft. In his senior season, Sheldon starting all 13 games and he set his career high in tackles—45, tackles for loss—15.5, and sacks. This earned him second-team All-American honors by the Associated Press.[8]

The games

A Texas team known for such football greats as Johnny Football came to ND on September 5, for a 7:30 p.m. game. Notre Dame played great football and won the game W (38-3). Malik Zaire was aggressive in the running game and outstanding in the passing game. Texas is always tough. Such a great performance made things look encouraging for Notre Dame's 2015 season.

Kizer's late TD rescues No. 9 Notre Dame at Virginia, 34-27

Nobody knows how tough Virginia can be as much as Coach Kelly, Malik Zaire, and DeShone Kizer. Zaire fractured his ankle late in the game and Kaiser came in off the bench with no warmups. Tommy Rees (Kizer) was back to save another ND game.

Notre Dame was losing. It was not long before backup quarterback DeShone Kizer threw a 40-yard touchdown pass to Will Fuller with 12 seconds left. Notre Dame beat Virginia W (34-27) in a thrilling finish. The season had rested on the back of Zaire. Kizer did a remarkable job in relief.

I watched Kizer also perform very well against Georgia Tech's Yellow Jackets at Notre Dame Stadium, and score a W (30-22) victory. He did the same at UMass even better at home the following week W (62-27). What a fine player!

Clemson Football Stops Notre Dame 2-Point Conversion to Clinch Win

On October 3, like everybody else, I heard the howling winds and the torrential rain when Notre Dame and Clemson were in the middle of a major tropical storm in South Carolina and we in Pennsylvania were feeling some of the same weather that the coaches and players on the field were experiencing.

Memorial Stadium in Clemson was getting pelted and whipped badly by the elements and it was a wonder that either team could perform at all. It would have been better if there was better weather but having said that, both teams did remarkably well.

Notre Dame was ranked # 6 and Clemson was ranked # 12. None of that seemed to matter to the players as they knew that with tough play, either team could win the game.

The bottom line on this critical game was that Clemson's talented QB, Deshaun Watson threw for two touchdowns, ran for a third and Clemson's defense stopped Freshman DeShone Kizer on a tying two-point conversion attempt as the 12th-ranked Tigers held on to beat Notre Dame by two points L (22-24). Clemson would not say no. They were tough as nails on both sides of the football. That probably is why they got to play for the BCS National Championship. In 2016, Watson and company beat Alabama for the National Championship.

Boston College and Notre Dame agreed to play in the (Holy War / Shamrock Series) again in 2015 on November 21, right before Thanksgiving at Fenway Park, a National Treasure Stadium. BC was unranked and Notre Dame was ranked # 5 and looking for a shot at the BCS National Championship.

BC had always been a spoiler and this again was their chance. The game started at 7:30 PM and it stayed close the whole game. The Irish Catholics from the CSC order beat the Catholics from the Jesuit order in the Holy Wars tradition W (19-16).

Notre Dame loves to win as much and perhaps even more than most teams. When the Irish met Stanford on November 28, with ND ranking in at # 13 and Stanford at # 4, both sets of fans knew nobody from the losing side would be able to find any consolation in a loss.

The Fighting Irish played very well as did Stanford. For the second time in what otherwise would have been an unblemished season, Notre Dame lost by two-points. The Cardinal were tough as usual—tough enough to beat ND L (36-38).

Having 2 two-point losses, and a great season. the # 8 ranked Notre Dame Fighting Irish won a berth to the Fiesta Bowl. The opponent would be Ohio State. The Buckeyes, coached by Urban Myer, had suffered just one loss during the season. Notre Dame entered the game a 6.5-point betting underdog.

The Fiesta Bowl 2016 ND v Ohio State

Some may say that it was Junior Ezekiel Elliot who single-handedly clobbered Notre Dame at the Fiesta Bowl. Elliot headed to the NFL before graduation in 2016. The tough running back, perhaps the best ever in Ohio State history, scored against the Irish on three short runs in the first half and proved he is the real deal.

He left ND defenders looking for relief again as he raced past them for a 47-yard score to open the second half. Elliott ran for 149 yards during the game and matched a Fiesta Bowl record with four touchdowns to close the curtain on his college career,

J.T. Barrett threw the ball for 211 yards and he also had 96 yards rushing in the highest-scoring game against Notre Dame's defense this season.

The Irish had some good moments behind freshman DeShone Kizer after the Buckeyes overly aggressive defensive end Joey Bosa was ejected for targeting in the first quarter. When ND's star linebacker Jaylon Smith, who was keeping things close for the Irish, left the game because of a knee injury. ND had a tough time keeping up with the blistering Buckeyes.

No excuses but even coach Brian Kelly offered: "The guy is so impactful on our defense…You lose a guy like that early on, it significantly affects what you're doing.

Ohio State had its way with Notre Dame's defense without Smith in the lineup, racing down the field for scores like a seven-on-seven drill. Notre Dame took advantage of Ohio State's Bosa-less defense a few times, although not enough to keep pace with the Buckeyes.

Kizer was Note Dame's key player on offense. He kept ND in the game. He connected with Chris Brown on a 4-yard touchdown pass to open the second half, pulling the Irish within a touchdown.

Kizer threw for 284 yards and two touchdowns on 22-of-37 passing but had an interception and lost a fumble. Like a lot of things in life, not everything goes well all the time.

If everything did not happen like it really did, things would have been better. If some of the anomalies could have been dialed back, it could have been a much different game. Nonetheless it was a hard-fought fine matchup. Having said that, like many Irish, I think it is about time for Notre Dame to win one against Ohio State. How about the next time!!

2016 Notre Dame Football Season Coach Brian Kelly

The 2016 Notre Dame Fighting Irish football team was again led by head coach Brian Kelly—in his seventh year. After a regular season in which the Irish lost just two games each by two points, with a number of starters back, Notre Dame was expected to compete well during the 2016 season. It did not happen

Coach Kelly had another fine recruiting class which bodes well for the future. Notre Dame accepted 23 commitments for 2016, including two 5-stars: Daelin Hayes and Tommy Kraemer. The class included student-athletes from 11 different states, and one Canadian province

Fall 2016 Coach Brian Kelly Year 7

2016 Results

1. at Texas	L 50–47 2OT	2. 1Nevada	W 39–10
3. Mich State	L 36–28	4. Duke	L 38–35
5. at Syracuse	W 50–33	6. at NC State	L 10–3
7. Stanford	L 17–10	8. Miami FL	W 30–27
9. at Navy	L 28–27	10. Army	W 44–6
11. Virg Tech	L 34–31	12. at USC	L 45–27

After a tough 4-8 season in 2016, it was nice to see a strong off-season. Coach Kelly added defensive coordinator Mike Elko and linebackers coach Clark Lea to his staff, along with the hiring of special teams coach and energetic recruiter Brian Polian. These are good signs for the future. Something had to be done and so far, so good.

With Kelly returning his focus to the offensive side of the ball and new offensive coordinator Chip Long brought in to help with the play-calling, he will be guiding a group that has arguably the nation's best offensive tackle in Mike McGlinchey, perhaps America's best offensive guard Quenton Nelson and two more returning starters on the offensive line in Alex Bars and Sam Mustipher up front.

The team should have plenty of speed and playmaking ability in the backfield and at wide receiver to spread the football around too.

Defensively Elko inherits a group that just needs to be put in a position to consistently succeed. Many criticized former defensive coordinator Brian Van Gorder for running a too complex scheme. Van Gorder had a tough time getting young players ready to play. Moreover, the system did not permit players such as Jaylon Smith to be in position to be productive behind the line of scrimmage.

Elko comes with a reputation of being a great communicator regarding his system and overall, the Irish should be highlighting a talented group of linebackers and defensive backs by enabling them to play faster.

247Sports has suggested that if guys like Daelin Hayes, Jerry Tillery, Khalid Kareem, Julian Okwara, Elijah Taylor, Jonathan Bonner and Jamir Jones blossom as they should with the new system. Notre Dame will go from a defense that struggled to get any kind of push to making consistent plays in the backfield.

Kelly is very pleased with the recruiting class which wrapped up February 1, as it will supplement a roster that was short on experience in 2016 but now has all those trials and tribulations to grow from. Fans are hoping the bad stuff is in the past.

The Fighting Irish 2017 recruiting class finished No. 11 nationally per the 247Sports Recruiting Rankings, which ties the second-best mark Kelly has had in seven full recruiting calendars in South Bend. That is good. only the 2013 class finished better at No. 5. Combine the 2017 efforts with the 2016 class (#13 in the nation) and it's a program should be able to win a lot of games.

Soon again, it will be time to play Notre Dame Football.

LETS GO PUBLISH! Books by Brian W. Kelly
(Sold at www.bookhawkers.com; Amazon.com, and Kindle.).

Great Players in Notre Dame Football The best players in any football prrgram

Great Coaches in Notre Dame Football The best coaches in any football prrgram

President Donald J. Trump, Master Builder: Solving the Student Debt Crisis!

President Donald J. Trump, Master Builder: It's Time for Seniors to Get a Break!

President Donald J. Trump, Master Builder: Healthcare & Welfare Accountability

President Donald J. Trump, Master Builder: "Make America Great Again"

President Donald J. Trump, Master Builder: The Annual Guest Plan

Great Players in Alabama Football From Quarterbacks to offensive Linemen Greats!

Great Moments in Alabama Football AU Football from the start. This is the book.

Great Moments in Penn State Football PSU Football, start--games, coaches, players,

Great Moments in Notre Dame Football ND Football, start, games, coaches, players

Four Dollars & Sixty-Two Cents—A Christmas Story That Will Warm Your Heart!

My Red Hat Keeps Me on The Ground. Darraggh's Red Hat is really Magical

Seniors, Social Security & the Minimum Wage. Things seniors need to know.

How to Write Your First Book and Publish It with CreateSpace

The US Immigration Fix--It's all in here. Finally, an answer.

I had a Dream IBM Could be #1 Again The title is self-explanatory

WineDiets.Com Presents The Wine Diet Learn how to lose weight while having fun.

Wilkes-Barre, PA; Return to Glory Wilkes-Barre City's return to glory

Geoffrey Parsons' Epoch... The Land of Fair Play Better than the original.

The Bill of Rights 4 Dummmies! This is the best book to learn about your rights.

Sol Bloom's Epoch ...Story of the Constitution The best book to learn the Constitution

America 4 Dummmies! All Americans should read to learn about this great country.

The Electoral College 4 Dummmies! How does it really work?

The All-Everything Machine Story about IBM's finest computer server.

Brian has written 105 books. Others can be found at amazon.com/author/brianwkelly

www.ingramcontent.com/pod-product-compliance
Lightning Source LLC
Chambersburg PA
CBHW070551100426
42744CB00006B/260